A HISTORY
OF THE
BRITISH
POLICE

A HISTORY
OF THE
BRITISH
POLICE

FROM ITS EARLIEST BEGINNINGS TO THE PRESENT DAY

RICHARD COWLEY

The
History
Press

First published 2011

The History Press
The Mill, Brimscombe Port
Stroud, Gloucestershire, GL5 2QG
www.thehistorypress.co.uk

British Library Cataloguing in Publication Data.
A catalogue record for this book is available from the British Library.

ISBN 978 0 7524 5891 5

Typesetting and origination by The History Press
Printed in Great Britain
Manufacturing managed by Jellyfish Print Solutions Ltd

CONTENTS

FOREWORD

I first joined the police in a county constabulary in 1968 and was instantly attracted to its history. In trying to find out more, it soon became clear that the only police history books available dealt purely with the Metropolitan Police, giving the impression that the whole of the country was policed from London and did what London did. It isn't, and it didn't. Provincial police forces evolved in their own way, for different reasons, and those reasons were largely ignored by the historians.

So little was thought of national provincial police history that the first real attempt at it, by Thomas Critchley, had only been published a year before I joined the constabulary. But in the forty years since, however, not much has changed, and the few books produced on national police history have been written by academics, concentrating on politics. There's nothing wrong with that, but I felt it required more.

This book is the culmination of all those years collecting and gathering.

ACKNOWLEDGEMENTS

Many people helped with this book in supplying illustrations and photographs, and I would like to thank them all. The copyright of all the photographs and illustrations remains with them, and I am extremely grateful for permission to reproduce them.

Individuals
Mr Peter Holyoake for photograph 66; Mr David Lemon for photographs 49 & 51; Mr Cyril Mason for photograph 60; Mrs J. Pedley for photographs 43 & 44; Mr B. Rowland for photograph 39; Mrs J. Underwood for photograph 50; Mr Alan Williams for photograph 56; Mrs Sue Williams for photograph 40; I would also like to thank the past superintendent of the Northern Police Convalescent Home (now the Police Treatment Centres) for permission to use the photograph of Miss Catherine Gurney (35). As always, Mr David Bailey of Northamptonshire Police has rendered invaluable service with his photographic techniques, and never once complained when I availed myself of his services, often with only minutes' notice.

Libraries, Museums, Picture Libraries & Record Offices
Tenterden and District Museum, especially Mrs Debbie Greaves, for photograph 33; Imperial War Museum for photograph 63 (GC244, LIC3573); Lancashire Local Studies Library, Preston, especially Ms Dorothy MacLeod, for photograph 34; Mary Evans Picture Library for photograph 46; Sheffield City Central Library for illustration 3; Northamptonshire Record Office, especially Miss Juliet Baxter, for illustrations/photographs 4, 12, 13, 14, 15, 17, 18, 26, 27 & 28. Crown copyright material reproduced under Click-Use PSI Licence number C2008000521.

British Police Forces
The British police forces have, as always, helped me enormously, so I would like to thank the chief constable of Cambridgeshire for photograph 62; the chief

constable of Cumbria Constabulary for photograph 68; the chief constable of
Essex Police, especially Ms Becky Wash, for photograph 23; the chief constable
of Gloucestershire Constabulary, especially Ms Maeve McNamara, for photograph 22; the chief constable of Greater Manchester Police, especially Mr
Duncan Broady, for illustrations 6, 10, 11 & 30; the chief constable of Hampshire
Constabulary for photograph 64; the chief constable of Kent Police, especially Ms
Anna Derham, for photograph 70; the chief constable of Lancashire Constabulary
for photographs 29 & 67; the chief constable of Lincolnshire Police for photograph 65; the chief constable of Norfolk Constabulary for photograph 72; the
chief constable of Northamptonshire Police for illustrations 1, 2, 7, 8, 9, 16, 25,
38, 42, 52, 53, 54, 55 & 61; the chief constable of North Wales Police, especially
Chief Superintendent Simon Humphries and Mr Martin Pendleton, for photograph 37; the chief constable of West Mercia Constabulary for photograph 20;
the chief constable of West Midlands Police, especially PC Charlotte Godfrey,
SC Sophie Kisiel and Mr Tony Rose, for photograph 48; the chief constable of
Wiltshire Constabulary, especially Inspector Stephen Bridge, for illustrations 19 &
21. Diagrams 24, 31, 69, 71 & 73 are by the author.

ONE

THE PREVIOUS SYSTEM

There hasn't always been a police force in Great Britain. Compared to some countries, Britain's system of organised police forces is a fairly modern invention. Indeed, the very word 'police' did not come into use until well into the nineteenth century. Before that, the term used was 'constable', and the parish constable, as the name implies, only looked after the law and order in his own village or parish, and nowhere else. And note that it was 'his' parish and not 'her' parish – all parish constables were men.

An organised police force did not come into existence in England until 1829. And when it did, this organised system was called the 'new police' to differentiate it from the system which used the parish constable and was then called the 'old police'.[1]

The old police system had grown up and evolved for nearly 1,000 years, and had been started by King Alfred the Great in the late ninth century. Having repelled the Norse invaders from what is now southern England, he wanted to give his country safe defences to guard against any more attacks from the Norsemen. Amongst his reforms was a policing system.

King Alfred divided the country into counties, or shires, for law-keeping purposes, and in each shire placed a Shire Reeve. *Reeve* was the Saxon word for a steward, or administrator, and over the years this name became corrupted to 'sheriff'. The sheriff's main occupation was to see that law and order were maintained, and that the shire enjoyed the peace that the king had provided for them – the King's Peace. Because he was directly responsible to the king, the shire reeve was chosen from the landowning class of men – the nobility and landed gentry of the day.

The shire was split into smaller territorial groups which contained about ten families and their land. These were called Tithings (from *tithe*, the Saxon word for 'ten'). Every freeman of each tithing that was 12 years of age or over had to give an assurance or pledge that he would personally answer for the good behaviour of every other man in his tithing. This meant that if any man committed a crime then everyone in his tithing was punished. So it was in the interest of every man to stop other men committing crimes. Every man, therefore, was a kind of policeman, and as the pledge that he had given was called a 'frankpledge', this system of policing was known as the System of Frankpledge.

The man elected by each tithing to be their spokesman at any court or official gathering was called the Tithingman or the Headborough (because he was the head or chief 'borhoe'; *borhoe* from the Saxon for 'pledge'). As the spokesman for the village, during the Saxon times, the tithingman came to be regarded as the chief person of the village.

After 1066, however, he came to be known by the new name that the Norman conquerors gave to him, and that name was Constable. To the Normans, the office of constable was originally one of high state, given only to the most trustworthy men, as the origin of the term betrays, *comes stabuli*, chief of the stables, keeper of the horses. By the time of the Norman Conquest, however, the term had been downgraded somewhat, but still meant any trustworthy administrative officer, exactly the same qualities as those needed by the tithingman.

The office of sheriff had also survived. However, by 1195, realising that only one sheriff per county was not going to be sufficient due to an expanding and more prosperous population, King Richard the Lionheart of England passed an Act of Parliament. He chose knights throughout the country, and into their hands placed fairly and squarely the task of keeping the peace in their respective counties. These knights were called either magistrates (from the Latin *magister*, meaning 'master'), or Justices of the Peace, and it was decreed that every county could have as many magistrates as it wished, spread over the whole county.

The parish constables were made directly responsible to the new local magistrates, and it was through the parish constable that the magistrates could pass down orders. So the parish constable became the link between the villagers and the magistrate, who was directly responsible to the king. But the parish constable was still not officially the policeman of his village – not until 1252, when, by an Act of Parliament in the reign of Henry III, the task of keeping the law and order in his village was placed upon his shoulders.

The parish constable was chosen annually by the villagers, mainly from the respectable tradesmen of the village, which meant that he still had his business to run during the day and was only a policeman during his spare time. He received no salary for his duties, only his expenses. So, in effect, the policing of the country was the responsibility of part-time unpaid amateurs.

The next great step in the development of the criminal justice system came with an Act of Parliament called the Statute of Winchester in 1285, in the reign of Edward I. This not only forced every able-bodied man between the ages of 15 and 60 to keep weapons for the maintenance of the King's Peace, but made extra provision for walled towns. During the nights, when the town gates were shut and presumably none of the parish constables was on duty, a nightwatchman was to be employed to arrest villains and suspected or suspicious persons. Thus the policing arrangements in the towns had an extra tier of police (the Town Watch) to that in the countryside.

The Statute of Winchester made no mention of the System of Frankpledge, so it is assumed that by then it was no longer used, and that everyone was content to leave the keeping of law and order to the parish constable. But the Statute of Winchester revived a technique of policing that had been in decline: Hue and Cry.

Hue and Cry was a very ancient custom. If a person was spotted who was believed to be guilty of a crime, either being committed there and then or at some time in the past, and was attempting to evade arrest, then it was required by law for every person who could to chase after the culprit, shouting and blowing horns if they had them. Those chasing the villain should also tell everybody to join in the chase until the person had been pursued and captured. All those who joined in the Hue and Cry were justified in capturing the fleeing criminal, using force if necessary.

In 1327, just forty-two years after the Statute of Winchester, King Edward III came to the English throne. An angry young man, determined to restore the power of law and order after his father's disastrous reign, he had to wait for three years before he could rid himself of the regent, Roger, Earl of Mortimer, and take control of government himself. But when he did, he quickly showed the skills that would make his reign one of the better ones of medieval England.

In the remarkably short space of time up to 1368, the offices and duties of the magistrates were examined and legally redefined by various Acts of Parliament. These included the establishment of their own court, the Quarter Sessions, so named because it was held every three months – an arrangement which was destined to last for over 600 years before any alteration came along, which was the Crown Court in 1971.

And so it was that by the fourteenth century the parish constable and the magistrate had become the two officials that ran the policing system of Great Britain. This was the 'old police' system, and it would last well into the nineteenth century.

Gradually over the years, parish constables had more and more duties placed upon them, especially in the Tudor times. However, many of these new duties were more concerned with civil administration than criminal behaviour. For instance, it was the parish constable's duty to see that the roads and bridges of the village were kept in good order, that the local tradesmen gave proper services and that the villagers went to church when they should.

The Breakdown of the 'Old Police'

This watering down of the original duties of the parish constable continued, and by the eighteenth century he had become more the representative of the local magistrate than of the villagers; the law and order side of his duties was secondary to the civil matters he had to attend to. The early eighteenth century, therefore, saw the start of the breakdown of the parish constable system as a criminal law enforcement system. This was not helped by a practice which gained ground quite speedily: the substitute system.

The men chosen as parish constables by the parish council did not wish to be unpaid policemen for a year, so there were men available who would undertake to be substitutes, and for a financial fee serve as parish constable for the year instead of the chosen man. This invariably led to the same man serving year after year, with the added disadvantage of advancing age and increasing incompetence – or even corruption. But if the substitute system caused the old police system to creak, then the real death blow was the Industrial Revolution.

Great Britain was the first country in the world to experience that great spurt of mechanisation that the historian Arnold Toynbee christened 'the Industrial Revolution'. Instead of people having work brought to them in their houses, enterprising men started to build factories, meaning the workers had to go to the factories to do their work. To accommodate all the workers who came, houses were built around the factories, and the villages started growing out to their boundaries and met with their neighbouring villages, which were growing just as quickly. Great towns and cities grew up, and as soon as that happened the parish constable system could not cope because it had been designed to work in small villages, not large towns.

It is always amusing to read in the newspapers and hear on television of small villages being described as 'sleepy', because the person who could say such a thing has obviously never lived in one; 'sleepy' is the very last thing they are. In a village, everybody knows everybody else's business, and there is always the seething undercurrent of village gossip going on. And that is the one essential ingredient that made the parish constable system work – and work well – for nearly 1,000 years.

If a crime occurred in the village, somebody would know who did it, including, of course, the parish constable himself, who also lived in the village and was obviously in touch with the grapevine as well. It was thus an easy task for the constable to arrest the culprit and take him before the local magistrate, who would then either bail him to a court or, if the crime was serious, commit him straight to prison to await trial.

Nevertheless, with the Industrial Revolution and the coming of the big towns, this village grapevine did not exist anymore, and people did not know each other's business. Crimes thus became undetected; criminals escaped justice; and

1 & 2 Staffs of office of a parish constable. As the parish constable was not in uniform, these staffs denoted his authority to act and were normally painted with the name of the parish for which the constable had jurisdiction. They were not meant as weapons of offence, but human nature being what it is, it is fortunate that these staffs cannot speak.

the crime rate escalated, which the part-time amateurs or decrepit substitutes of the parish constable system were powerless to control.

And no more so than in the biggest city of all: London. We know that crime was a big problem in London from the early eighteenth century onwards, and that people were worried about it. We know this because they wrote books about it, which have survived, where we can read their pleadings with the government to do something about it, such as introducing some form of full-time police force. Britain was the only country in Europe not to have full-time police – and very proud of it they were as well. The majority of people thought that a preventative police force was unconstitutional, and not what was wanted at all – too continental.

Instead of an organised police force, Britain relied on the deterrent principle to combat crime. That is why the punishments in Britain were extremely severe. This severity had started in 1723, when some poachers, who had blacked up their faces so as to make identification difficult, had been caught and then hanged under powers given by a new Act of Parliament which had just been passed to discourage lawlessness. This legislation, which then came to be nicknamed the 'Black Act' after the poachers, is infamous for introducing that most notorious of penal codes in the entire history of this country: the 'Bloody Code'.

Lasting for over 100 years, the Bloody Code would eventually list nearly 230 offences as punishable by death, including crimes such as impersonating a Chelsea pensioner, writing a threatening letter and consorting with gypsies. All of these were capital offences under the Bloody Code.

However, it was dawning on some men that this deterrent system was not actually reducing crime. The deterrent system only works if it is accompanied by a totally efficient and foolproof method of catching the wrongdoer, which would make people think twice before embarking on any crime, instilling into them the fear that being caught was inevitable. But the only means of catching criminals at this time was the old parish constable system, and this had been utterly emasculated by the advance of industrialisation.

Having no lead from central government, the only way open to people was to try to combat the enormous crime problem themselves. And so evolved the two major private crime-fighting initiatives associated with the eighteenth century. The first was the idea of the Felons' Associations, but being only of interest to a selected few, this plan was destined to peter out as the nineteenth century progressed and as the need for them decreased. The second initiative is perhaps the most well known – the Bow Street Runners – and is by far the most important, as it would eventually lead directly to the establishment of the 'new police'.

The Felons' Associations

Contrary to received and popular opinion, these associations were not private police forces, but were groups of prosperous people pooling their money so as to combat the exorbitant court costs of the time. The earliest known is probably the Bradfield Association in Yorkshire, started in 1737, followed by the Totley and Dore Association, also in Yorkshire, started in 1742.

During the eighteenth century, the system of bringing criminals to justice in law courts was getting more and more haphazard because of the deterioration of the parish constable system. If the offender was caught (and it was a big 'if'), the victim had to pursue his own claim through the courts because there was no official body to do it for him, which meant he had to pay all the expenses. Sometimes, because of this, deals were struck between the criminal and the victim for the return of the property intact for assurance of no prosecution (read about Jonathan Wild later). This was obviously completely unacceptable to right-thinking people.

Each association member paid an annual subscription which went into a central fund. Two basic services were offered: the first involved circulating reward notices for the return of the property or for information, and the second was to pay any ensuing court costs from the central fund. And, of course, the associations only provided this service to their own members; in other words, those who had something worth losing in the first place and who could afford the annual subscription. This made them totally out of reach to the average common working man and, as such, the associations were never very efficient as crime-fighting institutions or as deterrents against crime. So as soon as the organised police forces started appearing, first in London and then in the provinces where criminal prosecutions before the court cost the victim nothing, the associations declined quite quickly. Surprisingly enough, however, thirty-four associations are

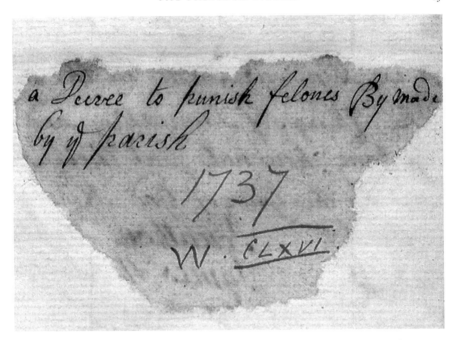

3 The oldest Felons' Association was the Bradfield Association in the West Riding of Yorkshire, formed in 1737. This is the association's first prospectus and membership list.

TERMS, or PROPOSALS,

FOR THE

MANAGEMENT

OF THE FOLLOWING

SUBSCRIPTIONS,

TO PREVENT

HORSE and SHEEP STEALING,

In the County of NORTHAMPTON;

And to Prosecute OFFENDERS.

I. THAT every Subscriber pays Ten Shillings for the Year, (to wit) from the first Day of *January*, 1781, to the first Day of *January* following; and that such Subscriptions be paid to Mr. JOHN HODSON, Attorney at Law, at *Wellingborough* in the said County, who is to continue Agent for the said Year.

II. THAT every Subscriber will keep proper Descriptions of his or her Horses Marks and Ages; and that on losing any, which are suspected to be stolen, he or she shall immediately give Notice to the said JOHN HODSON, in Person, or by Letter unsealed, when such Horse was first missing—the Place from whence lost—the Age and Description of the Horse—and what Road they may have Reason to think such Horse is gone, that Messengers may be sent in Pursuit.

III. THAT every Subscriber shall mark his or her Sheep with his or her usual Sheep-Brand; and on paying the Subscription-Money, deliver to the said JOHN HODSON the Mark or Form of the Brand he or she shall make Use of, and also on what Part of the Sheep placed; and that on losing any Sheep, which are suspected to be stolen, he or she shall immediately give Notice to the said JOHN HODSON, in such Manner as is mentioned in the second Article.

IV. THAT

4 The majority of the Felons' Associations faded away after the introduction of the paid police forces. However, thirty-four associations still exist, but purely as dining clubs. The Wellingborough Association, formed in 1781, is the oldest of these surviving associations.

still in existence today, but these are now nothing more than dining clubs, where the Annual General Meeting lasts for ten minutes and the dinner afterwards lasts for five hours.

The Bow Street Runners

More legend than fact is known about the Bow Street Runners because hardly any records have survived. During the Gordon Riots (anti-Catholic riots that rampaged in London for ten days in June 1780), the Bow Street Magistrates' Office was plundered and set on fire, thus losing all the records up to that date. Also, in 1839, when the Runners were disbanded, the records of the intervening years were deliberately destroyed because nobody thought them interesting enough to keep. However, we can make an intelligent guess of the history of the Runners based on other sources which have survived.[2]

Appointed in 1729 as magistrate for Westminster and Middlesex, with an office in what is now Leicester Square, Thomas de Veil was unlike his contemporary magistrates in that he did his own detective work. He had to. If he wanted to reduce the crime that he found around him, and having no organised and trained police force, he had no option but to do it himself. With an army background (he had been a captain and had seen action in Portugal), de Veil was made of stern stuff, and was not afraid of standing up to the criminal gangs that roamed London unchecked and that had previously intimidated other magistrates.[3]

It was through his direct influence, despite attempts on his life, that two of the most notorious gangs of London, the Wreathcock Gang (named after its leader) and the Black Boy Alley Gang, were broken up and brought to justice. He started making some inroads into the crime problem and was eventually awarded a government salary and a knighthood.

De Veil was the first person to make some attempt to reduce the enormous amount of crime that was endemic in London at the time. Having moved his office to Bow Street in 1739, his influence stretched over what are now the Home Counties, and he was the first detective to give help to provincial authorities. It is surprising, therefore, that no biography of him has been written and that he is not even in the *Dictionary of National Biography*. He died in September 1746.

Perhaps the reason why he does not have an entry is down to his personal habits, of which the prudish Victorian compilers of the *DNB* did not approve. If any female came to him for help but had no money to pay for his services, de Veil would extract his fee in kind, for which purposes he had a bedroom next to his office. Consequently, the number of illegitimate offspring he produced is unknown, but it has been estimated at as many as thirty.

After de Veil's death, an incompetent 80-year-old magistrate named Poulson took over. Not surprisingly, the crime situation started slipping back to its old ways. But in 1748, the well-known playwright Henry Fielding took over at Bow Street as magistrate. Having made little money from writing plays or as a barrister, Fielding was pleased to accept the Duke of Bedford's offer to be the Bow Street magistrate.

The Duke of Bedford was Secretary of State for the Southern Department, which in effect made him the Home Secretary, and he had been persuaded to give Fielding the job on the recommendation of a mutual friend, George (later Lord) Lyttelton. Fielding was determined to carry on de Veil's work.

So it was that one year later, in 1749, Fielding gathered together a few like-minded men, all ex-parish constables, to form a group to combat the ever-increasing crime problem, and to clear the streets of robbers and thieves. So successful did he become that he applied for, and received, financial help from central government. Although his men were originally called 'Mr Fielding's People', eventually the term 'Bow Street Runners' was applied to them.

So the Bow Street Runners were formed and received an annual salary. However, this was not enough to live on, but as a supplement there was the wonderful system called 'the Parliamentary Award'.

Due to the lack of any effective police force, the government paid a Parliamentary Award of money to anyone who brought a criminal to justice. This award was on a sliding scale; for example, theft at £10, burglary at £40. Unfortunately, this had led to some men taking advantage, the most notorious being Jonathan Wild, the thief taker. Wild had opened an office purporting to restore stolen property back to its rightful owner. The property had, of course, been stolen in the first place by the large gang of criminals organised by Wild himself. When Wild thought that members of his gang had committed a big enough crime to be worth his while, Wild 'grassed' on them to the authorities and thus collected the financial benefits. Even in those venal times this had been looked upon with distaste, and Jonathan Wild himself was hung in 1725, ostensibly for receiving a reward to restore stolen property.

The Bow Street Runners, however, worked the Parliamentary Awards system honestly and, because of this, investigated crime free of charge, which naturally encouraged the public to go to them.

Henry Fielding died in 1754, to be succeeded as magistrate by his half-brother John Fielding, who was blind. John Fielding increased and expanded the Bow Street detective groups, and started a series of horse and then foot patrols, mainly along the main roads into and out of London. He also founded a criminal record office and started a series of broadsheets giving names of criminals and news of crimes committed; these were the forerunners of the modern-day *Police Gazette*. By 1792, seven other offices of the Bow Street Runners had been started in London, and eventually, by the 1820s, it is estimated that the Bow Street patrols totalled about 450 men.

Although kindly looked upon by the government, the Bow Street Runners and patrols were still a private enterprise. In 1785 the government had made a half-hearted attempt to establish a police force in London. The Prime Minister, William Pitt the Younger, had introduced a bill into Parliament, but because this proposed separating the police away from the control of the magistrates, the bill was shelved in the face of great hostility, both from the public and from the magistrates who were due to lose their powers. It seemed that central government was content to let the situation continue, with the policing of London in the hands of private citizens.

Despite the Bow Street Runners' best efforts, however, the crime situation worsened, and other men were now drawing the attention of central government to it and the fact that there was no police force to combat it. The most famous of these was Patrick Colquhoun, a Glaswegian merchant living and trading in London. In 1797 he published his book, *A Treatise on the Police of the Metropolis*, where he drew up a blueprint for a London police force under unified control,

A

TREATISE

ON THE

POLICE OF THE METROPOLIS:

CONTAINING A DETAIL OF THE

VARIOUS CRIMES AND MISDEMEANORS

*By which Public and Private Property and Security are, at present,
injured and endangered:*

AND

SUGGESTING REMEDIES

FOR THEIR

PREVENTION.

The SEVENTH EDITION, Corrected and considerably enlarged.

BY P. COLQUHOUN, LL.D.

*Acting as a Magistrate for the Counties of Middlesex, Surry, Kent, and Essex.—
For the City and Liberty of Westminster, and for the Liberty of the Tower of London.*

Meminerint legum conditores, illas ad proximum hunc finem accommodare ;
Scelera videlicet arcenda, refrænandaque vitia ac morum pravitatem.
Judices pariter leges illas cum vigore, æquitate, integritate, publicæque utili-
tatis amore curent exequi; ut justitia et virtus omnes societatis ordines prevadant.
Industriaque simul et Temperantia inertiæ locum assumant et prodigalitatis.

LONDON:

PRINTED FOR J. MAWMAN, CADELL AND DAVIES, R. FAULDER, CLARKE AND
SONS, LONGMAN, HURST, REES AND ORME, VERNOR, HOOD, AND SHARPE,
H. D. SYMONDS, LACKINGTON, ALLEN, AND CO. SCATCHERD AND LETTER-
MAN, R. LEA, B. CROSBY AND CO. WYNNE AND SON, R. PHENEY, BLACKS
AND PARRY, J. ASPERNE ; AND WILSON AND SPENCE, YORK.

1806.

Printed by Bye and Law, St. John's Square, Clerkenwell.

5 Patrick Colquhoun's *A Treatise on the Police of the Metropolis* went through several editions, calling attention to the crime situation in London. This is the seventh edition, printed in 1806.

separating judicial and police functions. Although he failed to get the government interested, he himself succeeded in setting up the Marine Police in 1798,
which became the Thames River Police in 1800, to combat the huge smuggling
industry in and around the London docks. In this enterprise, Colquhoun had the
help of his friend Jeremy Bentham, who added his not inconsiderable influence
to the idea of police reform.

Bentham had helped to formulate the Utilitarian philosophy – 'the greatest
happiness for the greatest number' – and in 1789 was applying his philosophy to
police reform, when he wrote his great *Introduction to the Principals of Morals and
Legislation*. Bentham, his ideas and his disciples, were to come to dominate the
majority of the nineteenth century, especially when applied to legal and social
reforms.

With the voices of influential men now adding weight, the crescendo for police
reform grew as the eighteenth century turned into the nineteenth. Half-hearted
attempts to look at the situation were made by parliamentary committees in 1816
and 1818, but these came to nothing. However, in 1822 on to the scene came the
one man who would do something about it: Sir Robert Peel.

Eventual Action by the Home Secretary, Sir Robert Peel

Robert Peel became the Home Secretary in 1822. An astute politician, Peel was also pro-police. He had set up a police force in Ireland just eight years previously, when he was the Chief Secretary for Ireland in Lord Liverpool's government. Ironically enough, he had taken as his blueprint Pitt's failed bill of 1785.

Now promoted to Home Secretary, Peel could see for himself the crime situation in London and the attempts to control it. So in 1822 he personally established a committee to look into the matter, with himself as chairman.

As well as the Bow Street Runners and patrols, London still had its parish constables, appointed by the parish vestries. And it still had its magistrates, who in those days had administrative powers as well as judicial powers and were thus in charge of the parish constables. Peel knew he would face hostility from the magistrates because they feared their power was waning, and he also feared public hostility, no doubt simply because of the English aversion to change. So he was content to wait – for years if necessary.

As such, it was not until 1826 that he drew up a plan for a police force in London. Although resigning himself to biding his time, it was only one year later that his opportunity arose.

During 1827 there was such an enormous increase in crime which caused so much public unrest that Peel felt convinced that the time was right to make his move. In February 1828 his proposition for the appointment of a committee 'to enquire into the cause of the increase of the number of commitments and convictions in London and Middlesex for the year 1827; and into the state of the police of the Metropolis and the district adjoining thereto' was passed completely unopposed. Thus Peel's immense political genius showed when his real objective was wrapped up in a smokescreen.

The committee made its report within six months, in July 1828. It was all Peel wanted of it. The report recommended a full-time police force for London, the creation of an Office of Police under the direction of the Home Secretary and paid for by public funds, and a specially raised police rate.

The report, however, did not apply to the City of London, as that was always considered a special case, being entirely separated from Greater London. So the City carried on with its system of watchkeepers, nicknamed the 'Charleys', for an incredible ten years before events forced it to establish its own 'new police' force in 1839. But more of that later.

Based on this report, in April 1829 Peel introduced into Parliament 'A Bill for improving the police in the Metropolis'. It is astonishing to find that, despite years of public hostility and apathy for a full-time police force, the 1829 police bill was passed on Sunday 19 July, virtually unopposed, and with scarcely any debate.

Thus the Metropolitan Police Act 1829 was brought about by the political genius of Robert Peel, causing generations of policemen to be forever nick-

6 Sir Robert Peel (1788–1850).

named 'Bobbies' or 'Peelers', which is all very complimentary to Peel, but the credit was not his alone. Peel would not have achieved what he did without the earlier works of Thomas de Veil, Henry and John Fielding, William Pitt, Patrick Colquhoun and Jeremy Bentham.

It is a measure of how keen Peel was on police reform that, at the same time as all this was going on, he was thinking about the counties of the country as well. Consequently, he tried an experiment in the County of Cheshire of trying to breathe new life into the parish constable system.

His choice of Cheshire over any other county is interesting; why he chose it is not known, although he himself came from Bury in Lancashire, the neighbouring county. Nevertheless, Peel introduced the Cheshire police bill into Parliament and it was passed on Monday 1 June 1829, one month, it will be noted, before the passing of the Metropolitan Police Act. This Cheshire Constabulary of professional police officers thus predates the Metropolitan Police, and would be in operation for seven years before it came under any form of critical scrutiny by the Royal Commission of 1836. But more of that in Chapter 4.

Meanwhile, in the Metropolitan Police, the baton now passes to Charles Rowan and Richard Mayne. Although far less well known than Peel, both deserve as much credit, for if Peel was the 'architect' of the 'new police' in Britain, it was undoubtedly Rowan and Mayne who were the 'building contractors'.

TWO

1829–34

Sir Robert Peel had decided that he wanted two Joint Commissioners of the Metropolitan Police. The posts were not advertised and Peel decided not to accept applications for the positions. Instead, he wanted to appoint them himself and he had very definite ideas about the men he wanted. He was looking for men whose previous professions equipped them for what he believed to be the ideal mix for a police force.

First of all, he wanted a soldier who also knew about policing. For his second commissioner he wanted somebody with a knowledge of the law; in other words, a 'sensible lawyer'.[1]

Peel's beliefs had been formulated fifteen years earlier. In 1814, whilst Chief Secretary for Ireland in Lord Liverpool's government, he had been largely responsible for the establishment of the Irish Constabulary, where the politics of Ireland had necessitated a militarily structured police. Initially, therefore, he looked to Ireland for his soldier/policeman, hoping to find his man there. No suitable candidate appeared, so in June 1829 Peel offered the post of the 'soldier' commissioner to a certain Lieutenant-Colonel James Shaw, who declined.

His second choice, however, accepted. Charles Rowan was a colonel of the Oxfordshire and Buckinghamshire Light Infantry, the 52nd Regiment of the Line, and was a 'graduate' of the 'Shorncliffe Experiment'. This had been the brainchild of Sir John Moore, and was to be highly influential upon Rowan.

In 1803 General Sir John Moore was part of the army which was given the task of repelling Napoleon's expected invasion of England. At Shorncliffe Camp, near to Sandgate in Kent, he decided to reform his regiment, the 52nd, along with the 43rd and 90th. This would eventually lead to the system of Light Infantry, but although he was not to know it, it was Moore's ideas on regimental discipline and crime that would have the most lasting effect on the young Lieutenant Charles Rowan.

Amongst Moore's reforms was a system of regimental discipline, in which he laid down the concept that if the emphasis for his officers was on the prevention of indiscipline and crime at the outset, then there would be no need for punishment afterwards. It was this ideal, instilled at Shorncliffe, that Rowan would take through into later life. Rowan went on to fight at Waterloo with the 52nd, where a severe wound cut short his army career.[2]

The lawyer commissioner was easier to find. Recommended by 'leading members of the judiciary', Richard Mayne was a 32-year-old Irish barrister of Lincoln's Inn, who had been busy building himself a reputation. Mayne accepted the challenge and so became the second Joint Commissioner of the Metropolitan Police.[3]

It is not precisely known how Peel knew of Rowan and Mayne; he had certainly never met either of them, nor had they met each other, and why these two were chosen is one of the intriguing questions of police history. Happily, the two men hit it off straight away, and in the twenty-one years of co-operation between the two, no evidence exists of any serious disagreement between them.[4]

If Peel chose Rowan and Mayne without any prior knowledge, then his fluke of good fortune is to be marvelled at, because it is to Charles Rowan and Richard Mayne that the British police service arguably owes its greatest debt. From the inventive competence of these two springs the modern British police service, and there are many administrative innovations and procedures introduced by them in 1829 which are still recognisable in the police service of today.

Rowan and Mayne were sworn in as Joint Commissioners of the Metropolitan Police on Tuesday 7 July 1829, and they got to work immediately; in effect, they had to create a police force and its administration entirely from scratch. Although they were given a small secretarial staff, it was immediately realised that financial expertise was also needed. Thus was born the office of Receiver of the Metropolitan Police, which, in effect, is the treasurer and financial controller. Appointed on the very same day as the two commissioners, John Wray, another barrister, was the first Receiver. He retired in April 1860, to be replaced by Maurice Drummond.[5]

At first, the Joint Commissioners were given a room in the Home Office, but a permanent home was required. The resulting address has now become totally synonymous with the Metropolitan Police: 4 Whitehall Place, otherwise known as Scotland Yard.

Into Scotland Yard moved the two commissioners, ready to start work to organise the 'new police'. The term 'new police' was given at the time to mark the difference between the old system of parish constables and watchkeepers, and the Metropolitan Police system of professional, full-time organised men, whose only source of income was from being a policeman.

The organisation needed for the 'new police' was a gigantic task, as neither Rowan nor Mayne had any previous experience of police administration. Yet in an astonishing period of just twelve weeks (to the day), the Metropolitan Police was formed, equipped, organised and manned, so that at 6 p.m. on Tuesday

29 September 1829, the very first Metropolitan Police officers marched out of their stations on to the streets of London.

A look at the work achieved during these twelve weeks emphasises what a magnificent effort this was, and why the British police service owes such a debt to Rowan and Mayne. London was divided into divisions, each division into subdivisions, and each subdivision into the area patrolled by one police officer; these areas were called 'beats'.

Why they chose this name is not entirely known; suggestions include 'beating the bounds', the regular beat, a person's habitual round, the beat of the feet in slowly walking round – various suggestions have been made, but there is no proof either way. However, this term is still used today, 180 years later, to define the area patrolled by one constable.

Each division had to be provided with accommodation for use as police stations. Originally, there were five divisions, but a sixth was added working from Scotland Yard itself. These first divisions covered the centre of London, where it was considered imperative to get the 'new police' up and running. Eventually, however, as experience was gained, seventeen divisions were considered necessary to cover the whole of London right up to the outskirts, and it was realised that it would be at least a year before these remaining divisions were fully working.

Each division was designated by a letter, and by June 1830, all divisions were in place:

A Division	Whitehall
B Division	Westminster
C Division	Saint James
D Division	Marylebone
E Division	Holborn
F Division	Covent Garden
G Division	Finsbury
H Division	Whitechapel
I	not used
J	not used
K Division	Stepney
L Division	Lambeth
M Division	Southwark
N Division	Islington
O	not used
P Division	Camberwell
Q	not used
R Division	Greenwich
S Division	Hampstead

T Division	Kensington
U	not used
V Division	Wandsworth[6]

Each division had its station house, which quickly became known by the street it was in. Accommodation was also required for constables, both married and single, and by the end of 1829 nearly 100 houses had been leased by Wray for use as dormitories, which were called section houses; the word 'barracks' was never used.[7]

Due to Rowan's military background, the rank structure was modelled on his army experience. Each division was placed in the care of a superintendent, who had four inspectors under him. Each inspector was in command of four sergeants, who were each in charge of nine constables.

The names for the ranks of superintendent and inspector were from previously used terms in the 'old police' system. A superintending constable was in charge of several parish constables, and the term 'inspector' was used in Fielding's Bow Street system. The name of 'sergeant' was borrowed from the army, and for the lowest rank there could be no other name than 'constable', it being the oldest name for a law enforcement officer in the country. With a few additions along the way, these are the same ranks still in use today.

Sir Robert Peel had always maintained that the Metropolitan Police should not have direct officer entry, and would not be like the army and navy with their directly commissioned officers. The higher ranks should only be filled by promotion from the ranks below and not by some outsider merely because of his social standing. This concept was fully endorsed by Rowan and Mayne, and it was a policy they maintained. However, it only seemed to apply to the ranks up to superintendent.

The Metropolitan Police had to wait for an incredible 143 years, until 1972, to get its first commissioner (Sir Robert Mark) who had learned his trade by walking the beat as a constable (in the Manchester City Police). This same concept of directly appointed commissioners and chief constables was to be prevalent throughout the whole of the British police service, especially the county forces after 1839, and remnants of it could still be seen as late as the Second World War.

The uniform was also chosen by Rowan and Mayne, and they chose a dark blue, thereby condemning generations of policemen to be nicknamed 'the boys in blue'. Although faced with many suggestions from interested parties, among which were fantastic red creations with lots of braid and badges, they deliberately chose the understated dark blue swallow-tail coat and trousers, based on the men's fashions of the day, to emphasise that this was a civilian rather than a military force. The top hat was especially strengthened, not only to provide protection for the head, but so that it could be stood on to peep over high walls.

Each policeman was to have his own unique number on his uniform so that members of the public could identify him without having to ask his name. Because the tunics were buttoned up to the neck, the numerals, plus the man's division letter, were placed on the collar, first in cloth, later in metal. And because they were worn on the collar, they, not unnaturally, were referred to as 'collar numbers'.

But in the 1950s, when high-necked tunics were replaced by v-necked coats, shirt and tie, the numerals were placed on the shoulder epaulettes because there was no collar. So what were they called then? They remained 'collar numbers', and are still called that to this day, even though they have not been on the collar for over fifty years. The police service is nothing but conservative.

Another device adopted was the armlet, and this was as a direct result of the 'permanent uniform rule'. Peel, Rowan and Mayne were so fearful of the new force being seen as 'police spies' and 'agents provocateurs' that they decreed that the policemen should wear their uniform at all times. The London public, they reasoned, would want their policemen where they could see them, and if that meant permanent uniform, so be it.

This led to many complaints in the first few months, as members of the public had been refused help by policemen in uniform who, at the time, said they were 'off duty'. The result, introduced in late 1829, was the armlet, which was only worn when the officer was on duty.

Worn only by sergeants and constables, the armlet was a strip of cloth just under 2 inches wide (about 5 centimetres), with thin vertical stripes of blue and white. Originally it was worn around the right cuff by sergeants and around the left cuff by constables, but shortly after its introduction it was assigned to the left cuff for both ranks.

Since they also adopted the permanent uniform rule, the later provincial forces, both borough and county, also used the armlet device, although the provincial forces, especially the counties, tended to have horizontal rather than vertical stripes. In the 1938 film *Ask a Policeman* starring Will Hay, the horizontal stripes of a county police force can clearly be seen; whilst in one scene of the 1949 film *The Blue Lamp*, Jack Warner, playing PC George Dixon of the Metropolitan Police, is clearly seen fixing his vertically striped armlet to his left cuff.

With the relaxation of the permanent uniform rule, the wearing of the armlet was unnecessary, and the majority of provincial forces had ceased its use by the outbreak of the Second World War; but the Metropolitan Police persisted until 1968.[8] Thus armlets have not been seen on 99 per cent of the country's policemen for at least fifty years.

Yet quite often today, some cartoonists and artists insist on drawing policemen wearing armlets – some even putting them on both cuffs. Whether this indicates persisting folk memories or the artists' surprising lack of observation of the world around them is open to debate. However, there is still one force that wears the

7 The rattle was used to summon assistance or raise an alarm, but could, if the occasion required it, be used as another weapon on top of the truncheon. The provincial forces also used the rattles. Whistles replaced rattles in the Metropolitan Police in 1885, when it was found that rattles were audible over 700 yards, but whistles audible over 900 yards.

armlet – the City of London Police – so errant artists perhaps could be forgiven, although the City armlet is vertical stripes of red and white.

The pay structure of the Metropolitan Police had to be decided on. Superintendents were to receive £200 per year; inspectors £100; sergeants £1 2s 6d per week; and constables £1 1s per week, less 2s for 'free' accommodation. Today's equivalent values would be: superintendents £9,900 per year; inspectors £4,950 per year; sergeants £55.70 per week; and constables £52 per week, less £4.95 for accommodation.[9] Thankfully, this low level of payment has not persisted to the present day. Police salaries for 2010 were: superintendent £62,298; inspector £48,840; sergeant £36,519 (£702 per week); and constable £23,259 (£447 per week).[10]

So judging by the comparison with today's values, we can see that the Metropolitan Police was not a highly paid occupation. Because of this, it is surprising that so many skilled and semi-skilled tradesmen applied to join. It would have been expected for the bulk of the recruits to be from the labouring classes, as they would already be used to low pay and harsh conditions, and would have probably viewed the police, in the early days, as a social step-up.

Tradesmen, on the other hand, would already have been earning a decent wage in acceptable conditions, and some may have been taking a wage cut to join the police. To find so many skilled tradesmen being recruited is difficult to understand. Perhaps the novelty of the occasion overwhelmed financial apprehensions.

Nearly 1,000 men were recruited initially, but by early June 1830 the force had increased to over 3,000. Of these, 1,154 were labourers, but the rest were skilled tradesmen, consisting of 135 butchers, 109 bakers, 198 shoemakers, 52 tailors, 402 soldiers, 205 servants, 141 carpenters, 75 bricklayers, 55 blacksmiths, 20 turners, 152 clerks, 141 shop assistants, 141 superior mechanics, 46 plumbers and painters, 101 sailors, 51 weavers and 8 stonemasons.[11] But all these were from the working class, or what the Victorians would later call the 'respectable' working class. Where is the middle class? Where are the solicitors, the bankers, the schoolteachers and so on? The low police salaries were clearly the greatest factor, and perhaps the middle class thought that working for the police was socially below them, something that only the servant class did. It was this perception that it was a working-class service that would bedevil the British police until well into the twentieth century.

The enforcing of laws by working-class men on other working-class men seemed to be acceptable. But that raised the intriguing prospect of the working-class police trying to enforce laws on their 'social superiors'. And as we shall see, this would prove totally excruciating for the police for many a long year.

Although not dealing with practicalities, the *General Instruction Book* was to be a model of its kind, so far as it went. 'It must be understood,' wrote Rowan in the introduction, 'that the principal object to be attained is the Prevention of Crime. To this great end every effort of the Police is to be directed.' These were sentiments that had already been voiced by the pioneers of policing reform, namely the Fielding brothers and Patrick Colquhoun. Rowan, however, gave them added impetus by the lessons he had learned from his days at Shorncliffe.

The *General Instruction Book* was a combined effort between the two commissioners and was in two parts: Part 1 dealt with the organisation and the theoretical duties of policemen, and was obviously written by Charles Rowan; Part 2 dealt with the legal powers of a constable as defined by common law and relevant Acts of Parliament, and this was obviously the work of Richard Mayne. Copies of it were printed and circulated to all members of the force by Saturday 26 September, three days before the magical first day.[12]

Thus was the Metropolitan Police established and organised in 1829 and 1830. Looking back, it appears to be an easy, straightforward task. But what followed was far from easy, because the new force had to face the London public, and hostility to the new force was immediate, all-embracing and violent. Opposition to the police was on two levels: from the social and political hierarchy, and from the working class.

8 Oil lamps with sliding shutters were used on night duty. Several models appeared, but this one was designed by Philip Bicknell, chief constable of Lincolnshire, 1856–1902, containing the flat surface at the top for heating a cup of coffee or tea.

Sir Robert Peel was a Tory and was Home Secretary in the Duke of Wellington's Tory government. So the Metropolitan Police was a Tory creation. In November 1830, however, the Tory government suddenly resigned, to be replaced by a Whig government under Earl Grey. This meant a Whig Home Secretary just fourteen months after the establishment of the Metropolitan Police. The Whigs had been bitterly opposed to any form of organised police; indeed, there was a supposed manifesto pledge to disband the force.

The new Home Secretary, William Lamb, 2nd Viscount Melbourne, even though he was a political and ministerial novice, could see that to disband the Metropolitan Police was probably not the wisest of things he could do. But he could make life difficult for Rowan and Mayne, who now, without Peel's backing, were very vulnerable – and make life difficult he did.

Due to the feelings of the times, agitation for social reform was growing and public disquiet was mounting throughout 1831; in that year the National Political Union of the Working Classes was founded. Throughout London, public disorder was being fomented by the National Political Union, which increased when it advertised a large meeting to be held on Monday 7 November 1831 at White Conduit House, Pentonville. Knowing that Melbourne would probably use this meeting as an excuse to attack, ridicule and belittle the Metropolitan Police if it was unable to control the expected crowds, Rowan decided that he would play politics as well. He wrote to all London magistrates in a circular, suggesting that special constables be sworn in to deal with the expected disturbance. The recruitment of special constables on an ad hoc basis had been made possible under the newly passed Special Constables Act (1 and 2 William IV, Chapter 41), which Melbourne had steered through Parliament on 15 October, and which put the resulting special constables directly under the control of the London magistrates, and not the commissioners. This was obviously a direct critical gibe at Rowan and Mayne.

Rowan's tongue-in-cheek bluff worked. The meeting was cancelled. But unbeknown to Rowan, Melbourne had ordered two London magistrates, Frederick Roe and Allan Laing, to attend the meeting.

The establishment of the Metropolitan Police had not replaced the previous system, it was initially a supplement to it. The London magistrates, therefore, being supposedly in charge of the parish constables, were opposed to the 'new police' as they saw them gradually taking all their powers away from them. And there was nobody more opposed than Frederick Roe.

Even though the meeting had been cancelled, Roe demanded of the superintendent of the division, which included Pentonville, the Metropolitan Police manpower dispositions had the meeting gone ahead. The superintendent duly obliged. However, obviously wishing to pick a quarrel, Roe complained to Melbourne of the superintendent's attitude.

Letters winged backwards and forwards, but Melbourne's indecision left the matter unresolved, the whole crux of the matter being, of course, to determine who would be in charge of London's police: the Metropolitan Police commissioners or the London magistrates. This matter would eventually be resolved – in the commissioners' favour – but a lot would happen in the meantime.

The following year, 1832, the chief magistrate at Bow Street passed away and Melbourne, possibly being deliberately provocative, replaced him with Frederick Roe. Rowan and Mayne now faced years of sustained dual attack from Melbourne and Roe.

Working-class opposition to the Metropolitan Police was also prolonged and violent. The Metropolitan Police had been established because of the rising crime rate – the 1827 crime figures resulted in Peel's committee of 1828. A rising crime rate meant either more criminals or the same number of criminals committing more crime, or a combination.

Either way, criminals were on the streets and had been used to 'getting away with it' for a long time. Now suddenly faced with a body of properly organised men who were trying to stop them getting away with their crimes, it is no wonder that mayhem ensued.

The working classes reacted with the only weapon at their disposal: assaults, both verbal and physical. Immediately, posters and broadsheets were circulated calling for the abolition of 'Peel's Bloody Gang' and the 'Blue Lobsters' (presumably from the colour of the uniform). Press campaigns railed against the 'secret' activities and the 'tyranny' of the new police.[13]

Reports of physical assaults on policemen in the early years are many. For instance, one policeman was held down whilst a horse-drawn cab was driven over him. Another policeman was deliberately lured into a pub and then systematically beaten up by a professional bare-knuckle pugilist.[14] Strangely enough, no figures for assaults on the police are readily available for these early years. The earliest published statistics are for 1869–72, during which time there were a total of 15,933 attacks, an average of 3,983 a year over the four years, equating to a Metropolitan policeman being assaulted once every two years.[15]

Sometimes, physical assault took on a more traumatic character, and had the potential to turn into murder. The first Metropolitan Police officer to be murdered on duty occurred just nine months and one day after the force had been on the streets. On Monday 28 June 1830, in Somers Town, PC Joseph Grantham, aged 31, died from a massive brain haemorrhage after being kicked in the head. He had been set upon when he had tried to separate two drunken Irishmen who were haggling over a woman. This incident received little press coverage, but what little it did get was in the vein that Grantham had got what he deserved. Nobody stood trial for the murder as the coroner's inquest did not indict anyone, although the culprits' names were well known.

The second Metropolitan Police officer to be murdered on duty was PC John Long. Whilst patrolling with PC John Newton in Gray's Inn Road on Monday 16 August 1830, they became suspicious of three men. They followed them to Mecklenbergh Square and challenged them. In the ensuing struggle, PC Long was stabbed to death. PC Newton immediately gave chase and eventually caught the man, a well-known criminal called William Sapwell.

His accomplices, although traced, were found not guilty due to lack of evidence, but Sapwell was found guilty and was hanged in the presence of a large crowd. One heartening note in all this is that as Sapwell was hanged, the crowd, through feelings of disgust at the crime, preserved total silence.[16]

Meanwhile, as all this was going on, the force was facing its own teething troubles, which had to be rectified at the same time as it was providing its service to the public. Not the least of the problems was the huge turnover in men. By 1831, 1,250 men had resigned voluntarily and 1,989 had been dismissed, 80 per cent of them for drunkenness; and of the original intake only 850 remained.[17] This turnover, of course, put great strains on whatever training there was.

The histories of the Metropolitan Police – and there are legions of them – make no mention of the training, or lack of it, in the first two years of its existence. All the policemen on the beat had was the *General Instruction Book*, but this contained only vague generalisations about 'having a perfect command of temper' and 'doing his duty in a quiet and determined manner', and so on.

All very well and good, but the *General Instruction Book* had been written by two men who had not the slightest idea what a policeman on the beat needed to know; it contained no practical advice. For a start, they did not even realise how much fortitude it would take merely to wear a uniform in public, the sense that everyone's eyes are upon you, noting your every movement and ready to complain if you are seen doing anything 'wrong'.

Rowan and Mayne also did not include practical advice on how to deal with the constant stream of queries from members of the public, who demanded instant answers and expected a magic wand to be waved to rectify everything immediately. There was no advice, either, on the practicalities of arrest; for a start, who can you arrest? What do you do? What do you say? No doubt the second part of the *General Instruction Book*, written by Mayne, the barrister, helped somewhat on this, but on the whole, practical advice to the policemen faced with the public every day was in short supply.

Once over this hurdle, however, the policeman was then faced with an even bigger task: taking the case to court. The policeman had to be his own prosecuting counsel in court, meaning he had to present his own evidence and make out his own case, thus coming up against professional talkers in the shape of solicitors and barristers.

Giving evidence in court is a daunting task at the best of times, but when faced with hostility from all sides, from both the accused and the defence, then a policeman needs great strength of character and a belief in his evidence in order to convince magistrates that his side of the story is the correct one. No doubt he quickly found out that the defence lawyers were not interested in getting to the truth of the matter; all they were interested in was getting their client off the charge, which is an entirely different thing. If the policeman lost the case, he could probably lay himself open to counterclaims of false arrest, and so on.

It is an astounding thing to realise that this system (of police being the prosecutors as well as the investigators/accusers) was probably peculiarly British, and the only legal system like it in Europe. Sir John Maule, in 1880, had been appointed as the first Director of Public Prosecutions, but that was only for the more important cases. Prosecution of the minor cases was still in the hands of the police, until the creation of the Crown Prosecution Service (CPS) in 1986, following the Prosecution of Offences Act 1985. But since the Criminal Justice Act of 2003, the CPS now prosecutes all cases going to court, except very few minor ones which are still in the hands of the police.

In 1829 the lack of practical advice meant that the policemen of the Metropolitan Police, having nothing previous to go on, were literally 'having to make it up as they went along', and had to gain experience of the job very quickly indeed. For this, they and the force deserve credit. Some men, of course, feeling the strain, realised that the work of a policeman was not for them and turned to drink, thus the high percentage of dismissals for drunkenness.

Therefore, given the struggles that the force had in gaining experience, at exactly the same time as maintaining a service to the public and trying to reduce crime, is it any wonder that mistakes were made? Some of these mistakes, of course, were easily put right, but others were not.

Due to the worries about social unrest still being incited by the National Political Union (NPU), in February 1833 Superintendent Andrew McLean of P Division ordered Sergeant William Popay to attend meetings of the NPU in plain clothes, and report back on all he heard. Posing as a painter, Popay quickly became one of the leading 'revolutionaries' because of his violent anti-police rants. And for three months he got away with it. That is, until May 1833, when he was spotted by a genuine NPU member, George Fusey, hobnobbing with police-men in one of the police section houses.[18]

As soon as this was made public there was a tremendous public uproar. All the old chestnuts were trotted out again: 'police spies', 'agent provocateurs' and the like. For once, the NPU found itself in the enviable position of being 'flavour of the month', with public opinion squarely behind them. Wishing to capitalise on this, a great demonstration was arranged to take place in Coldbath Fields on Monday 13 May 1833.

The meeting took place and the inevitable happened. During the general free-for-all, PC Robert Culley was stabbed to death. The red-hot feelings abroad during that month meant that the inquest on Robert Culley actually brought in a verdict of justifiable homicide. The coroner was so astounded that he refused to accept it, but the jury was adamant and, after a stand-off of several hours, the coroner reluctantly agreed. This verdict was later overturned by a higher court, however, and Robert Culley's widow received private and public subscriptions and £200 from the government.[19]

Being faced with this and the Popay affair, two separate inquiries were established. The Popay inquiry conceded that the occasional employment of policemen in plain clothes was acceptable, but would not condone police spies. William Popay was dismissed. The Coldbath Fields inquiry was entirely differ-ent, with Sir Robert Peel himself sitting on it, who immediately summoned the Home Secretary, Lord Melbourne, to give evidence before a Select Committee. Melbourne was 'grilled' and did not come out of it with grace.

The Select Committee's report, in 1834, made three recommendations: first, that the London magistrates have their judicial and administrative powers sepa-rated; second, that all existing police systems in London be incorporated into the Metropolitan Police, under the control of the commissioners; and third, that the City of London be incorporated for police purposes into the Metropolitan Police. These recommendations were shelved at that time, but, five years later, were to reappear when the Police Act of 1839 was gestating.[20]

There remained just one more incident, and a serious one at that; one which nearly wrecked the Metropolitan Police and which has been described as 'Rowan and Mayne's darkest hour'.[21] It stemmed directly from the hostility from the Home Office and the London magistrates.

Although Earl Grey resigned as Prime Minister in July 1834 and Lord Melbourne succeeded him, the new Home Secretary was Melbourne's brother-in-law, John William Ponsonby, 1st Lord Duncannon. He was worse than Melbourne had been. Being naturally drawn to Roe because of their mutually abiding detestation of the Metropolitan Police, both joined forces to engineer the resignations of Rowan and Mayne. Then, suddenly, they were presented with a perfect opportunity.

On Thursday 19 June 1834 a prostitute, Ruth Morris, arrested in D Division for being drunk and disorderly, was banged up for the night. All run-of-the-mill stuff which happens with monotonous regularity, but in the morning she alleged that she was raped by Inspector Squire Wovenden of the night shift. Superintendent James Lazenby refused to accept the complaint as it was obviously untrue, but reported the matter upwards to the commissioners.

Mayne, recognising a powder keg when he saw it, took the complaint seriously and decreed that Wovenden should be charged before a Magistrates' Court like anybody else would have been. But Ruth Morris refused to testify and thus Wovenden did not stand trial. Because of this, Duncannon and Roe, in cahoots, issued a magistrates' warrant for Wovenden's arrest, over the heads of Rowan and Mayne, and Wovenden was sent for trial to the assizes.[22]

In those days there were two juries: the examining jury (the Grand Jury, sitting privately) and the determining jury (the Petty Jury, sitting in open court). The evidence in all cases was examined by the Grand Jury first, and only if they found a prima facie case would they then pass it through to the court to be heard in front of the Petty Jury.

Wovenden's Grand Jury looked at the evidence, decided that there was no case, and dismissed it by marking the papers 'No True Bill' (or sometimes, the word used was *Ignoramus* – Latin for 'we know not'). Rowan and Mayne then held their own internal inquiry, finding that Wovenden and Lazenby had committed no impropriety, and that they were only the victims of Roe's vindictiveness. These findings they sent to Duncannon, who, being hand-in-glove with Roe, sent them to him. Roe retaliated by demanding the dismissal of both Wovenden and Lazenby, both Peninsular War veterans and good policemen, hoping that this would cause the resignation of Rowan and Mayne, which was his real purpose.

Rowan and Mayne found themselves in the most difficult dilemma of their partnership so far. Loyalty to two good policemen indicated that they should resign. But if that happened, the whole Metropolitan Police would undoubtedly have been in jeopardy from a hostile Whig government and, who knows, perhaps would have crumbled away to dust. Rowan and Mayne took a difficult decision in line with Bentham's utilitarianism of the day: the 'greatest good for the greatest number'. Either it was Wovenden and Lazenby or the whole 3,000 men of the Metropolitan Police.

Wovenden and Lazenby were both dismissed and, despite numerous attempts to reverse this decision, they were never reinstated. Roe, sensing victory and that the commissioners 'were on the ropes', followed up by demanding a reduction in the pay of the superintendents. The finances for the Metropolitan Police had partly been borne on parish rates, and the parish vestries were, in effect, Chief Magistrate Roe's constituents. Therefore, any reduction in payment would have advanced his popularity.

On Monday 17 November 1834 the king dismissed the Whig government under Melbourne as Prime Minister and reinstated the Tory Sir Robert Peel. Peel was in Rome at that time, so the Duke of Wellington took the reins. Three weeks later, however, on Wednesday 10 December 1834, Wellington handed back the premiership to the man who had started it all off, Sir Robert Peel.[23] Out went Duncannon as Home Secretary, being replaced by a personal friend of Robert Peel, Henry Goulburn, who would make a non-abrasive Home Secretary and, in later years, an even better Chancellor of the Exchequer.[24]

Rowan and Mayne breathed collective sighs of relief. They had weathered the storm of political opposition and, despite one or two little later digs from Roe, were never seriously attacked or challenged in their positions again.

Working-class opposition was, however, an altogether different thing, and that continued unabated, as indeed it still does today. It is a fact that in the seventy years between 1829 and 1899, 165 Metropolitan Police officers lost their lives, 52 of these as a direct result of assaults whilst on duty.[25]

Charles Rowan and Richard Mayne are to be lauded in their achievement. Within five years, a disciplined, organised police force was carved from virtually nothing that had gone before. The Metropolitan Police was to be proved far from perfect in the later years, but nobody can deny that it set the standard and provided the norm and the model for subsequent British police forces, both county and borough. By 1835 the system had been tested by experience and thus, amended and tweaked, it was sent out into the country. And for that, the British police service must be eternally grateful.

THREE

1835

Sir Robert Peel was not to last long as Prime Minister. Having taken office in December 1834, by April 1835 he was out, replaced by none other than Lord Melbourne. However, in August 1841 he was back again when Melbourne was himself ousted.[1] During those six years of Melbourne's ministry, the two men who occupied the Home Office were to have a profound effect upon the policing of Great Britain, the first of them especially so. From the same family as the Dukes of Bedford, Lord John Russell, although of Whig persuasion, inherited a Metropolitan Police that he knew he had to keep.

Having weathered and survived all kinds of birth pangs and teething troubles, the Metropolitan Police was definitely here to stay. Lord John Russell knew this purely by reading the report into the Popay incident, and the 1834 Select Committee report into the Coldbath Fields episode, which had naturally looked dispassionately at the Metropolitan Police: 'Your Committee conclude with this expression of their Opinion; viz. that the Metropolitan Police Force, as respects its influence in repressing crime and the security it has given to persons and property, is one of the most valuable modern institutions.'[2]

The Great Reform Act had been passed in 1832, and although the Prime Minister was Earl Grey and the Home Secretary Lord Melbourne, it was in fact Lord John Russell, as MP for Tavistock, who was the chief architect of the legislation and who steered the bill through Parliament. Thus voting reform was very prominent in Russell's thoughts and, after the success over the parliamentary voting, it was natural that he would now turn his eyes to the boroughs of the country.

The result was the Royal Commission on Municipal Corporations, which was 'to inquire into the existing state of the Municipal Corporations in England and Wales and to collect information respecting the defects in their constitution'; it was appointed on 18 July 1833. This Royal Commission, according to Sidney and Beatrice Webb, was one of the two 'Royal Commissions of these years … to stand out as models of investigation, upon the results of which English

Local Government was reorganised'.[3] (Incidentally, the other one was the Royal Commission on the Poor Law of 1834.)

The twenty Royal Commissioners visited the 178 listed boroughs of the country with the task of finding out the exact state of the municipal corporations; in other words, how the boroughs governed themselves. But, quite naturally, the question of what police systems were being used by the towns was also looked into.

Although springing from the same root piece of legislation (the Statute of Winchester 1285), police in the provincial towns had been forced to evolve in a slightly different way to the countryside parishes. Whereas in rural areas the old system of parish constables, magistrates and presentments to Quarter Sessions survived to 1839, and even to 1856 in some places, by the early 1830s the growing towns of a rapidly industrialising Britain had their own system of local government, and therefore of policing themselves.

In the middle of the eighteenth century, industrialisation in Britain had begun to turn certain towns into large sprawling conurbations teeming with factory workers. The system of magistrate and parish constable began to fail as the old system could not cope with the new conditions. The Statute of Winchester had also introduced the system of Watch and Ward (*ward* was Old English meaning 'to guard a place') in the towns, in addition to that of the parish constable. But these systems could not bear the strain of a life which at the time of the establishment of the parish constable system was unknown – the Industrial Revolution had brought chaos to policing as well as to local government.

Over the intervening 548 years there had been no lead from central government; it was generally left to individual towns to see to their own street cleaning, maintenance and lighting, as well as to the policing of their boroughs. It was a collection of concerned people, in deciding they had to do things for themselves, who applied to Parliament to give them the power under a local Act to levy rates in order to maintain the services in their particular township. These purely local, or Improvement Acts, were administered under the guidance of local commissioners, who could be a separate body from the mayor and corporation. Most of these local commissioners gave precedence to paving, lighting and street cleaning, but a policing concern was never very far behind. The local commissioners implemented the Statute of Winchester by employing watchmen to guard the town during the night, which involved calling the hours in a loud voice. Unfortunately, many of these watchmen were old and infirm, and were only employed as an alternative to keeping them on the parish poor rate.

Thus, by the 1830s, policing in the boroughs of Britain was a huge mishmash of nightwatchmen under Improvement Act commissioners and daytime parish constables appointed by the corporation under their powers as *ex officio* magistrates. In short, a complete mess.

This was the picture which emerged from the Royal Commission, and Lord John Russell was itching to put it right. His first concern was the enfranchisement of the new middle classes, made rich by the Industrial Revolution. Thus, by injecting 'new blood' he intended to bring about the reform of the government of each borough by taking it away from the hereditary local bigwigs. By this means he hoped to introduce a countrywide, uniform system of local government.

Introduced into Parliament in June 1835, the bill based upon the Commission's report proposed sweeping changes to local government in 178 boroughs of the country. Although the bill passed through the House of Commons relatively unscathed, when it reached the Lords it was given a battering.

Representatives of the boroughs that were threatened by the bill lobbied every peer they could find, and at one point it looked as though the bill would be rejected. But despite the compromises that had to be made, the bill eventually passed on to the Statute Book as the Municipal Corporations Act 1835 (5 and 6 William IV, Chapter 76) on Wednesday 9 September 1835. These compromises, however, made the 1835 Act so vague on police matters that the consequences were not to be resolved for at least another hundred years.

The main thrust of the Act said that every one of the 178 boroughs listed should hold political elections amongst the newly enfranchised free men of the borough, and so elect a Town Council. Into the hands of this Town Council would be placed the responsibility of governing the borough.

So far, so good. But Lord John Russell was also kept mindful of the policing situation in these boroughs, which, as the Royal Commission had found out, was woefully inadequate.

The Act, therefore, contained the coda that from this newly elected Town Council a subcommittee must be formed, which was to be called the Watch Committee tasked with establishing a 'new police' force (along the lines of the Metropolitan Police) for their boroughs. The Watch Committee was to consist of no more than a third of the members of the Town Council, with the mayor as *ex officio* chairman, who would also be sworn in as a magistrate.

As regards elections for the Town Councils, the boroughs lost no time in complying as they were only too pleased to implement it, their concern being to place their administrations on a more democratic footing. However, on the policing side, things were not to be that straightforward. For a start, the 1835 Act made no mention of the Home Secretary (other than requiring quarterly reports), unlike the 1829 Metropolitan Police Act, which made the Home Secretary, in effect, the Police Authority for the Metropolitan Police. And surprisingly, there was no mention either of a chief or head constable. All the 1835 Act said was that the Watch Committee must within three weeks of its first meeting appoint 'a sufficient number of fit men' to be sworn in to act as constables who would 'keep the peace by day and night and prevent robberies'.[4]

Into the lap of the Watch Committee, therefore, was laid unequivocally the responsibility for appointing and dismissing constables and the framing of regulations. In appointing their constables, the Watch Committee designated one of them to be in charge of the rest, if only to facilitate administration and management of the force; however, there was no legal requirement for them to do so.

That then raised the question 'Who was in charge?' Was it to be the Watch Committee, or the 'chief' constable that the Watch Committee had themselves appointed to head the other constables? Upon this question, the Act remained silent. From the battering the bill had received in the Lords, the result was a hastily contrived and ill-thought-out piece of legislation, and, not being primarily concerned with police reform, such questions as to who would control the borough police forces were completely overlooked.

The vagueness of the 1835 Act surprisingly did not lead to any testing law cases to resolve the issue until many years later. It was not until 1930, during the case of Fisher *v.* Oldham Corporation, that it was decided that police officers of the Oldham Borough Police, in arresting a man called Fisher (falsely, as it happened – hence the lawsuit), were acting by virtue of the common and statute law, and not by authority of the Oldham Watch Committee.

And as late as 1959, the Nottingham Watch Committee suspended their chief constable, Aethelstan Popkess, for refusing to disclose the reasons for the action he took in dealing with a criminal case. After many arguments, the Home Secretary, 'Rab' Butler, told the Watch Committee that their actions were unacceptable by dint of interfering with the chief constable's duty in enforcing the criminal law.

The Watch Committee eventually reinstated their chief constable, but the whole question had been brought out into the open. This was one of the incidents that precipitated the Willink Committee and eventually the great Police Act of 1964, which finally codified in black and white, 129 years later, the exact position of all the parties concerned. But more of that in Chapter 12.

Nevertheless, in the hundred-odd years before these two incidents, the relations between Watch Committees and their chief constables seemed not to have caused any undue friction anywhere. Perhaps this was down to the great British genius of compromise, and the tendency to muddle through come-what-may. Also, because there was little, if any, interference from the Home Office, and certainly no follow-up by central government to check there was compliance with the police provisions of the 1835 Act, we get three different types of reaction. Some boroughs implemented the Act completely; some did so partially; others totally ignored it.

The 178 boroughs in the Municipal Corporations Act are listed in the next few pages, together with the dates of the establishment of any Watch Committee and police force that can be directly attributable to them:

Aberystwyth Borough Police *nothing traceable*

Abingdon Borough Police *formed* 1 April 1836

Andover Borough Police *formed* 1836

Arundel Borough Police *formed* 10 February 1836

Banbury Borough Police *formed* March 1836

Barnstaple Borough Police *formed* 1836

Basingstoke Borough Police *formed* 1836

Bath City Police *formed* 6 February 1836

Beaumaris Borough Police *formed* 1836

Beccles Borough Police *formed* 1840

Bedford Borough Police *formed* 1835

Berwick-upon-Tweed Borough Police *formed* 1835

Beverley Borough Police *formed* 1 January 1836

Bewdley Borough Police *formed* 1836

Bideford Borough Police *formed* 22 August 1836

Blandford Forum Borough Police *formed* 1 February 1836

Bodmin Borough Police *formed* 1836

Boston Borough Police *formed* 6 February 1836

Brecon Borough Police *formed* 1829

Bridgnorth Borough Police *formed* 8 January 1836

Bridgwater Borough Police *formed* 10 November 1839

Bridport Borough Police *formed* 18 February 1836

Bristol City Police *formed* 22 June 1836

Buckingham Borough Police *formed* January 1836

Bury St Edmunds Borough Police *formed* March 1836

Calne *nothing traceable*

Cambridge Borough Police *formed* 21 January 1836

Canterbury City Police *formed* 7 March 1836

Cardiff City Police *formed* January 1836

Cardigan *nothing traceable*

Carlisle City Police *formed* 1836, or maybe 1827?

Carmarthen Borough Police *formed* 1831

Caernarvon *nothing traceable*

Chard Borough Police *formed* 1839

Chepping Wycombe Borough Police *formed* 1849

Chester City Police *formed* 1 January 1836

Chesterfield Borough Police *formed* 7 January 1836

Chichester City Police *formed* 1836

Chippenham *nothing traceable*

Chipping Norton Borough Police *formed* 1836

Clitheroe Borough Police *formed* 1 July 1887

Colchester Borough Police *formed* 25 February 1836

Congleton Borough Police *formed* February 1836

Coventry Borough Police *formed* 7 March 1836

Dartmouth or Clifton-Dartmouth-Hardness *nothing traceable*

Daventry Borough Police *formed* 1836

Deal Borough Police *formed* 18 January 1836

Denbigh *nothing traceable*

Derby City Police *formed* February 1836

Devizes *nothing traceable*

Doncaster Borough Police *formed* 1836

Dorchester Borough Police *formed*
29 January 1836

Dover Borough Police *formed*
20 January 1836

Droitwich Borough Police *formed* 1836

Durham City Police *formed*
2 February 1836

East Retford Borough Police *formed*
1 January 1836

Evesham Borough Police *formed*
12 January 1836

Exeter City Police *formed* 18 January
1836

Eye Borough Police *formed* 1840

Falmouth Borough Police *formed* 1836

Faversham Borough Police *formed*
21 October 1839

Flint *nothing traceable*

Folkestone Borough Police *formed*
1836

Gateshead Borough Police *formed*
1 October 1836

Glastonbury *nothing traceable*

Gloucester City Police *formed*
26 February 1836

Godalming Borough Police *formed*
1836

Godmanchester *nothing traceable*

Grantham Borough Police *formed*
9 February 1836

Gravesend Borough Police *formed*
1836

Great Grimsby Borough Police *formed*
27 April 1846

Great Torrington Borough Police
formed 1836

Great Yarmouth Borough Police
formed January 1836

Guildford Borough Police *formed*
20 January 1836

Harwich Borough Police *formed*
January 1836

Hastings Borough Police *formed*
1 June 1836

Haverfordwest Borough Police *formed*
1835

Helston Borough Police *formed* 1836

Hereford City Police *formed* 1 January
1836

Hertford Borough Police *formed*
12 January 1836

Huntingdon *nothing traceable*

Hythe *nothing traceable*

Ipswich Borough Police *formed*
1 March 1836

Kendal Borough Police *formed*
11 January 1836

Kidderminster Borough Police *formed*
1835

King's Lynn Borough Police *formed*
8 January 1836

Kingston upon Hull Borough Police
formed 2 May 1836

Kingston upon Thames *nothing
traceable*

Lancaster Borough Police *formed* 1824,
but reformed 1835

Launceston (otherwise Dunheved)
Borough Police *formed* 1836

Leeds City Police *formed* 2 April 1836

Leicester Borough Police *formed*
10 February 1836

Leominster Borough Police *formed*
February 1836

Lichfield *nothing traceable*

Lincoln City Police *formed* September
1829

Liskeard Borough Police *formed* 1836

Liverpool City Police *formed*
9 February 1836

Llandovery *nothing traceable*

Llanidloes *nothing traceable*

Louth Borough Police *formed*
12 February 1836

Ludlow Borough Police *formed* 1836

Lyme Regis Borough Police *formed*
1829

Lymington Borough Police *formed*
1836

Macclesfield Borough Police *formed*
19 January 1836

Maidenhead Borough Police *formed*
27 January 1836

Maidstone Borough Police *formed*
1836

Maldon Borough Police *formed*
5 January 1836

Marlborough *nothing traceable*

Monmouth Borough Police *formed*
1836

Morpeth *nothing traceable*

Neath Borough Police *formed* 1836

New Windsor Borough Police *formed*
5 March 1836

Newark Borough Police *formed* 1836

Newbury Borough Police *formed*
January 1835

Newcastle-under-Lyme Borough
Police *formed* 1 November 1834

Newcastle upon Tyne City Police
formed 2 May 1836

Newport (Isle of Wight) Borough
Police *formed* 1837

Newport (Monmouthshire) Borough
Police *formed* 1 February 1836

Northampton Borough Police *formed*
11 January 1836

Norwich City Police *formed*
22 January 1836

Nottingham City Police *formed* 1841

Oswestry Borough Police *formed*
12 February 1836

Oxford City Police *formed* 1 January
1869

Pembroke Borough Police *formed* 1856

Penryn Borough Police *formed* 1836

Penzance Borough Police *formed* 1836

Plymouth City Police *formed* 1836

Pontefract Borough Police *formed*
19 January 1836

Poole Borough Police *formed* 1835

Portsmouth City Police *formed*
21 March 1836

Preston Borough Police *formed* 1815

Pwllheli Borough Police *formed*
March 1857

Reading Borough Police *formed*
21 February 1836

Richmond Borough Police *formed*
1848

Ripon City Police *formed* November
1838

Rochester City Police *formed* 1837

Romsey Borough Police *formed* 1836

Ruthin *nothing traceable*

Rye Borough Police *formed* 1838

Saffron Walden Borough Police *formed*
1835

Salisbury City Police *formed* 27 April
1838

Sandwich Borough Police *formed*
c. 1856

Scarborough Borough Police *formed*
January 1836

Shaftesbury *nothing traceable*

Shrewsbury Borough Police *formed*
5 February 1836

South Molton Borough Police *formed*
1836

Southampton City Police *formed*
6 March 1836

Southwold Borough Police *formed*
1840

St Albans City Police *formed* 23 July
1836

St Ives Borough Police *formed* 1836

Stafford Borough Police *formed*
  October 1840
Stamford Borough Police *formed*
  2 January 1836
Stockport Borough Police *formed*
  23 March 1870
Stockton-on-Tees *nothing traceable*
Stratford-on-Avon Borough Police
  formed 1835
Sudbury Borough Police *formed* 1835
Sunderland Borough Police *formed*
  5 October 1837
Swansea Borough Police *formed*
  4 April 1836
Tamworth Borough Police *formed*
  1840
Tenby Borough Police *formed c.* 1840
Tenterden Borough Police *formed*
  c. 1856
Tewkesbury Borough Police *formed*
  29 January 1836
Thetford Borough Police *formed*
  11 February 1836

Tiverton Borough Police *formed* 1836
Totnes Borough Police *formed* 1836
Truro Borough Police *formed*
  December 1838
Wallingford Borough Police *formed*
  13 January 1836
Walsall Borough Police *formed* 6 July
  1832
Warwick Borough Police *formed*
  26 September 1846
Wells *nothing traceable*
Welshpool *nothing traceable*
Wenlock Borough Police *formed* 1836
Weymouth and Melcombe Regis
  Borough Police *formed* 1846
Wigan Borough Police *formed*
  6 January 1836
Winchester City Police *formed* 28 July
  1832
Wisbech Borough Police *formed* 1835
Worcester City Police *formed*
  18 January 1833
York City Police *formed* 28 April 1836[5]

From this list it can be seen that forty-seven boroughs ignored the Act in 1836, although twenty-three of these did form forces later. This leaves 131 who established their borough police forces in 1835 or 1836 – or ostensibly formed forces.

As there was no coercive follow-up by central government, it is unknown what the quality of these forces was. There may be evidence that some of the boroughs simply took on their old watchmen and carried on entirely as before, not making any attempt to organise a 'new police' force for their boroughs, and thus not having the expense either.[6] However, the proportion of boroughs that did this is simply not known because nobody has done research into this question before.

On the other hand, there is plenty of evidence from the published histories of these forces (see Bibliography) that many of the boroughs, in availing themselves of this 'new broom' legislation, sacked all their old watchmen and started afresh with newly appointed young men as constables. Unfortunately, nobody has looked at this, so we do not know this proportion, either.

It will be noted that in the above list, many of what we would call large industrial towns are missing, such as Birmingham, Manchester, Bradford and so on. This is simply because in 1835 they had not been granted charters of incorporation and

9 PC9 James Stowe of the Northampton Borough Police in the uniform worn between 1835 and 1851. Note the similarity of the uniforms of Manchester and Northampton, which was virtually a standard pattern throughout the country.

10 Manchester was not incorporated as a borough until October 1838, and thus formed a Watch Committee in January 1839. But the magistrates that ran the 'old police' system refused to recognise them. Consequently, Manchester policing was in chaos until the government intervened and the Manchester City 'new police' was established in October 1842, under Edward Willis. This photograph is of the 'new police' parading for duty in the mid-1840s.

11 Manchester City Police 'relaxing', although the horizontally striped armlet is clearly visible, denoting that the officers should have been on duty, which was the whole point of the armlet.

were not therefore affected by the Municipal Corporation Act. All these had to wait until they were granted municipal status at a later date.

The Borough of Clitheroe may be unique in that it was affected by the 1835 Act and was therefore entitled to form its own force – but did not do so until 1887, fifty-two years later. In the meantime, Clitheroe borough appears to have been policed by the Lancashire County Constabulary.

By the early months of 1836, borough police reform seemed to have been accomplished. However, no inspection or inquiry into these forces was ever made, so the government was unaware of the twenty-four boroughs ignoring the Act. And of the others that were complying, the government did not know what proportion of them were anywhere near to being effective.

As no research has been done, we do not know the answer to that question today, and Lord John Russell definitely did not know the answer in 1836. The backsliding and ineffective borough forces were therefore allowed to continue up until the greatest shake-up of them all – the 1856 County and Borough Police Act, which brought the annual inspections.

Nevertheless, by 1836 Lord John Russell could look at the country and, thanks to legislation, know that London was being policed properly, and could assume the boroughs of the country were being policed properly too. All that remained now was to get the counties policed adequately, and this is what he set about doing. In this he was alleviated of most of the burden by the man whose thinking seemed to sum up the large part of the nineteenth century – Edwin Chadwick.

FOUR

1836–39

Edwin Chadwick was a protégé of Jeremy Bentham, and it is Jeremy Bentham who, as one of the leading philosophers of the day, had put his societal weight behind police reform in London in the 1780s. Inspired by Bentham's utilitarianism, Chadwick, in 1829, published an article in the *London Review* on 'Preventive Police', which brought him the acquaintance and friendship of Bentham.

Bentham's association and authority with influential members of the government had secured Chadwick the post of Chief Commissioner to the Royal Commission on the Poor Law, the one so admired by Sidney and Beatrice Webb. Chadwick, however, knew the MPs well enough to be aware of Lord John Russell's thinking on police reform.

With his 'Preventive Police' article behind him, Chadwick proposed to Lord John Russell that a Royal Commission be made into the state of the police in the country, to see what reform was needed. Russell warmed to the idea and accepted it immediately.

Russell was of the opinion that three commissioners should be enough. He then acutely demonstrated his knowledge of human nature by asking the idea's proposer, Chadwick himself, to head the inquiry, thus ensuring the maximum enthusiasm for the task. The second commissioner was to be the man who arguably knew more about police administration in the country at that time than anyone else, Charles Rowan, Metropolitan Police Commissioner. The third and final commissioner proposed by Russell was to be 'a country gentleman', in the shape of a certain Charles Shaw Lefevre from Devonshire.[1]

With all three commissioners chosen, the Royal Commission 'for the purpose of enquiring for the best means of establishing an efficient constabulary force in the counties of England and Wales' started its deliberations in late 1836. The Commission took a wide range of evidence and opinion, not only from persons of quality, but from the extreme low levels of society as well. And why not? If you are going to understand why crime happens and then attempt to stop it, you pick the brains of criminals – you don't just ask country landowners.

The Commission interviewed many convicted criminals, who gave them 'hints and wrinkles' on how to break into houses and what measures would stop them from doing so. The Commission also heard of many illegal practices that only criminals knew about, and what sort of policing activities would make them think twice about committing crime. Having gathered all this information, the Commission then turned its attention to the existing policing arrangements in the country.

This turned up a whole hotchpotch of policing systems around the country at that time, the most important being the Cheshire experiment. This had been introduced by Sir Robert Peel in 1829, by the Cheshire Police Act (10 George IV, Chapter 97), as an experiment to be followed and observed, and if it had proved of any worth then it probably would have formed the basis of a nationwide system. In the event, it was not to be, as Peel was superseded in the Home Office by the markedly anti-police Lord Melbourne in November 1830. However, the system continued operating, which is why it came under the scrutiny of the Royal Commission of 1836.

The Cheshire experiment tried to breathe new life into the parish constable system. Professional 'high constables' had been appointed by the county magistrates in the hundreds of the county, who were then placed in charge of professional 'assistant' parish constables in their district, who also had been appointed by the magistrates.

Twenty pages of the Commission's final report were devoted to the Cheshire experiment, which they said 'was an experiment made with a view to the application of a general measure to other counties of England and Wales'.[2] Describing the experiment as an 'honourable failure', the Commission said that it had not lived up to the hopes of 1829. The Cheshire experiment failed mainly because it did not have a 'chief' constable in charge to co-ordinate it all; in other words, there were nine 'high constables', each having his own small force below him, and in effect this gave nine individual police forces in the county.

In addition, the system relied too heavily on the whims of the magistracy to introduce it. Magistrates are, after all, human and have their weaknesses, foibles and fears, and some were found to be too easily swayed by factors other than the preservation of law and order. This is why, on the whole, the Royal Commission looked upon the Cheshire experiment as an 'honourable failure'.

The ailing parish constable system was also scrutinised by the commissioners, who appeared to be none too impressed with the whole set-up. It is one of the ironies of police history that a Commission which subjected the whole rural police to much-needed scrutiny, the first of its kind in the country, the deductions from which could have laid foundations for a modern, forward-looking police system, resulted in such completely ill-judged conclusions.

The Commission took three years to issue its report, which it did in March 1839, and painted an appalling picture. It reported that crime was rampant throughout the nation, and the means of prevention, detection and dealing with it were virtually non-existent. In short, the Commission urged the introduction of a rural constabulary, but in doing so made very controversial recommendations.

The Commission recommended that there would be one single police force for the whole of the country, organised along the lines of the Metropolitan Police. The Metropolitan Police commissioners should organise the force, under rules approved by the Home Secretary, and this force should be paid for by one-quarter of the annual cost coming from the national Exchequer, three-quarters coming from county rates.

The only power that would be given to local magistrates was the authority to apply to the Metropolitan Police commissioners for an allocation of policemen to their particular area. The county magistrates would maintain some semblance of local control by having the power to dismiss any policeman they thought unsuitable for their area. Apart from that, the local magistrates would have no say in the administration of the police within their county.

This last recommendation was clearly because Chadwick had been none too impressed by the magistrates' powers in the Cheshire experiment. He also wanted to sever the link between magistrates and the police. Chadwick argued that magistrates should not have administrative and directive powers over the police, whilst at the same time keeping their judicial powers. He wished to stop the practice, which was capable of being easily abused, of having people appearing before magistrates in a court of law who had been presented before them by the police who were magistrate controlled. He said that the whole success of the Metropolitan Police had been because the link between the Metropolitan Police and the London magistrates had been disconnected.

Although there were three commissioners and Chadwick had obviously been influenced by Charles Rowan on the effectiveness of the wondrous Metropolitan Police, the report appears to have been written only by Chadwick himself. It has been criticised for seemingly presenting only Chadwick's selection of the collected evidence and for putting forward his own ideas on police reform that he had formulated before the Commission had even started.[3] Be that as it may, however, although Chadwick does voice a genuine concern over the dual role of the magistrates, he seems to misunderstand completely the situation in the world around him.

He must have known that the county magistrates had been the administrators of their counties, and thus had been used to dealing with all aspects of local government for several hundreds of years. Yet, in all seriousness, he now proposed that county magistrates should have no control over the police force which would be operating within their counties – a police force controlled by and consisting of Londoners at that. Such ignorance of human nature and misreading of his times is astonishing.

Lord John Russell, being of the magisterial class himself, must have read Chadwick's report with some concern; it was so controversial that he knew the county magistrates would fight it tooth and nail if a bill based upon the report was ever presented to Parliament. He knew that county magistrates would never give up 500 years' worth of their powers, especially on the say-so of one so lowly born as Chadwick (born in Longsight, Manchester, son of a journalist[4]). As such, he conducted his own private survey amongst the magistrates in early 1839.

He found that about half the county magistrates would support a similar resolution to the one passed by the Shropshire bench as early as December 1838. 'We are in favour,' said Shropshire, 'of a body of constables appointed by the magistrates, paid out of the county rates and disposable at any point of the shire where their services might be required.'[5] Also, in February 1839, the Lancashire magistrates stated that they would wholeheartedly support the 'new police' in their county and had sent a circular to that effect to every bench of magistrates throughout the country.

Lord John Russell was worried. He knew a police bill based on the Chadwick report would meet immense opposition, but yet, in the spring of 1839, he needed a rural constabulary – fast. Revolution was in the air.

The People's Charter, with its six demands of Parliament for working-class social reform, had been drafted in 1838 by William Lovett and Francis Place. The Chartists, as they were called, planned to culminate their petition to Parliament with a vast 'People's Convention' in London; if their demands were rejected then the convention would organise a national strike.

The convention did indeed take place in February 1839, but immediately internal squabbles began to tear the Chartists apart. Today, with hindsight, we can say that Chartism was a generic term and the movement really consisted of local groups agitating against purely local grievances – a national Chartist movement was more or less impossible. The split in the movement was inevitable, and the various factions went back to their separate areas in a highly belligerent mood.

Violent extremism was now a distinct possibility, and disquieting reports were coming in from all over the country that Chartism could soon erupt into turbulent social disorder. And no more so than in the big industrial cities of the Midlands and the North, especially Birmingham, where rioting and heavy loss of property occurred during early July.

The Birmingham magistrates, having no city police force, had to resort to the military and to requesting a contingent of Metropolitan Police from London. This last action was later regretted by the Birmingham magistrates, who would say that they believed the intervention of the Metropolitan Police had made matters worse.

As Birmingham, Bolton and Manchester were not incorporated boroughs under the Municipal Corporations Act, they did not have a 'new police' force, and still relied on their old systems of local commissioners. Concerned by more

Whitehall
2ᵈ February 1839

Sir,

I am directed by Lord John Russell to inform you, that the Magistrates of the County of Salop, at the last General Quarter Sessions of the Peace held in and for that County, agreed to the following Resolution, viz⁵:

"That in consequence of the present inefficiency of the Constabulary Force, arising from the great increase of Population, and the extension of the Trade and Commerce of the Country, it is the opinion of this Court, that a Body of Constables appointed by the Magistrates, paid out of the County Rate, and disposable at any point of the Shire where their Services might be required, would be highly desirable; as providing in the most efficient manner for the prevention as well as detection of Offences, for the security of person and property, and for the constant preservation of the public Peace."

Lord John Russell requests that you will submit this Resolution to the Magistrates of the County of Northampton, at the next Court of Quarter Sessions over which you preside, and request their attention to it, — and that you will afterwards report their opinion on the subject referred to in the Resolution to Lord John Russell.

I have the Honor to be
Sir
Your obedient Servant
F. Maule

The Chairman
of the Quarter Sessions
for the County of
Northampton

12 & 13 Lord John Russell's circular to the county magistrates, February 1839.

At a General Meeting of the Magistrates of the County of Lancaster, called pursuant to the directions of the Lord Lieutenant of the said County, to take into consideration a Communication from Her Majesty's Secretary of State for the Home Department as to the Establishment of an efficient Constabulary Force in the said County, and to enable His Lordship to reply to such Communication by the Authority and on the behalf of the said County, held at the Court House in Preston on Thursday the 31st day of January 1839.

Present;

The Honorable Richard Bootle Wilbraham.
Sir Peter Hesketh Fleetwood Baronet.

Thomas Batty Addison Esqr.	Henry Tempest Esqr.
William Catrow Esqr.	Adam Hodgson Esqr.
James Nowell Farington Esqr.	William Chadwick Esqr.
Thomas Robert Wilson France Esqr.	James Whitaker Esqr.
William Marshall Esqr.	John Holt Esqr.
Peter Ainsworth Esqr.	William Wallace Currie Esqr.
Henry Ashworth Esqr.	William Smith Esqr.
John Bentley Esqr.	Samuel Lees Esqr.
William Garnett Esqr.	Edmund Grundy Esqr.
James Blanchard Esqr.	James Foulds Esqr.
Clement Royds Esqr.	Paul Moon James Esqr.
Henry Hargreaves Esqr.	William Gerard Walmsley Esqr.
Robert Josias Jackson Norreys Esq.	Reginald Hargreaves Esqr.
Thomas John Knowlys Esqr.	John Ormerod Esqr.
Lawrence Rawstorne Esqr.	William Newson Wood Esqr.
William Earle Esqr.	John Earnshaw Esqr.
John Lister Esqr.	Cornelius Bourne Esqr.
James Pedder Esqr.	Lawrence Heyworth Esqr.
William Birley Esqr.	John Bourne Esqr.
John Heys Esqr.	Joseph Feilden Esqr.
Joseph Bushell Esqr.	Charles Townley Esqr.
Richard Edward Alison Esqr.	Peregrine Edward Townley Esqr.
William Ince Anderton Esqr.	Joshua Thomas Horton, Clerk.
Abraham Wood Esqr.	Robinson Shuttleworth Marton, Clerk.
John Frederic Foster Esqr.	Robert Atherton Rawstorne, Clerk.
Shakespear Phillips Esqr.	and
Richard Walker Esqr.	

Moved by Sir Peter Hesketh Fleetwood Bart, and seconded by Colonel Rawstorne, that the Honorable Richard Bootle Wilbraham do take the Chair.

Moved by Sir Peter Hesketh Fleetwood Bart, and seconded by Thomas John Knowlys Esqr., and resolved unanimously that it is the Opinion of the Magistrates of this County here assembled, that a more efficient, and well re-gulated Constabulary System would add to the un-interrupted Enjoyment of the Liberty of the Subject, as well as to the Security and Protection of Persons and Property.

Resolved that a Copy of the above Resolution be transmitted to the Lord Lieutenant by the Chairman.

Signed) R Bootle Wilbraham
Chairman

Resolved that the Thanks of this Meeting be given to the Honorable Richard Bootle Wilbraham for his Services in the Chair.

14 & 15 The Lancashire magistrates' circular.

threats of Chartist violence, the Whig government needed to act, and during 1839, after frenzied activity in Parliament, Birmingham, Bolton and Manchester all received police enabling acts.

These, however, were unusual, and reflected the seriousness of the times. So serious, in fact, that these measures were introduced by the Whig government under Lord Melbourne – that same Lord Melbourne who had so opposed the Metropolitan Police in 1829. The government, by these enabling acts, circumvented the establishment of a Watch Committee and directly appointed a Chief Commissioner of Police to each borough, giving him the power to form a police force immediately.

Bolton acted first, under Commissioner Simpton, and formed its force on 18 February;[6] Manchester on 17 October under Commissioner Sir Charles Shaw;[7] and Birmingham on 20 November with Commissioner Frances Burgess.[8] These three forces were established hurriedly because of Chartist riots, thus because of the public disorder problem, not any crime problem. It is this key point that later historians seized upon, but more of that later.

The threat of public disorder because of Chartism occupied the Whig government during the spring and summer of 1839. As Home Secretary, Lord John Russell knew that if serious Chartist riots did break out in the countryside, away from the big cities, he had no means to deal with them. The only means available for riot suppression at that time was the full-time army, if available, or the part-time militia or yeomanry (the nearest modern equivalent would be the Territorial Army – militia being infantry and yeomanry being cavalry), and they took time to mobilise. In any case, the military did not have the civil power of constables; that is, the ability to arrest and to bring before a court. So in other words, he needed a rural constabulary.

Consequently, Russell introduced the County Police bill into Parliament on Wednesday 24 July, but in order to have any chance of getting an Act on to the Statute Book, he had to dispense with the idea of one national police force administered from London. He knew that had he introduced a bill based purely on the conclusions of the 1836 Royal Commission, he would have run up against a brick wall.

The Tory Party was in opposition, and it is conceivable that the vast majority of Tory MPs were themselves county magistrates. Regardless of the riotous inclination of the country at the time, they would not for one minute have been in favour of any diminution in the powers of their colleagues on the county benches.

Opposition to the bill was, however, inevitable, and came mainly from the young Benjamin Disraeli, MP for Maidstone, who was purely trying to make his presence felt, having less than two years' service in the Commons.[9] It was also Disraeli who was one of the three members to vote against the Birmingham Police bill going through Parliament at the same time.[10] Nevertheless, concerns about Chartist violence were much too difficult to overcome, and despite many politicians pontificating about 'police spies', the bill was passed into law on Tuesday 27 August 1839, becoming known as the County Police Act 1839 (2 and 3 Victoria, Chapter 93).

Due to the political pressures of the age, this Act did not make police forces compulsory and rejected the idea of a national police force run from London. Instead, the Act gave powers to the county magistrates to establish a rural constabulary for their county (or any part of it), if they so wished. There was no compulsion upon them to do so, hence the 1839 County Police Act quickly becoming known as the 'permissive' Act. The county police would be funded from its county police rates, and the Home Secretary was empowered to make rules and regulations for any force so established, therefore bringing any such force under greater Home Office control than the borough forces under their politically elected Watch Committees.

The County Police Act 1839 was Lord John Russell's swan song as Home Secretary. Three days after the Act was passed, Russell was transferred to the post of Secretary of State for War and the Colonies. Replacing him at the Home Office was Constantine Henry Phipps, the 1st Marquess of Normanby.

For the first time in over 500 years, the County Police Act 1839 gave the counties the opportunity to establish a police system that was tailored to fit contemporary conditions. As with the boroughs, some counties acted immediately, some partially and some completely ignored it.

FIVE

1839–56

Not only was 1839 a momentous year for the counties of the country, it was significant for the policing of London as well. Although the Metropolitan Police had been established in 1829, a complete break had not been made with the other policing systems of the capital. The year 1839 was to change all that.

By the late 1830s, the Metropolitan Police had overcome the teething problems that a brand new methodology always has to endure, and was seemingly coming to be regarded as a force for the good rather than the reverse, if the comments of the 1834 Select Committee into the Coldbath Fields episode are anything to go by. And because there were no serious problems in the meantime, by 1838 Lord John Russell, as Home Secretary, was again looking at the policing of London.

Besides the Metropolitan Police, he saw the remnants of the old police systems of the London magistrates: the Thames River Police, which had been started by Patrick Colquhoun in 1800; the Bow Street Runners; and finally the old system of watchkeepers, the legendary 'Charleys'.

Russell wanted to tidy up. The Metropolitan Police was here to stay; it had proved its worth and was a properly organised police service. He wanted to extend it to all of London by absorbing all these old systems into the far more efficient one. With that in mind, he wrote to the City, saying that it was only right to inform them that the government believed the City policing arrangements ought to be under the jurisdiction and control of the Metropolitan Police commissioners and, at that very instant, was drafting an Act of Parliament to do exactly that. The City aldermen and Court of Common Council were horrified.

To go into all the detail of what happened next would be tedious and serve no purpose. Suffice it to say that the City of London respectfully declined to be policed by the Metropolitan Police and wanted its own independent force. As such, after much frenzy, which included a petition to Queen Victoria herself, the City of London Police bill was presented to Parliament, subsequently becoming law as the City of London Police Act 1839 (2 and 3 Victoria, Chapter 44).

On Monday 11 November 1839, the City of London Police was established, being made entirely independent from the Metropolitan Police (although following the latter's model), which it still is to this day.[1]

One curious thing about this is that Daniel Whittle Harvey, at that time MP for Southwark, hoped to become the first Commissioner of the City of London Police, but wanted to remain an MP at the same time. The nonsensical nature of this ambition was firmly quashed when the Act was passed containing a clause forbidding any such thing. In the event, Harvey resigned as MP and became the first Commissioner of the City of London Police when the force was formed.

It was also enacted that the chief officer of the City of London Police should be *ex officio* a magistrate, as in the Metropolitan Police. He could not, therefore, hold the office of constable at the same time and, because he was not a constable, he could not be called a 'chief' constable. He was thus called a commissioner, making the City of London Police and the Metropolitan Police the only two police forces in the land to have commissioners rather than chief constables.

With the City of London sorted, it was now an easy task to mop up the remnants. By the Metropolitan Police Act 1839 (2 and 3 Victoria, Chapter 47), the boundaries of the Metropolitan Police district were extended to a 15-mile radius from Charing Cross; the River Police was converted into the Thames Division of the Metropolitan Police; the old constables of the London magistrates were abolished; and the Bow Street Runners were disbanded.

This last enactment made some very experienced detectives redundant. The majority went into the Metropolitan Police, but there was one, Henry Goddard, who became the first chief constable of Northamptonshire, which had formed its force on 4 January 1840 under the auspices of the County Police Act 1839. Goddard is believed to be the only ex-Runner who took up such a position. Goddard died in 1883, but the last surviving Bow Street Runner of all was Peter Shonfield, who died in 1894 aged 85.[2]

With the consolidating 1839 Act, the development of the policing of London was complete, and firmly in the hands of the Metropolitan Police and the City of London Police. No more would the happenings in London influence the police development in the rest of the country, except in one or two ways which will be mentioned when the occasion calls for it.

When the Metropolitan Police had been established there were no fears of civil mayhem, and so the Metropolitan Police had been created because of the amount of crime in London. But it was the advent of Chartism which had caused the passing of the 1839 County Police Act. In other words, it was the fear of social calamity and working-class insurrection caused by civil disorder, street brawling and general rioting, and the desire to suppress these, that had produced the need for county constabularies.

Up until the 1960s, this had been the prevailing, indeed the only, school of thought about the establishment of police forces in the country, and for want of a

16 Henry Goddard, first chief
constable of Northamptonshire,
the only Bow Street Runner to be
appointed as a chief constable when
they were disbanded in 1839.

better term was called the 'orthodox' or 'consensus' model. The consensus school
is mainly associated with police historians Charles Reith and Leon Radzinowicz,
but Jenifer Hart, Thomas Critchley, David Ascoli and J.J. Tobias have all made
contributions. The main thrust of this argument is that between 1829 and 1856,
police forces were established in answer to the perceived threat of an escalating
incidence of crime and public disorder outbreaks. Thus the police were established with the full consent of the public and, as a result, 'quickly won control
over the mob, held crime within acceptable limits, and won the confidence and
lasting admiration of the British people'.[3] And Robert Reiner, in his book *The
Politics of the Police*, adds a small proviso by saying that although there was initial
opposition, the people eventually consented to be policed as the benefits of a
'benign police institution became apparent to all'.[4]

   In 1967 Allan Silver, an American Professor of Sociology, challenged this view
and took it further when he said that the police, as well as crime and riot control,
were established by the ruling class as an instrument to maintain their dominance
and to force social control, and middle-class manners, on to the working class (or
'dangerous class'). Thus he constituted the 'conflict' school.

   This idea was taken up by Robert Storch, an American Professor of History,
who has become the main 'conflict' historian up to the present. He adds that the
working class objected to the police being thrust upon them in their everyday
life (the terms he uses are 'domestic missionary' to 'act as an all-purpose lever of

urban discipline') and violently objected in the form of anti-police riots. And when these riots proved futile, they responded with actual physical assaults upon the police, either individually or when in a group. Assaults on police, he says, became 'chronic' and 'endemic'.[5]

This needs to be explored further. In establishing their police forces, the magistrates of the counties were surely taking notice of the world around them, and in a police force they saw a way to improve that world. They knew what laws were then current and they also saw that no one was enforcing those laws.

It is doubtful whether the old parish constables ever interested themselves in bringing to justice the local drunk, the local prostitute, the local poacher or the army of 'sturdy beggars' at that time plaguing the countryside. Yet all these people were offenders against the laws then in use, and the laws in existence in the 1830s reflected both the landed classes' concerns as well as those of the thinking/respectable class.

Poaching was covered by the Night Poaching Act 1828 (8 George IV, Chapter 69) and the Game Act 1831 (1 and 2 William IV, Chapter 32), and subsequently by the Night Poaching Act 1844 (7 and 8 Victoria, Chapter 29) and the Hares Act 1848 (11 and 12 Victoria, Chapter 29). Intoxicating liquor had always been tightly controlled, especially by the Victorians who were to become paranoid about drink and the working classes. By 1840, several liquor licensing laws were in force: the Liquor Act 1532 (5 and 6 Edward VI, Chapter 25), the Intoxicating Liquor Act 1830 (1 William IV, Chapter 64), the Beerhouses Act 1834 (4 and 5 William IV, Chapter 85) and the Beerhouses Act 1840 (3 and 4 Victoria, Chapter 61).[6]

However, the 'catch-all' law in use at that time was undoubtedly the Vagrancy Act 1824 (5 George IV, Chapter 83). This Act was passed to combat the mayhem and havoc caused by the discharge of soldiers and sailors after the Napoleonic Wars, who roamed the countryside thieving, living on their wits and causing all kinds of social alarm whenever they showed up. It 'was intended to prevent wasters and sturdy beggars from wandering about the country and committing sundry questionable acts by which an easy livelihood might be gained'.[7] The Act was split into three classes: Idle and Disorderly Persons; Rogues and Vagabonds; and Incorrigible Rogues.

To be classed as an Idle and Disorderly Person, one had to commit any one of seven offences: begging; soliciting prostitutes; being an uncertificated pedlar; refusing to work as an able-bodied person and thus being chargeable on the parish; being in receipt of poor relief and absconding etc; giving false names to obtain poor relief; women neglecting illegitimate children.

To be classed as a Rogue or Vagabond, there were fifteen offences to choose from: being convicted twice of being 'idle and disorderly'; violently resisting arrest as 'an idle and disorderly person'; fortune telling; begging by exposing wounds; collecting alms under false pretences; sleeping rough; exposing obscene publications; exposing the person with intent to insult a female; having house-breaking implements; having an offensive weapon; being found on enclosed premises; loitering with intent to commit a felony; absconding and leaving the family chargeable on the Poor Laws; gaming in a public place; trading in prostitution.

To be an Incorrigible Rogue, only three offences were given: committing any of the fifteen offences as a Rogue and Vagabond having already been convicted of being a Rogue and Vagabond; violently resisting arrest as a Rogue and Vagabond; absconding from any place of confinement.[8]

The parish constable was only called in after an offence had been committed. The 'new police' were different. They were a patrolling, preventative police who went looking for offences; the Vagrancy Act was ready made for them, with virtually anything that the working class did deemed to be an offence that was not already covered by the Game Laws and Liquor Acts. It also gave the easiest power of arrest in the book ('Any, Any, Any' – any person may arrest any person committing any offence). The ordinary working man was thus faced with a regime that he had not encountered for a long time, if at all.

Is it any wonder, then, that he objected and retaliated in the only way he knew how – the only way at his disposal – physical violence, by assaulting the policeman who had just caught him doing something which he had been getting away with for years without capture or punishment? Some men, of course, accepted the inevitable and came quietly, but others did not. The police forced compliance with the existing laws, and if this means describing them as 'domestic missionaries' and 'all purpose levers of social discipline', then so be it.

It is exactly the same today. The police enforce the law; some accept it, many do not and start 'kicking up'. The evidence for this can be seen in any police reality television programme. Things have not changed much in 170 years. This is not policing by consent, this is policing by force, forcing compliance with the law. That is why in the 1830s it was called a police *force* – somewhat of a clue there.

So at the moment there is a choice of two models of police establishment, the 'conflict' and the 'consensus'. However, there are 'for' and 'against' arguments for both models, and much more research will have to be done before any definitive answer comes up, especially with regard to the 'evidence' used by Storch, when he cites the number of assaults on police and anti-police riots. The seven instances that Storch gives of anti-police riots, which occurred in Lancashire in 1839 and 1840 and which he exemplifies as evidence of the ideological clash between the working class and the police, definitely need examining.

Since at some point during these seven riots, and because the police were involved, the wrath of the mob was directed towards the police, Storch calls them anti-police riots. However, in every single one of the seven instances, the riot occurred as a result of a policeman doing a lawful act, which the recipient tried to resist and which then escalated violently and quickly as his (drunken? – four out of the seven instances started off in a public house) comrades came to his assistance spoiling for a fight, and having the opportunity to do so without fear of legal reprisal in the anonymity of the crowd.

Thus, although there was a riot and violence was directed at the police, it was not an anti-police riot (an ideological clash between the police and working-class men that occurred purely and solely because of 'the very presence of the police'); this was a clash of personalities between the policeman doing a lawful act (although probably misjudged and ill-timed) and the recipient who objected. No ideology was involved. Had the policemen not attempted to carry out their duty, no riot would have occurred, which is contrary to Storch's theory that riots occurred simply because of the mere presence of the policemen.[9]

The latest book on the conflict model is by Robert Storch himself in collaboration with David Philips, *Policing Provincial England 1829–1856: The Politics of Reform*. No significant book has recently appeared advocating the consensus model directly. However, strangely enough, of the force histories that are available of the counties voluntarily establishing forces, the authors seem to concentrate on crime and public disorder as being the reasons for establishment, thus falling into the consensus model. Yet, much more research must be done on these two models before a definite answer as to how the police were established can be found. And if an answer is arrived at, then it would, in all likelihood, turn out to be a dissatisfying and predictable mixture of both theories.

The 'permissive' County Police Act had been passed in August 1839 and enabled county magistrates to form police forces for their county only if they wanted to, as there was no follow-up coercion from central government (hence 'permissive'). And as with the boroughs of the country after the 1835 Municipal Corporations Act, the counties acted in exactly the same way: some implemented it totally, some only partially and some ignored it completely.

By placing the power to form a police force firmly into the laps of the county magistrates, central government declined to give any lead into how the police service should develop, considering it a local and not a central government issue. All central government was prepared to do was circulate the Code of Rules and Regulations of the Metropolitan Police in the hope that this would provide a model for any county force that cared to ask for them. Also, as Lord Normanby had replaced Lord John Russell as Home Secretary, these rules became known as Lord Normanby's Rules and Regulations. Lord Normanby was not anywhere near as competent as Russell, and the Duke of Wellington called Normanby's appointment to the Home Office 'a very bad, and very foolish appointment'.[10] It was to be this lack of any coherent policing policy from Normanby and his successors, along with the indifference of central government towards the county forces, that would bedevil the British police service for at least fifty years.

As far as is known, the list below is the chronological order of the forces established under the 'permissive' 1839 Act. Some dates are disputed between those

RULES,

Made by the MARQUESS *of* NORMANBY, *one of Her Majesty's Principal Secretaries of State, pursuant to the 3rd Section of the 2 & 3* VICT., *cap. 93, for Establishing an Uniform System for the* GOVERNMENT, PAY, CLOTHING, ACCOUTREMENTS, *and* NECESSARIES *for* CONSTABLES *appointed under that Act.*

Whitehall, 1st December, 1840.

QUALIFICATIONS.

CHIEF CONSTABLE.

His Age must not exceed Forty-five Years.

He must be certified by a Medical Practitioner to be in good Health, and of sound Constitution, and fitted to perform the Duties of the Office.

He must not have been a Bankrupt, nor have taken the benefit of the Insolvent Act.

He must be recommended to the Secretary of State by the Magistrates in whom the Appointment is vested, as a Person of general good Character and Conduct.

SUPERINTENDENT OR INSPECTOR.

His Age must not exceed Forty Years.

He must be not less than 5 feet 7 inches high, without his Shoes.

He must be a man of General Intelligence, able to read and write well, and to keep Accounts :

And must be certified by a Medical Practitioner, to be free from bodily complaint, and of a strong Constitution.

SERJEANT OR CONSTABLE.

His Age must not exceed Forty Years.

He must be not less than 5 feet 7 inches high, without his Shoes.

He must be able to Read and Write, Intelligent and Active, and certified to be free from bodily complaint, and of a strong Constitution ; and recommended as of irreproachable character and connexions.

If a Candidate for any of the above Offices, has been previously employed in any branch of the public Service, Civil or Military, he shall not be eligible for appointment, unless he produces satisfactory Testimonials of his conduct in such Service ; and a person who has been *dismissed* from any Police Force, shall not be eligible for appointment in any other Police Force.

Note.—On the Special Recommendation of the Chief Constable, with the Approval of two Justices, as to the peculiar fitness for Appointment of a Person exceeding the limited Age, or under the standard height, the Secretary of State will consider whether the case may not be made an exception to the Rules.

17 The first page (of three) of the Marquess of Normanby's Rules circulated to any county that asked for them.

REGULATIONS,

by the MARQUESS *of* NORMANBY, *one of Her Majesty's Principal Secretaries of State, pursuant to the 16th Section of the 3 & 4* VICT., *cap. 88, for the* GOVERNMENT *of the* LOCAL CONSTABLES *appointed under that Act.*

Whitehall, 1st December, 1840.

APPOINTMENT OF CONSTABLES.

No person shall be appointed a Local Constable who shall be a Gamekeeper, Wood-Ranger, Bailiff, Sheriff's Bailiff, or who shall be a hired servant in the employment of any person, or who shall keep or have any interest in any house for the sale of Beer, Wine, or Spirituous Liquors; and if any person who shall be appointed a Constable, shall at any time after such appointment, become a Game-keeper, Wood-Ranger, Bailiff, Sheriff's Bailiff, or shall act in any of the said capacities, or shall sell or have any interest in the sale of any Beer, Wine, or Spirituous Liquors, such person shall thereupon become and be incapable of acting as such Constable, and shall forfeit his appointment of Constable, and also all fees or allowances payable to him as a Constable,—and the Chief Constable shall not insert in the list to be made out by him and laid before the Justices acting in and for any Petty Sessional Division of the County at one of their Special Sessions, holden for hearing Appeals against the Poor Rates, the names of any persons so disqualified.

PAY, OR, FEES AND ALLOWANCES.

The Local Constable is to receive, for the service of Summonses and execution of Warrants, and for the performance of such other occasional duties as may be required of him, such Fees and Allowances only and under such regulations, as shall from time to time be settled by the Justices of the County in General or Quarter-Sessions, and approved of by one of Her Majesty's Principal Secretaries of State.

He shall not upon any occasion, or under any pretence whatsoever, take Money or other Gratuity from any person for any act done by him by virtue of his office of Constable, without the permission in writing of the Chief Constable, or of the Justices in General, or Quarter, or Petty Sessions assembled.

GENERAL INSTRUCTIONS.

All Summonses are to be served, and Warrants executed, as soon as practicable. If the party against whom a Summons or Warrant has been delivered to any Constable cannot be found within the Parish, Township, or Place for which such Constable is appointed, or if for any other cause the Constable is unable to serve the Summons, or execute the Warrant, he will report to the Chief Constable that such Summons or Warrant is in his possession, with the cause why the same has not been served or executed, and he will give to the Chief Constable, or to such other Constable as the Chief Constable may name, all the information he

18 The first page (of four) of the Marquess of Normanby's Regulations, which accompanied the Rules.

given in *The British Police. Police Forces and Chief Officers 1829–2000* by Stallion and Wall; *A History of Police in England and Wales* by T.A. Critchley; and the article 'Who Was First?' in the *Journal of the Police History Society*.[11] Wherever possible, however, the dates are as given in the individual force histories, and are the dates on which the county magistrates passed a resolution in Quarter Sessions to form a police force. The county magistrates, not the Home Secretary, were the local authority for their county, and so it is the date of the acceptance and adoption by the magistrates of the 1839 Act that must be taken, and no other.

This is a tentative list which will only be rectified by further research. Although the actual dates of establishment may be disputed, the names of the counties voluntarily establishing police forces are not:

1	Wiltshire	Wednesday 13 November 1839
2	Gloucestershire	Monday 18 November 1839
3	Norfolk	Friday 22 November 1839
4	Essex	Monday 25 November 1839
5	Durham	Tuesday 10 December 1839
6	Worcestershire	Friday 13 December 1839
7	Lancashire	Wednesday 18 December 1839
8	Leicestershire	Saturday 21 December 1839
9	Cumberland	Tuesday 31 December 1839 (Derwent Division only)
10	Hampshire	unknown date in December 1839
11	Shropshire	unknown date in December 1839
12	Northamptonshire	Saturday 4 January 1840
13	Bedfordshire	Tuesday 28 January 1840
14	Nottinghamshire	unknown date in April 1840
15	East Suffolk	Thursday 5 March 1840
16	Warwickshire	unknown date in March 1840 (Knightlow Division only)
17	Denbighshire	unknown date in May 1840
18	Montgomeryshire	Tuesday 25 July 1840
19	East Sussex	unknown date in September 1840
20	Staffordshire	unknown date in 1840
21	Hertfordshire	unknown date in January 1841
22	Isle of Ely	Tuesday 9 February 1841
23	Glamorganshire	unknown date in 1841
24	Carmarthenshire	Tuesday 25 July 1843
25	Cardiganshire	Tuesday 2 January 1844
26	West Suffolk	Tuesday 7 January 1845
27	Rutland	Thursday 29 June 1848
28	Surrey	Wednesday 1 January 1851

29	Cambridgeshire	Tuesday 25 November 1851
30	Berkshire	Saturday 9 February 1856
31	Somersetshire	Wednesday 21 May 1856[12]

But we must not be naive. Although many of these county forces were constituted properly, with adequate manpower, command structure, proper buildings and so on, there were some that were not. Rutland, for instance, consisted of only two men when it was established. Cumberland only covered its Derwent Division (centred on Keswick). Similarly, Warwickshire covered only the hundred of Knightlow, which is on the extreme east of the county, bordering Leicestershire and Northamptonshire, and containing the towns of Warwick and Coventry. Staffordshire only covered the south of the county, until October 1842 when it was extended to cover the whole. So to assume every one of these initial forces was efficient in manpower, equipment and funding would be very wrong.

Despite the debate over 'consensus' and 'conflict', we are still left with the fact that in the last two months of 1839, ten county police forces were established. And that meant ten chief constables were appointed.

Section 4 of the 1839 Act specifically mentions the appointment of a chief constable, thus emphasising that the chief officer of a county constabulary holds the appointment of constable, rather than magistrate. Section 6 of the Act places squarely upon the chief constable the power to appoint, dismiss and discipline the constables, as well as to determine their respective duties and patrol areas, or as the Act puts it, their 'general disposition'.

In this, the 1839 Act gave county chief constables powers that the borough chief constables did not have. The 1835 Municipal Corporations Act had placed the governance (including appointment and dismissal) of their borough force into the hands of the politically elected Watch Committees, and not those chosen by the Watch Committee to be their 'chief' constable. The 1839 Act did no such thing. The power to run the county force was placed into the hands of the chief constable and not the magistrates in Quarter Sessions, who as the Police Authority only held the financial power

19 A drawing made in September 1841 of PC107 James Dewey of the Wiltshire County Constabulary. This pattern seemed to be the standard adopted by the county constabularies, although not all counties embraced the use of the armlet of either horizontal or vertical stripes. The headgear would be a top hat which would have been strengthened, not only to provide protection but to provide a platform on which to look over high walls.

and not operational power. Right from the start, therefore, the county chief constables were on a different constitutional basis from the borough chiefs, with the county chiefs having the backing of parliamentary legislation, whilst the borough chiefs did not. This anomaly was not rectified until the great Police Act of 1964. In the meantime, this difference between the two is shown by the contrasting treatment of Victor Bosanquet and Benjamin Carlton.

Victor Bosanquet was the chief constable of Monmouthshire and had been since 1893 with no major 'clashes' between him and his Police Authority (the Standing Joint Committee, the successor to the magistrates in Quarter Sessions). In 1926, during the General Strike, Bosanquet started legal proceedings against two miners' leaders who had led a column of 2,000 from one of the collieries to Newport.

The procession was stopped from entering Newport and Bosanquet brought legal action against the two leaders. This was dismissed, but Bosanquet appealed. The Standing Joint Committee, which was Labour controlled, tried to get Bosanquet to withdraw the appeal. Bosanquet refused, and in July 1926 the Standing Joint Committee demanded his resignation, which was supported by forty-two votes to twenty-eight by the Monmouthshire County Council (also Labour controlled).

Flatly refusing to resign, Bosanquet argued that operational decisions were his and his alone, and were nothing to do with the politically controlled Police Authority. Although this left friction between the two, the Standing Joint Committee was powerless, and Bosanquet continued on as chief constable for another ten years, until 30 August 1936, when he died whilst holding office after forty-three years of service as chief constable.

In contrast, in 1923 the Canterbury City Watch Committee demoted its chief constable, Benjamin Carlton, to sergeant. He had been charged with four cases of alleged 'corrupt practice' under the Police Regulations 1920, mainly concerning obtaining free rides with the local bus company. As he pleaded guilty, the Watch Committee decided to be lenient and offered demotion rather than dismissal. Carlton was demoted but took the ignominy of serving as a sergeant after being the chief constable for only a few months.

The very first county chief constable to be appointed was Richard Reader Harris of Worcestershire, who was appointed on the same day as the force was established, Monday 18 November 1839. Wiltshire's Samuel Meredith was appointed on Thursday 28 November. As with the establishment of the forces, although approval of the chief constable was required by the Home Secretary, it is the date of appointment by the county magistrates which is the correct date and not the date of approval by the Home Secretary.

With the establishment of county police forces, the county magistrates were faced with something new, and if ratepayers' money was to be spent on it, it should be correct right from the start. It was expected that some counties would

20 Richard Harris, the very first chief
constable to be appointed under the
'permissive' County Police Act of 1839. He
was appointed to the Worcestershire County
Constabulary on Monday 18 November 1839.

21 Samuel Meredith, the second chief
constable to be appointed, of Wiltshire
County Constabulary, on Thursday
28 November 1839.

22 Anthony Lefroy, first chief constable of
the Gloucestershire County Constabulary.

23 Admiral John McHardy, first chief
constable of the Essex County Constabulary.

go for police experience in their first chief constable. The first chief constable of Gloucestershire, Anthony Lefroy, was exactly that, as he was an Inspector of the Irish Constabulary. But Samuel Meredith of Wiltshire had no police experience whatsoever, as he was a commander in the Royal Navy. Perhaps the thinking of the appointing magistrates was that their police force would be run along military lines, and therefore an army or naval officer, of the same socially superior gentry class, was the best man to have, rather than a policeman with previous experience.

The backgrounds of the first chief constables to be appointed are indicative of this thinking:

Worcester	Richard Harris	Inspector, Metropolitan Police
Wiltshire	Samuel Meredith	Commander, Royal Navy
Gloucestershire	Anthony Lefroy	Inspector, Irish Police
Norfolk	Richard Oakes	Lieutenant Colonel, 1st Life Guards
Essex	John McHardy	Captain, Royal Navy
Durham	John Wemyss	Major, 2nd Dragoon Guards
Lancashire	John Woodford	Captain, Rifle Brigade
Leicestershire	Frederick Goodyer	Inspector, Metropolitan Police (previously chief constable of Leicester Borough Police)
Cumberland (Derwent Division)	Samuel Eve	nothing known
Hampshire	George Robbins	Captain, Army
Shropshire	Dawson Mayne	Captain, Royal Navy (brother to Richard Mayne, Metropolitan Police Commissioner)
Northamptonshire	Henry Goddard	Bow Street Runner
Bedfordshire	Edward Boultbee	Captain, Honourable East India Company
Nottinghamshire	S. Walker	Major, Army
East Suffolk	John Hatton	Inspector, Irish Constabulary (then appointed in Staffordshire)
Warwickshire (Knightlow Hundred)	George Baker	Captain, Army
Denbighshire	John Denman	civilian, nothing known
Montgomeryshire	John Newcombe	Major, Army
East Sussex	Henry McKay	Lieutenant Colonel, 6th Inniskilling Dragoons
Staffordshire	John Hatton	appointed from East Suffolk in 1842
Hertfordshire	Archibald Robertson	Captain, Army
Isle of Ely	Frederick Hampton	Captain, Army
Glamorganshire	Charles Napier	Captain, Rifle Brigade

Carmarthenshire	R. Scott	Captain, Army
Cardiganshire	William Freeman	Captain, Army
West Suffolk	George Griffiths	Major, Army
Rutland	Thomas Garton	civilian, nothing known
Surrey	H.C. Hastings	Captain, Army
Cambridgeshire	George Davies	Captain, Royal Navy
Berkshire	James Fraser	Colonel, Army
Somersetshire	Valentine Goold	Irish Constabulary

This list is as complete as possible at the moment, which speaks volumes. Even after 170 years, there are still gaps in our knowledge. Virtually every aspect of social life in Britain has been put under the scrutiny of historians – except the police. British police history is very much an under-researched field and the number of police history books remains remarkably low. The British police service is one of the essential ingredients of a civilised society and is in evidence every day of the year, right in front of our very eyes, yet the knowledge of its history is ashamedly low or even non-existent. It is time for our historians to act.

So, of the chief constables of the first voluntary thirty-one forces, as far as is known, only six had previous police experience; the rest were officers of the army and navy. This would put them on a social par with the appointing magistrates, as these were the days of purchased commissions. The magistrates thought that army and navy officers, from the ruling class, already had the experience of ordering and administering uniformed men and so this expertise could be directly applied to another uniformed body, albeit civilians.

In applying for and accepting appointments, this list would suggest that army and navy officers did not consider the 'new police' beneath their social station. By that time, the success of the Metropolitan Police had vindicated any criticisms of the experimental nature of the 'new police', and although the higher classes saw policemen as only on a par with the servant class, nevertheless, to be a chief constable appeared to be socially acceptable. It appears, therefore, that the concept of the rural police was considered with approval in some respects, judging by the quality of the men chosen to be the pioneering chief constables.

As the nineteenth century wore on, the county chief constables seemed invariably to come from the magisterial class, whilst the borough chief constables tended not to. More often than not, the borough chief constables were promoted from the (working-class) men who had started out as constables on the beat, whilst their county colleagues were appointed straight to their office by virtue of their social background.[13]

The geographical location of these voluntary forces also raises questions. Wiltshire and Gloucestershire were the first two forces formed, but why did their immediate neighbours of Dorsetshire, Somersetshire, Oxfordshire and Berkshire not do so? Were they not affected by Chartist riots or plagued by vagrants?

Northamptonshire was not especially threatened with any real Chartist problems, yet formed its force in January 1840.[14] Why was this so? It may indicate that counties not threatened by civil violence were as much concerned with crime and enforcement of law as with anything else, and in the 1839 Act saw some means to deal with it. But if that is solely the case, why the flurry of eighteen forces being established in 1839 and 1840 when the threat of violent civil riots was real, and only ten being established in the succeeding sixteen years until 1856 when this threat was receding?

Throughout the 1840s Chartist violence was perceived to be waning and in its death throes. The last great Chartist rally was held in London in April 1848, and although subsequently having a few flutters here and there, Chartism was not as panic-inducing as it once was. But if Chartism was no longer a threat, surely crime was still prevalent? Only ten 'new police' forces were established between 1840 and 1856, so magistrates could not have been that concerned about crime or with enforcing compliance with the law by the working classes. Maybe, then, the magistrates were more concerned with civil disorder than with crime. Or maybe there is another traditional highly influential factor – money.

The county forces that were set up were financed by local rates, and after 1840 fears were being voiced by, and to, the county magistrates about the cost of the county force. There are several instances of county magistrates being urged by county ratepayers either to abolish or reduce the county force on account of its cost. Durham, for example, at the January 1842 Quarter Sessions, received petitions from 172 of its 240 parishes for the complete disbanding of its county force.[15] And in Bedfordshire, the 1841 summer Quarter Sessions received similar deputations from numerous parishes.[16]

The perceived need to get cheaper police brought about the two last wheezings of the parish constable system. To pay parish constables only when needed was first proposed by Thomas Law Hodges, a Tory country gentleman in Kent. When in August 1841 the Melbourne Whig ministry fell, to be replaced by the Tory ministry of Sir Robert Peel, with Sir James Graham replacing Lord Normanby as Home Secretary,[17] unsurprisingly the Peel ministry was interested in police reform.

Based on Hodges' scheme, the Parish Constables Act 1842 (5 and 6 Victoria, Chapter 109) was passed on 12 August 1842. In effect, it required the county magistrates in petty sessions in each parish to draw up lists of those men who could be sworn in as parish constables should the occasion arise, but only to act in their own parish and only when needed, thus saving money on a permanent county constabulary. The Act also ordered that lock-ups be provided throughout the county for the temporary confinement of prisoners, and that superintending constables were to be appointed who would be paid out of county rates and who would be in charge of the lock-ups, newly built or provided under the Act.

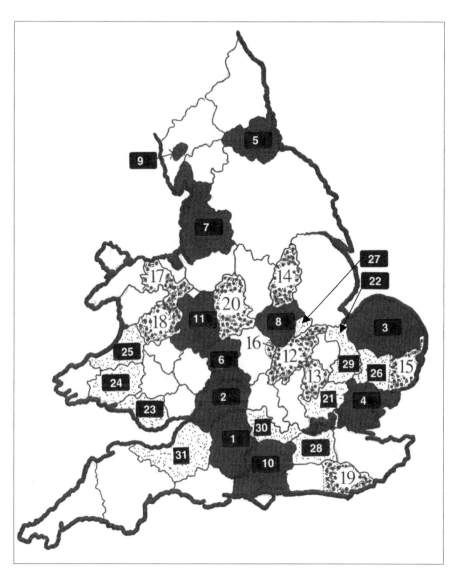

24 Map of England and Wales showing the thirty-one voluntary forces, 1839 to 1856.
Numbers 1–11 formed in the autumn of 1839; numbers 12–20 formed in 1840; and numbers
21–31 formed between 1841 and 1856.

It is not known how many counties took up this Act, as no returns were ever made. However, we do know that in Kent, where it all started, the system was deemed to be such good value for money that when an attempt to set up a county force under the 1839 County Police Act was made, it was defeated by thirty votes in favour of the parish constables.[18]

No further attempts at police reform were made until 1850, when, under the ministry of Lord John Russell with Sir George Grey as Home Secretary, an amending Act to the 1842 Parish Constables Act was made. Again inspired by the Kent Quarter Sessions, the Parish Constables Act 1850 (13 Victoria, Chapter 20) enabled the magistrates in Quarter Sessions to appoint divisional superintendents for all petty session divisions, who would be in charge of the superintending constables of the lock-ups and the parish constables themselves.

However, the parish constables under the 1842 Act were not volunteers; in effect, they were conscripted. Therefore, it was a conscripted police force and conscription seldom works. Nevertheless, before all this was discovered, the divisional superintending constable system was widely adopted by those counties not having the 'new police' forces of the 1839 County Police Act.

The 1850 Act was implemented fully in Buckinghamshire, Derbyshire, Herefordshire, Kent, Lincolnshire, Northumberland, Oxfordshire, West Sussex and all the Ridings of Yorkshire. It was not implemented in Berkshire, Devonshire, Dorsetshire and Somersetshire. Not having implemented the 1839 Act either, they still continued with the old parish constable system.[19]

In effect, in 1850 England had three parallel policing systems going on at the same time, and it might have stayed like that had it not been for one man. Starting in December 1852, the ministry of Lord Aberdeen was destined to last less than three years, but during that time, there was one man in government who, by his drive and vigorous qualities, would shake the country out of the puzzling clutter of policing systems which had been allowed to develop.

Described by one police historian as an 'ebullient genius',[20] Lord Palmerston became Home Secretary in December 1852, and so became responsible for a police service fragmented for several reasons. These included the partial implementation and non-enforcement of the 1835 Municipal Corporations Act in the boroughs; only patchy adoption of the 'permissive' 1839 County Police Act; only some counties opting for the superintending constable system of the Parish Constables Acts of 1842 and 1850; and some counties not adopting either, but still relying on the ancient parish constable system.

Palmerston's attention was drawn to the police question by a letter from Lord Fortescue, a Devonshire magistrate, dated January 1853.[21] Spurred on by this to investigate, he uncovered for himself the whole mishmash of the police service that he had inherited. Palmerston could see the total nonsense of it all and it took no great imagination to realise that criminals might well be sheltering in those counties not having a full-time preventive or patrolling police force. Indeed, just such a thing had already happened. Three years earlier, a brutal murder had been carried out at Frimley by a notorious gang who were using unpoliced Surrey as a haven between 'efficiently' policed Hampshire and London. In fact, it was this incident which led directly to the Surrey County Constabulary being established.[22]

The Select Committee on Police was appointed by Palmerston in 1853, the secretary being Edwin Chadwick. Chadwick, it will be remembered, had also been involved in the Royal Commission of 1836, and the 1853 Committee gave him an opportunity to review the happenings of the intervening years.

The picture was not encouraging. Of the 178 boroughs of England and Wales, thirteen had never formed any sort of police force even though the 1835 Municipal Corporations Act had required them to do so, and many of the existing borough forces were totally inadequate in terms of manpower in ratio to the population. The counties were no better either. Only thirty-one of a total of fifty-six had implemented the 1839 County Police Act and, of these, some had inadequate manpower and were not covering the whole of their counties.[23]

The counties which had adopted the Parish Constables Acts were also examined and evidence taken on the efficiency of the system. The most devastating criticism of the superintending constables system came from John Dunne, who had himself been a superintending constable in Kent, but had been appointed as chief constable of Norwich City in 1851 (and who, as Sir John Dunne, would be one of the longest serving chief constables, with fifty-two years' service with three forces).

Dunne found his parish constables (who were not volunteers, but 'pressed') disinclined to serve, refractory, hopeless, occasionally obstructive and inclined to sabotage inspections of public houses by tipping off landlords beforehand. His 'force' lacked professionalism and was prone to insubordination. There was no co-ordination between the petty sessions magistrates and the Quarter Sessions, who were each trying their hands at 'empire building', to the detriment of the system.[24]

Dunne was not alone in his criticisms; many of the divisional superintendents were of the same mind. These criticisms, and the eventual confession from the Buckinghamshire magistrates that the superintending constable policing of its county was not working and perhaps a more embodied and consolidated police force under the 1839 County Police Act would have been better, meant that the 1853 Select Committee looked upon the superintending constable system as unviable.[25]

As expected, the Select Committee's report was a comparison of those counties and boroughs that had 'new police' forces against those that did not, with the superintending constables system and unpoliced areas emerging unfavourably.[26] Although the question of a national police force again reared its head, Chadwick by this time had changed his mind, saying that he now considered it undesirable. However, he appears to have left his options open. The sixth recommendation of

25 A police sabre, issued in many county forces, especially to the men stationed in the most rural and isolated beats. This one is dated 1867.

the report suggested that the smaller borough forces be amalgamated with their surrounding counties and the larger boroughs share some kind of management system with their counties, even to the extent of having the same chief constable. Had this recommendation been carried through (in the event, it was not), it would have been much easier subsequently to form a national force if it was considered necessary for some reason – or Chadwick changed his mind again.

Recommendations seven and eight of the report are the most important. The committee advocated that police forces should now become compulsory in every borough and county of England and Wales, and that central government should provide financial aid to those forces, without interfering with their local management.

The cost for the 'voluntary' forces of 1839–56 had fallen entirely upon the local county ratepayers, and it was realised that it was probably this lack of financial aid from central government which had caused the 1839 Act not to have been adopted by more counties. The 1853 Select Committee thus included a financial aid provision as one of the mainstays of their report.

Armed with the Select Committee's report, Palmerston drafted a proposed police bill during the late winter of 1854. His new-found enthusiasm, though, seemed to take over and his bill made far greater changes than was recommended by the Select Committee.

They were drastic propositions: boroughs with less than 20,000 population would lose their independent police force and be policed by their surrounding counties and the remaining boroughs would come under greater Home Office control; the five smallest counties were to be forcibly amalgamated with bigger neighbours for police purposes – and to top it all, there would be no government financial aid.

Not surprisingly, these propositions met with storms of opposition from the boroughs, and Palmerston was rapidly forced to water them down. But even his second attempt failed because his original ideas were not reduced far enough. No doubt he would have tried again, but fate took a hand when, in February 1855, Parliament was prorogued and Palmerston became Prime Minister after the ensuing General Election. His replacement at the Home Office, Sir George Grey, continued with the police question, and in early 1856 introduced the third police bill into Parliament.

Being much closer to the report of the Select Committee, now three years old, Grey's police bill stood a far better chance of success from the outset than Palmerston's two efforts. Grey proposed that police forces should indeed become compulsory, with each being maintained in an efficient manner. In order to achieve this efficiency, Grey adapted one of the Benthamite ideals of Chadwick in establishing an Inspectorate of Constabulary, which would inspect every force annually, with the incentive of a government grant of one-quarter of the annual cost of pay and clothing being given to efficient forces. Grey left the borough forces alone, except to say that boroughs with populations under 5,000 would not be entitled to receive the government grant. In this way, of course, he applied pressure on these small borough forces to amalgamate with their counties.

But even Grey's bill came up against opposition. From its first introduction into the House on Tuesday 5 February 1856, the bill was continually barraged with criticism and objection, mainly from the municipal corporations of the sixty-four small boroughs who stood to receive no government grant.

Whatever the corporations might have thought, however, the Members obviously thought differently. The Borough of Banbury, for instance, had presented their Member, Henry Tancred, with a petition opposing the bill, but in the event he voted against his constituents' wishes and supported the Whig government.[27] Tancred, a Liberal, was not alone. The bill was passed on Monday 10 March and received the Royal Assent on Monday 21 July 1856, becoming known as the County and Borough Police Act 1856 (19 and 20 Victoria, Chapter 19).

In short, the 1856 Act had four main points:

1 Every county and borough must maintain a police force
2 This police force must be 'efficient'
3 And to ensure this efficiency, every force will be inspected annually by a newly created Inspectorate of Constabulary
4 And if found efficient by the Inspectors, central government would pay one quarter of the annual cost of pay and clothing (called the 'Exchequer Grant'), whilst the other three quarters, plus the cost of the other expenses, coming from the local rates

The 1856 Act did not apply to the Metropolitan Police or to the City of London Police. It did not apply, either, to Scotland which had its own specific Act of Parliament to cover the establishment of a Scottish Inspectorate of Constabulary.

Canals, Railways & Docks Police

Due to the industrialisation going on in this period, canals, railways and docks became part of the British infrastructure. Every company running such an operation quickly came to realise that a police force was needed because of the amount of thieving of their property that was going on.

However, as these men were employees of a private company, their powers were limited in the eyes of the law. Consequently, railway companies were allowed to appoint their police forces as special constables, under the Special Constables Act 1831 (1 and 2 William IV, Chapter 41), thus giving them police powers when faced with crime. The appointment of canal police was made possible by the Constables on Canals Act 1840 (3 and 4 Victoria, Chapter 50). These police forces were established because of crime, although some railway police forces used their men to work the signals as well.

Due to the fact that they were established early on, in some parts of the country the canal police, along with the railway police, are older than the county forces through which the canals and railways run. Eventually, over the years, the individual railway and canals companies amalgamated to form ever bigger companies, and their police forces followed suit. This process came to its logical conclusion in 1962 when the only national police force in Great Britain was constituted: the British Transport Police.

As far as can be found, these are all the railway and canal police forces that have existed, plus their dates of operation:

Stockton and Darlington Railway Police	1825– ??
Liverpool and Manchester Railway Police	1830– ??
London and Birmingham Railway Police	1833– ??
Great Western Railway Police	1835–1947
Taff Vale Railway Police	1836–1922
Hull and Selby Railway Police	1836–1872
Eastern Counties Railway Police	1836–1862
London and South Western Railway Police	1839–1922
West London Railway Police	1840–1920
Midland Railway Police	1844–1922
North British Railway Police	1844–1922
Eastern Union Railway Police	1844–1862
Furness Railway Police	1844–1922
Caledonian Railway Police	1845–1922
North Staffordshire Railway Police	1845–1922
London and North Western Railway Police	1846–1922
Great Northern Railway Police	1846–1922
London, Brighton and South Coast Railway Police	1846–1922

Lancashire and Yorkshire Railway Police	1847–1922
South Devon and Cornwall Railway Police	?? –1849
Glasgow and South Western Railway Police	1850–1922
North London Railway Police	1853–1922
South Eastern Railway Police	1854–1920
Rhmney Railway Police	1854–1922
North Eastern Railway Police	1854–1922
London, Tilbury and Southend Railway Police	1854–1912
Scottish North Eastern Railway Police	1856–1866
London, Chatham and Dover Railway Police	1857–1920
Pembroke and Tenby Railway Police	1859–1897
Metropolitan Railway Police	1863–1934
Cheshire Lines Committee Police	1865–1948
Great Eastern Railway Police	1862–1922
Somerset and Dorset Joint Railway Police	1862–1948
Metropolitan District Railway Police	1868–1934
Bristol and Exeter Railway Police	?? –1876
Barry Railway Police	1884–1922
Hull and Barnsley Railway Police	1885–1922
Port Talbot Railway and Dock Police	1894–1922
Cardiff Railway Police	1897–1922
Great Central Railway Police	1897–1922
South Eastern and Chatham Railway Police	1920–1922
Brecon and Merthyr Tydfil Junction Railway Police	?? –1922
London, Midland and Scottish Railway Police	1923–1947
London and North Eastern Railway Police	1923–1947
Southern Railway Police	1923–1947
London Transport Police	1934–1958
South Yorkshire Canal Police	1895–1948
Aire and Calder Navigation Police	?? –1948
Grand Union Canal Police	1929–1950
Lee Navigation Police	?? –1948
British Transport Commission Police	1948–1962
British Transport Police	1962–present

Alongside all of this, each port and docks complex also found it necessary to form a police force. Again, over the years these have been absorbed into either the British Transport Police or the Port of London Authority Police, although there are some, given at the end, which are still in existence in their original form:

West India Dock Police	1802–1838
London Dock Police	1805–1864

East India Dock Police	1807–1838
Commercial Dock Police	1810–1865
Saint Katherine's Dock Police	1823–1864
Gloucester and Berkeley Docks Police	1827–1948
East and West India Dock Police	1838–1901
Southampton Harbour Board Police	1838–1968
Hull Docks Police	1840–1893
Grand Surrey Dock and Canal Police	1855–1865
London and Saint Katherine's Dock Police	1864–1901
Surrey Commercial Docks Police	1865–1908
Bute Docks Police	1865–1897
Milwall Docks Police	1868–1908
Barry Dock Police	1884–1922
Port Talbot Railway and Dock Police	1894–1922
London and India Docks Police	1901–1908
Swansea Harbour Police	?? –1922
Belfast Harbour Police	1825–present
Falmouth (Harbour) Docks Police	1870–present
Larne Harbour Police	1877–present
Port of London Authority Police	1908–present
Dover Harbour Board Police	1920–present
Port of Bristol Authority Police	1929–present
Port of Felixstowe Police	1975–present
Port of Liverpool Police	1976–present
Isle of Man Harbour Police	?? –present

The whole history of the policing of transport in this country is so huge that it cannot be given here and demands books all to itself. And so it has: *The Railway Policeman. The Story of the Constable on the Track* by J.R. Whitbread; *A Force on the Move: the Story of the British Transport Police 1825–1995* by Pauline Appleby; and *The Keepers of the Door: The History of the Port of London Authority Police* by Glyn Hardwicke.

SIX

1856–74

The remaining counties which had not formed their county constabularies were now legally bound to establish one, and an efficient one at that. And this they did, in the flurry of 1856 and 1857, to ensure that when they were scrutinised by the new Inspectors of Constabulary, they would receive actual hard cash from the government for doing so. The dates of the formation of forces are:

32.	North Riding of Yorkshire	Tuesday 14 October 1856
33.	Flintshire	unknown date in November 1856
34.	West Riding of Yorkshire	Saturday 29 November 1856
35.	Dorsetshire	Tuesday 2 December 1856
36.	Lincolnshire	Thursday 1 January 1857 (all three parts, Lindsey, Kesteven and Holland)
37.	Westmorland	Tuesday 6 January 1857
38.	Breconshire	Tuesday 6 January 1857
39.	Cornwall	Tuesday 6 January 1857
--	Cumberland	Tuesday 6 January 1857 (extended to whole county)
40.	Devonshire	Tuesday 6 January 1857
41.	East Riding of Yorkshire	Tuesday 6 January 1857
42.	Radnorshire	Thursday 8 January 1857
43.	Kent	Wednesday 14 January 1857
44.	Herefordshire	Monday 19 January 1857
--	Warwickshire	Thursday 5 February 1857 (extended to whole county)
45.	Buckinghamshire	Friday 6 February 1857
46.	West Sussex	Thursday 26 February 1857
--	Liberty of Peterborough	Tuesday 10 March 1857
47.	Derbyshire	Tuesday 17 March 1857

48.	Monmouthshire	Monday 23 March 1857
49.	Oxfordshire	Wednesday 25 March 1857
50.	Northumberland	Wednesday 1 April 1857
51.	Caernarfonshire	Thursday 9 April 1857
52.	Anglesey	Monday 20 April 1857
53.	Cheshire	Monday 20 April 1857
54.	Huntingdonshire	unknown date in April 1857
55.	Pembrokeshire	Tuesday 9 June 1857
56.	Merionethshire	Wednesday 30 September 1857

Although the three parts of Lincolnshire (Lindsey, Holland and Kesteven) all had separate forces, they were all considered as one county and had just the one chief constable. Similarly, the Liberty of Peterborough, which was formerly in Northamptonshire, formed its own, separate force in 1856, but was still considered part of Northamptonshire and so shared the same chief constable, an arrangement which continued until 1931.

Having witnessed thirty-one counties set up forces voluntarily, these new twenty-five also cast an eye over what sort of a job the original thirty-one chief constables had made of it, and their observations must have determined whether they chose police officers or army or navy officers. These are the men chosen, and there are no prizes for guessing the ratio of army and navy officers to policemen:

North Riding of Yorkshire	Thomas Hill	Captain, Army
Flintshire	Peter Browne	civilian, nothing known
West Riding of Yorkshire	Charles Cobbe	Lieutenant Colonel, The Buffs
Dorsetshire	Samuel Cox	Lieutenant Colonel, Army
Lincolnshire	Philip Bicknell	Captain, The Black Watch
Westmorland	John Dunne	Superintending constable
Breconshire	Edmund Gwynne	Lieutenant, Army
Cornwall	Walter Gilbert	Colonel, Army (and Baronet?)
Cumberland	John Dunne	sharing with Westmorland
Devon	Gerald de Courcey Hamilton	Sub-Inspector General of Police, Australia
East Riding of Yorkshire	Bernard Layard	Lieutenant Colonel, Army
Radnorshire	James Telfer	Captain, Royal Artillery
Kent	John Ruxton	Captain, King's Royal Rifle Corps
Herefordshire	James Telfer	sharing with Radnorshire
Warwickshire	James Isaac	Metropolitan Police
Buckinghamshire	Willoughby Carter	Captain, Army
West Sussex	Frederick Montgomerie	Captain, Army

Liberty of Peterborough	Henry Bayly	District Inspector, Irish Constabulary, sharing with Northamptonshire
Derbyshire	Willoughby Fox	Irish Constabulary
Monmouthshire	Edmund Herbert	Major, Army
Oxfordshire	Charles Owen	Captain, Army
Northumberland	Alexander Browne	Major, Army
Caernarfonshire	Thomas Ellis	Lieutenant, Army
Anglesey	David Griffith	Captain, Army
Cheshire	Thomas Smith	Captain, Army
Huntingdonshire	George Davies	Captain, Royal Navy, sharing with Cambridgeshire
Pembrokeshire	Anthony Stokes	Captain, King's Shropshire Light Infantry
Merionethshire	H. Lloyd-Clough	Captain, Army

Of the twenty-four chief constables appointed (although Dunne, Bayly, Telfer and Davies each held two forces 'in plurality'), only four had previous police experience; four have unknown backgrounds but the remaining sixteen were all army or navy officers. The tendency of the counties to choose military officers over experienced policemen lasted well into the twentieth century, which led to a few problems along the way, which will be explored later.

The baton now passes to the Inspectorate of Constabulary, because by the 1856 County Police Act, the responsibility for the welfare of the policing of England and Wales had been placed well and truly into their hands. So it is to Her Majesty's Inspectors of Constabulary that the attention now turns.

As soon as the Inspectorate started in 1856, the inspectors themselves gave the English and Welsh police the most thorough scrutiny ever, even greater than the 1836 Royal Commission and 1853 Select Committee. What they found was most discouraging, as was to be expected considering the potpourri of policing systems that had been bequeathed to them.

Right from the start the inspectors identified six major flaws in the policing of the country, which they thought, when rectified, would place the policing of the country on a sure footing. So from 1856, the policy of the Inspectorate was geared to fulfilling these six main aims.

However, it would take the Inspectorate until 1890 to succeed in them all, and it was certainly not plain sailing all the way. It was a tough job and they very nearly failed. This period consisted of two phases: from 1856 until 1874 and from 1874 until 1890.

The implementation of the 1856 Act, and the choice of the Inspectors of Constabulary, was left to Sir George Grey as Home Secretary. His choice for the first inspector, William Cartwright, was seemingly unorthodox, as Cartwright himself had never been a policeman and had never held the office of chief constable. But was Grey astute in his choice?

William Cartwright was from the county landowning family of baronets of Aynho in Northamptonshire, and was steeped in the ways of local government. After army service (he had fought in the Peninsular War and at Waterloo), he had been chairman of Brackley Board of Guardians since 1833, Deputy Lord Lieutenant of Northamptonshire since 1846 and chairman of Northamptonshire Quarter Sessions since 1851.

Allied to this, the Cartwright family as a whole had a reputation for being 'pro-police'. William's father, William Ralph Cartwright, at that time a Tory MP, had been the magistrate who had proposed that Northamptonshire adopt the 1839 'permissive' Act and form a county police force in January 1840; he subsequently sat on the committee of magistrates which acted as the county Police Authority.[1] William Cartwright himself had unsuccessfully applied to be the first chief constable of Essex in 1839,[2] and William's son Aubrey, as MP for South Northamptonshire, would be one of the Members agitating for police superannuation reform and would sit on the 1875 Superannuation Select Committee.[3]

Grey was certainly aware of the Cartwright family's reputation regarding the 'new police'. He was also aware of Cartwright's experience and skill in local government, a quality which was absolutely essential because Grey and his contemporaries believed that the government of the police lay firmly in the province of local rather than central government. The 1853 Select Committee's report[4] had stressed this, and even Palmerston was firmly attached to 'the principle of local self-government'.[5]

Indeed, as Carolyn Steedman argues, the 1856 Act itself actually strengthened the powers of the magistrates by defining existing petty-sessional divisions as police units and thereby placing the magistrates 'firmly at the apex' of local policing.[6] It was this local structure that would, in time, easily lead to police officers being used for local civil administrative functions such as Weights and Measures Inspectors, Common Lodging House Inspectors and the like. It was Grey himself who would write to his first inspectors that they must 'secure the goodwill and cooperation of the local authorities'.[7]

The feeling that the Home Office considered policing to be a local government function in the period 1856 to c. 1874 is shown most in the question of consolidation of the smaller borough forces with their surrounding counties. The refusal of the Home Office to get involved with consolidation questions was not an 'abnegation of responsibility', writes Steedman, 'but a clear refusal to interfere in the financial and legal structure of local government'.[8] In any case, she adds, this feeling was further reinforced by most parliamentary private secretaries having already been in local government themselves as deputy lieutenants, chairmen of Quarter Sessions and magistrates. It was this clear refusal of the

26 William Cartwright, the first
Inspector of Constabulary to be
appointed.

Home Office to provide any coherent police policy from central government
that was to be the hallmark of the period 1856 to 1874, and which was to present
the inspectors with the opportunity to formulate their own policies based on
local government structures.

Cartwright, therefore, with his unique mixture of local government experience and police interests, must have seemed to Grey like a godsend. Within nine
days of the passing of the Act, Cartwright had been snapped up at an annual salary
of £700.[9] Grey's trust was not misplaced. Cartwright was the most influential of
the first three inspectors,[10] and arguably of all time. So much so that in his obituary in 1873 he was described as 'the policeman's friend'.[11]

Section 15 of the 1856 Act stipulated that a maximum of three inspectors could
be appointed. Grey initially appointed only two. Cartwright's appointment warrant is dated Friday 1 August 1856, and is preserved in the Northamptonshire
Record Office.[12] Grey's second choice was more conventional.

John Woodford, a nephew of Sir John Woodford of Keswick, the general of
the Peninsular War, had been chief constable of Lancashire since the force was
formed in 1839.[13] His success in establishing and maintaining the administration,
discipline and strength of purpose necessary to mould a body of men into a

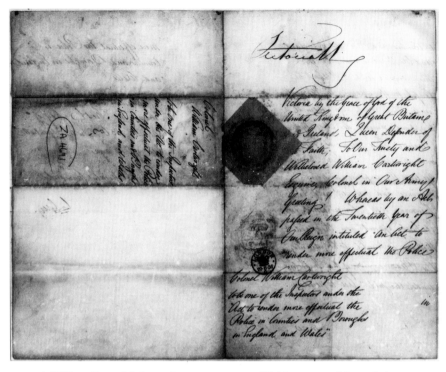

27 & 28 William Cartwright's appointment warrant as HM Inspector of Constabulary.

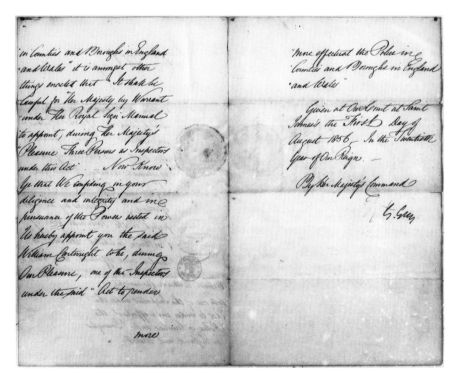

coherent constabulary, which at that time was the second largest force in the country after the Metropolitan Police, led Woodford to be regarded as the country's 'top policeman'.[14]

The fact that Grey, as Home Secretary, then left the implementation of the 1856 Act to his two new inspectors is shown by Cartwright himself in the very first annual report of the inspectors for 1856–57.[15] As the inspectors had been appointed in the late summer and autumn, and wished to start work straight away, the inspection year started on 1 October and lasted until 29 September (in other words, the old legal Quarter Day, Michaelmas Day). Thus, inspectors' reports overlap two calendar years, an annoying practice that persisted until 1959, when Sir William Johnson finally saw sense and made all subsequent reports for calendar years.[16]

In his first report, Cartwright clearly stated that England and Wales were to be split into two districts by Woodford and himself. They then decided between them that such large areas would be impossible to cover, and that, inevitably, a third inspector would have to be appointed to split the country into three districts rather than two. This idea was communicated to Grey, who complied.

Again, Grey's choice of third inspector was conventional. Edward Willis was chief constable of Manchester City, and had been since 1842; previous to that he had been Woodford's deputy of the Lancashire force.[17] Woodford was thus well aware of Willis' capabilities, and doubtless was very influential on Grey over the new appointment, which took place on Tuesday 20 January 1857.[18]

England and Wales were divided by the inspectors into three districts. The Northern District, under Woodford, consisted of the counties of Cheshire, Cumberland, Durham, Lancashire, Northumberland, Westmorland and the three Ridings of Yorkshire, plus all the boroughs within these counties.

The Midland District, under Cartwright, consisted of Bedfordshire, Buckinghamshire, Cambridgeshire, Derbyshire, Essex, Hertfordshire, Huntingdonshire, Leicestershire, Lincolnshire, Norfolk, Northamptonshire, Nottinghamshire, Oxfordshire, Rutland, Shropshire, Staffordshire, Suffolk (East and West), Warwickshire, Worcestershire, Anglesey, Caernarfonshire, Denbighshire, Flintshire, Merionethshire and Montgomeryshire, plus all the boroughs.

The Southern District, under Willis, consisted of Berkshire, Cornwall, Devonshire, Dorsetshire, Gloucestershire, Herefordshire, Kent, Monmouthshire, Somersetshire, Surrey, Sussex (East and West), Wiltshire, Breconshire, Carmarthenshire, Glamorganshire, Pembrokeshire and Radnorshire, plus all the boroughs.

Cartwright in his first report states how he approached his task. Journeying round his district in the first months of 1857, he made a preliminary study of the existing forces and offered advice to those new forces being established under the 1856 Act. In this cursory survey, he found that only fifteen of his twenty-five counties already had forces in existence – and of those fifteen, he considered only nine to be efficient.

29 John Woodford, the second Inspector of Constabulary to be appointed.

Returning to his home at Flore House, near Northampton, he employed clerks (for which he was given expenses)[19] to maintain correspondence with the Quarter Sessions of his counties and the Watch Committees of his boroughs. His official inspection was then made in the summer months of 1857, when he and the other two inspectors visited and considered the efficiency of every police force in the land.

Upon the definition of 'efficiency', the 1856 Act was reticent. The only concrete instruction that it gave to the inspectors was under Section 15, which issued them with powers to 'inspect the State of the Police Stations, Charge Rooms, Cells or Lock-ups, or other Premises occupied for the Use of such Police'. The question as to the adequacy of police buildings, which, as Steedman points out, 'had been noticeably lacking in previous years',[20] at least gave the inspectors a tangible starting point and was one which they 'were to pursue with tenacity for the next ten years'.[21]

But the Act was strangely quiet on what else constituted 'efficiency', except for Section 16 which provided for the issue of a Certificate of Efficiency to every force found to be in a 'State of Efficiency in point of Numbers and Discipline'. The definition of efficiency, therefore, was left to the inspectors themselves to decide.

The conclusion they arrived at addressed the twin issues of Section 16 (i.e. numbers and discipline) and consisted of asking four questions of every individual police force:

30 Edward Willis, the third Inspector
of Constabulary to be appointed.

1 What is the absolute strength of the force?
2 What is the ratio of policemen to population?
3 What is the quality of supervision exercised over the men?
4 What degree of co-operation is given to neighbouring forces?[22]

On the question of the ratio of policemen to population, the inspectors were not
entirely in the dark. The 1839 'permissive' Act (unlike the 1856 Act) had actually
stipulated a ration of at least one policeman per thousand people in the counties.[23]
This was at least a starting point, and was taken as the norm by the inspectors.
But this was for counties. Surely towns and large cities had to be different?
Woodford approached Grey. 'The Home Secretary,' replied Grey, in a letter of
Tuesday 21 October 1856:

> could not give any sanction to the rule that a police force is to be considered suf-
> ficient in point of numbers if it is in the proportion of one man to a thousand, and
> he thinks that although it is possible that in some places that might be a sufficient
> number, experience has shown that in towns with a large population a larger pro-
> portion is requisite.[24]

Grey's seemingly non-committal reply stopped short at giving a direct order and
placed the onus squarely back on the inspectors, implying that they had to make
up their own minds on this point, as well as every other.

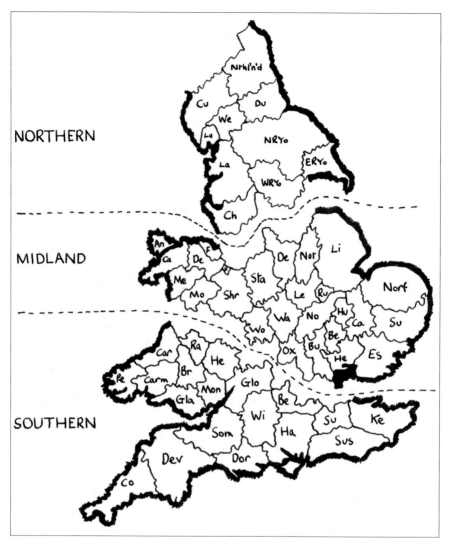

31 The three original inspection districts as decided by the Inspectors of Constabulary themselves in 1856. Woodford took the Northern District, Cartwright took the Midland District and Willis took the Southern District. These districts would vary over the years.

In the middle months of 1857, the inspections began. All three inspectors, writes Jenifer Hart, worked very hard initially, 'visiting almost every station and lock-up, taking many days over even small forces'.[25] The length of the inspections varied, however. Woodford, for instance, took thirteen days to inspect Lancashire, even though he had been the chief constable just a few months previously.[26]

It was relatively easy for the inspectors to address themselves to their four questions. The ratio of police officers to population could be arrived at by a simple long division sum using the 1851 census figures.[27] If in the inspector's opinion the ratio was not correct, then he could bring influence to bear upon the Police Authority by the subtle threat of withholding the Exchequer Grant. The inspectors did not use a legal 'sledgehammer', indeed they could not, because the 1856 Act did not give them one – it only gave them the power to recommend, not to coerce. But this seemed to work well in some instances. 'There is ample evidence,' writes Parris, 'of the influence of the Inspectors in rendering forces efficient.'[28] For example, Devonshire County increased its manpower to an efficient state in 1856–57 after a direct recommendation from Willis.[29] Likewise, Shrewsbury Borough in 1856–57 after Cartwight's recommendation[30] and Sunderland Borough in 1861–62 after Woodford's.[31]

On the discipline aspect of the four questions, the inspectors tested the efficiency by ensuring that 'a force should have enough superior officers to supervise the constables on duty continuously and regularly'.[32] The lack of supervision, especially in the boroughs, was frequently mentioned by the inspectors in their reports,[33] but again there is ample evidence that they addressed this problem and achieved success. Radnorshire County, in 1857, appointed a second superintendent because Cartwright had said that it was 'impossible for the present Superintendent to supervise the constables of the whole county in an efficient manner'. At a salary of £80 per year, plus £40 horse allowance (which is equivalent today to £3,450 and £1,725), the financial strain on a tiny county with limited resources must have been tremendous.[34] Nevertheless, Cartwright's recommendation was carried through.[35]

Northamptonshire County introduced another tier of supervision in 1857 with the creation of six police sergeants, a rank hitherto unknown in the force. This was Cartwright's direct influence (after all, he lived in the county). Cartwright was a great believer in sergeants anyway: 'there is no rank more valuable to the well working of a force.'[36]

The internal discipline of a force was also directly correlated to inter-force co-operation. The 'conference point' system, where one constable from one force met with a constable from a neighbouring force for the mutually beneficial swapping of information, could not work if numbers and discipline were lacking in either force.[37]

Overall, the inspectors were flexible and did not apply rigid, unswerving rules. Each force was looked at in the context of its own locality. So the efficiency was judged by considering the needs of the locality in ordinary conditions and not in exceptional periods of unrest; and the adequacy of the police to combat crime, not to exterminate it completely (which they knew was impossible anyway); and the average level of co-operation between forces, and not the extreme cases of non-co-operation.[38] This flexibility did not antagonise or create jealousies amongst the police authorities by treating forces in similar circumstances differently to others. On the contrary, says Jenifer Hart, the fact 'that a great deal was achieved by persuasion, testifies to the good sense and the tact of the inspectorate, or at any rate the first three Inspectors'.[39] Anyway, she adds, 'they were far from being ogres'.[40]

Each inspector wrote a separate report, but all three documents were prepared for Parliament together and were presented in one volume. The first inspectors' report was published in the autumn of 1857, and detailed minutely the results of the closest scrutiny that the English and Welsh police service had been subjected to up until that time. The results were hardly encouraging.

The idea that the country possessed a standardised and homogenous police system was completely exploded by the first annual report of the Inspectors of Constabulary (hereafter referred to as the 'First Report'). Each inspector gave his detailed comments for every single force and the variance over the whole police service was marked and noticeable. Individual forces were found to be different in pay, outlook, leadership, efficiency, status and even in the uniform itself – Lancashire County, for example, had a rifle-green uniform,[41] as did Shropshire County, where the police were nicknamed 'Paddy Mayne's Grasshoppers' after the chief constable Irishman Dawson Mayne, brother to Richard Mayne.[42]

The inspectors found themselves confronted with a massive task, although they were thankful to find that in some instances they were not facing the problems alone. Some police authorities were just as keen as the inspectors to maintain an efficient force, and it was Cartwright who could write in his first report 'generally' of the 'earnest desire on the part of the authorities to make their respective forces as efficient as possible'. This keenness showed when, in his 'official' inspection in 1857, he 'had the satisfaction to find that the counties which had been deficient in numbers, or in other respects, were so increased and improved, as to be efficient' – a stark contrast to his earlier 'unofficial' inspection when only nine of his twenty-five counties were satisfactory. Cartwright had found Shropshire inefficient for 1856–57, but in his first report he could write that the county 'has, since the 1st of October last, placed its force upon an efficient footing'. In effect, therefore, only tiny Rutland County was inefficient in Cartwright's district.

The county constabularies, in any case, were never to be any problem. In Woodford's Northern District, only the East Riding of Yorkshire was inefficient, and in Willis' district, only Cornwall, Herefordshire and Monmouthshire were unsatisfactory. Five of these six (Shropshire included) would be reported efficient in the following year,[43] leaving only Rutland outstanding until 1861–62,[44] after which few counties were ever in danger of losing their Exchequer Grant – and none ever did.[45]

However, if there was no problem with the counties, there certainly was with the boroughs. It was the boroughs that would be the thorn in the Inspectorate's side for many years to come.

'There is no doubt,' writes Henry Parris, 'that want of numbers and discipline was the main deficiency in 1856.'[46] In some cases the larger cities were adequately policed. Birmingham, for instance, had a ratio of police to population of 1:646, Liverpool 1:393 and Manchester 1:540.[47] Other cities definitely did not have sufficient policing. St Ives in Cornwall, for example, had a ratio of 1:6,500[48] and Pwllheli stood at 1:3,000,[49] because these two towns only had one constable in them. Of the 208 boroughs in England and Wales by then having police powers, 65 had populations under 5,000 (the small boroughs), whilst 57 had more than 20,000 population (the large boroughs), leaving 86 (the medium boroughs) with populations in between.[50] Cartwright's district had twenty-four small boroughs, and forty-four large and medium; Woodford had only two small boroughs, with forty-three large and medium; and Willis had twenty-five small boroughs, and fifty-two large and medium, all these boroughs having police forces. The discrepancy of eighteen is the number of boroughs which, although holding police powers, had consolidated and had agreed to be policed by their surrounding counties (for example, Bury St Edmunds at 13,900 population and Wenlock at 18,728).[51]

Cartwright was the only one of the inspectors to make a substantial general report in the First Report, as well as reports on individual forces. In fact, it was well over six pages long. Willis' general report was less than two pages and Woodford made no general report at all, confining himself to specific comments on each individual force. Whether this was accidental or deliberate, or whether it was agreed between the three, with Willis and Woodford acquiescing to (the socially superior?) Cartwright, we do not know, there being no evidence either way. Be that as it may, Cartwright's report remains a substantial statement of the policy of the inspectors after the first inspection and before they launched themselves into their second year.

As well as the obvious work to be done in elevating and maintaining the unsatisfactory boroughs to a point of efficiency in numbers and discipline in line with the four questions, other unforeseen subjects had surfaced which were equally needy of comment, if not outright reform. In all, Cartwright made twelve points, six of which were substantial and six minor, although still needing attention.

In his minor six comments, Cartwright drew attention to:

1 The difficulties in policing detached parts of counties
2 The unsuitability of forming separate autonomous police districts within the same county
3 The benefits of police officers transferring between forces being able to take their superannuation contributions with them, which, up until that time, was impossible
4 The benefits of appointing police surgeons
5 The need for more detective officers
6 The need to keep the *Police Gazette* (a newspaper containing criminals' names, habits and so on) secret within the police force, which it had not been

By the Police Acts of 1857, 1858 and 1859, which modified the 1856 Act, comments one and two were clarified; comment three would be attended to by the 1875 Select Committee on Superannuation (see below) and the remaining three would be rectified within the course of a few years.[52]

However, it would be Cartwright's six major points, identified right from the very birth of the Inspectorate, which would provide the main tasks for the inspectors in the years to come, in their aim of achieving an efficient police service.

These six major tasks were:

1 The raising to, and maintenance in, efficiency of the unsatisfactory borough police forces

2 The eradication of the tiny borough police forces

3 The provision of a sensible, settled pension scheme given as of right, rather than discretionary

4 Unified national pay scales

5 The provision of decent, purpose-built police stations, accommodation, cells and lock-ups

6 To extend the use of police officers in civil social legislation (such as relieving officers under the poor laws, weights and measures inspectors, and the like)

Each of these six main aims needs clarification:

1 The raising to, and maintenance in, efficiency of the unsatisfactory borough police forces

Henry Parris classifies the boroughs of this period into three: large (over 20,000 population); medium (between 5,000 and 20,000 population); and small (under 5,000).[53] All the large boroughs (fifty-seven of them) had existing police forces at the time of the first inspection, and the great majority of them were to be deemed efficient within two years. There were, however, four notable backsliders (Ashton-under-Lyne, Oldham, Stockport and Macclesfield) all still inefficient by 1870, whilst Sheffield slipped out of efficiency between 1862 and 1865.

The proportion of inefficient medium borough police forces was higher than that of the large boroughs. But there was one avenue that the medium boroughs could take which would ensure efficiency, and that was consolidation. A consolidated borough was one which could legally organise its own force, but chose to be policed by the surrounding county. After 1858/59, all counties were efficient (except Rutland, but that did not have a medium-sized borough within its borders in any case) so consolidated boroughs were, by definition, being policed efficiently. Therefore, consolidation meant that the borough could be efficiently policed with no extra rate burden to pay for maintaining an independent force. Cartwright would always advocate the advantages of consolidation, and, in his report for 1857/58, reproduced in full letters from the magistrates of fourteen boroughs, all singing the praises of their own consolidation agreements.[54] The number of consolidated boroughs rose to fifty-eight (out of 223) by the inspection year 1869/70.[55]

Not all medium boroughs wanted to consolidate, however. Parris discusses the reasons – there could be many.[56] Local pride must enter into it: the 'family feeling' within the borough for its very own police force was often extremely strong, sometimes manifesting itself in wonderfully extravagant chrome-badged and bedecked helmets (for example, Rochdale[57] and Guildford[58]). In the case of Sunderland, civic pride and resentment of outside interference was so acute that the Watch Committee wrote to the Home Secretary saying that it did not want the Exchequer Grant for 1856/57. The Home Secretary replied that this would not get them out of inspection, which subsequently found them efficient. When faced with hard cash, however, the Watch Committee finally accepted the grant of £996 15s 6d, although there were still some of its members viewing the grant 'with some suspicion'.[59]

Another reason for the refusal of a medium borough to consolidate was that there could be a genuine argument for fewer police. Also, a newly created borough did not want to take a seemingly retrograde step, bypassing their own policing back to the county from which they had just 'escaped'. And perhaps more pertinent, men representing the local licensing, brewing and trading interests had seats on the Watch Committee, and thus had power over police administration, which they would not have had under a county chief constable.

The urging towards efficiency of these straying large and medium boroughs would be pursued with vigour by the first inspectors as a priority – 'urging' being the operative word, because they had no coercive powers at all. Neither did the Home Secretary. Once politically elected, the Watch Committee of a borough was omnipotent, and the Home Secretary had no influence whatsoever – he could not even prevent a Watch Committee taking on a man who had been dismissed from another force for misconduct.[60] Legislation did not exist, either, to enable the Home Secretary to coerce police forces to amalgamate. Borough police forces were local government organisations over which central government had no control, save only the threat of withholding the Exchequer Grant.

So if no powers existed to compel change and there was no lead from central government – which refused to interfere with local government – then the inspectors deserve credit for achieving what they did. 'Their independent status,' argues Parris, 'enabled the Inspectors to act on their own initiative, to report with considerable candour, and to urge their views with vigour.'[61] Although the reduction in efficiency of these large and medium boroughs was less marked than in the counties, 'nevertheless, reduction was significant, sixty three in 1857 to eighteen in 1870'.[62]

2 The eradication of the tiny borough police forces

The small boroughs (that is, those under 5,000 people) were the despair of the inspectors after 1856. Cartwright in his policy statement in the First Report articulated his objections:

> It is impossible to over-rate the difficulties these small boroughs have in keeping up an independent force, as in a force of two or three men no sort of discipline or classification can be maintained, and it being impractical to establish any superannuation fund: the men in the force are generally old, and unfit for their work from physical infirmity, and represent more the old style of watchmen than police officers of the present day. In like manner, by non-consolidation, the county force is seriously weakened, as the superintendent or inspector of the division is not generally allocated in these boroughs, most of which are head-quarters of county petty-sessional divisions, and consequently the centre of the divisional force, besides being the most advantageous spot for the public for placing the standard weights and measures for the division of the county.

It took no great imagination to realise that these virtually unpoliced enclaves were havens for criminals. Surprisingly, under Section 8 of the 'permissive' County Police Act 1839, a county police officer did not have jurisdiction in any of the boroughs within his county's borders, unlike the borough constable who had jurisdiction in the surrounding county.[63] Criminals were thus able to escape to the safety of the borough boundaries and 'cock-a-snoot' at the pursuing forces of law and order. As long as they committed no crime within the borough itself, the one or possibly two borough constables were unable, unwilling or too frightened to touch them. It was exactly the same situation, although on a lesser scale, that had necessitated the 1853 Select Committee and the 1856 Act in the first place.

In the First Report, there were twenty-four small boroughs in Cartwright's district and twenty-five in Willis'; Woodford was lucky in having only two (Richmond and Hedon). Of course, not all small boroughs were so bloody-minded and some eagerly consolidated with their counties (for example, Beccles with a population of 4,398, Godmanchester with 2,337 and Retford with 2,934) as the advantages became obvious.

The inspectors must have realised that they had no powers, either coercive or persuasive, over the small boroughs that refused to consolidate because, by definition, being under 5,000 in population they stood to receive no Exchequer Grant anyway. However, right at the outset, the inspectors 'were optimistic enough to think that such folly could not last and that the smaller boroughs would amalgamate voluntarily with the surrounding forces'.[64]

3 The provision of a sensible, settled pension scheme given as of right, rather than discretionary

This was considered so important by Cartwright that he devoted one whole page (out of six) to this question. His report is reproduced verbatim:

> One of the most important points I have to bring to your notice is that of the super-annuation funds in the boroughs. The question has been brought forward in almost all of the principal boroughs in my district, and as their authorities are most anxious to establish such a fund, I have been frequently urged to lay this subject before you in my annual report.
>
> The advantages of a superannuation fund are so obvious, that I need not dwell upon them, more than to state, that by its establishment the police officers in the force are given a security that not only will they receive their due when active and in health, but when worn out in the service they will have a fund to support them in their latter days. They also look upon it as a sort of friendly society, to which they have contributed, which gives it a greater value than having a mere gratuity to receive. Without such fund, men are constantly shifting from one force to the other, much to the detriment of the forces; but when they have paid for a certain period towards the superannuation fund, they have a deep interest in the funds of the force, which binds them to remain in it for the mutual advantage of both boroughs and themselves.
>
> The great difficulty arises in those boroughs that have not formed a superannuation fund, and have men who have served in them upwards of 15 years, or approaching to that period; this renders it impossible to form a fund under the second section of the 11th & 12th Vict. c.14, as under that section sums are to be deducted from every constable, and after 15 years' service each constable, if 50 years of age, is entitled to retire, receiving half the amount of his full pay; thus, when there are constables of that age in such boroughs, they become entitled at once to the advantage of a retiring pension, without perhaps having paid towards it for any time; and in such forces there are constables approaching 50 years of age, whose pension would soon break a newly established fund. The question is of so much importance that I have brought it under your notice, and I venture to enquire whether, in the formation of new superannua-tion funds, the same rule which governs county superannuation funds might not be equally applicable to boroughs ...

Cartwright was concerned over the lack of borough superannuation funds. The county constabularies, under the Police Act 1840 (2 and 3 Victoria, Chapter 93), Section 11, were obliged to form funds, which were secured from insolvency by being tied in with the county police rate under Section 11 of the 1856 Act. By an Act of 11 and 12 Victoria, Chapter 14, Section 2, town councils were enabled but not compelled to form superannuation funds for their employees (which included the police). Only a handful ever did,[65] and in 1857 the vast majority of the boroughs had no pension funds whatsoever. Cartwright wanted a uniform pension scheme for both borough and county forces.

The fight for a unified, decent pension as of right was seen by the inspectors as a major plank for the provision of a settled, contented and efficiently working police service.

4 Unified national pay scales
Cartwright wrote:

> It has been my endeavour to recommend an assimilation of pay in the grades in different counties, so that there should be no encouragement to good men to leave their force for higher pay in another, after they have been drilled and made useful officers in any county or borough in which they have served for any lengthened period.

The thinking behind this was self-explanatory, as the difference in wages between forces, counties and boroughs was marked. Steedman quotes a recruiting weekly net wage of 14s 1d for Buckinghamshire in 1868 as opposed to a net wage anywhere between 17s 1d and 18s 1d for Staffordshire, and in 1867 there was a staggering 9s difference between Hereford City, at 10s per week, and a medium-sized borough at 19s.[66]

5 The provision of decent, purpose-built police stations, accommodation, cells and lock-ups
Cartwright knew the importance of providing humane prison cells and lock-ups, as well as the boost to morale of well-built and designed police stations. He had found in his district that the lock-ups 'require considerable attention, a great many being at present totally unfit to receive any human being'. This commitment to building new lock-ups, which, Carolyn Steedman has pointed out, the inspectors 'were to pursue with tenacity for the next ten years',[67] was the only one of the six main aims of the Inspectorate in which central government actively assisted right from the start. It was Willis in his 1858/59 report,[68] exulting the fact that more purpose-built police stations were appearing, who referred to 'a new book of plans for police stations formally supplied by the Home Office'.

So why did central government take a specific interest in this area of the inspectors' work? Was this unique interest directly attributable to the latest fashionable thinking of the sanitary movement currently in vogue? The Public Health Act was only eight years old, and the Commissioner of the General Board of Health, up until 1854, was none other than Edwin Chadwick, one of the architects of the 1856 County and Borough Police Act. Although Chadwick was dismissed in 1854, his successor John Simon, as Medical Officer to the General Board of Health, 'followed up the work of Chadwick … and began his assiduous efforts to create a healthy Britain'.[69]

6 To extend the use of police officers in civil social legislation

Right from the very outset, all three inspectors gave support to policemen having administrative functions.[70] They, like the local authorities, had seen the 'new police' as the most convenient and cheapest executive force to hand, and local by-laws would place more and more upon their shoulders. Indeed, the 1856 Act (under Section 6) had empowered local magistrates to give policemen these duties, and in the early months of 1857 there had been a rush to appoint police officers as Weights and Measures Inspectors, Common Lodging House Inspectors[71] and, the job nearest and dearest to Cartwright's heart, that of Relieving Officer under the Poor Laws.

Thus, by the end of the first inspection year in September 1857, the inspectors had clearly identified the areas where reform, encouragement and pressure were needed in the drive towards an efficient police service. Five of these six aims were never to vary, but the remaining one (that of civil administrative duties) was to be tempered somewhat over the years, as the police service gradually became confident enough to assert itself into wanting to do more 'real police work rather than local authority administration'.[72]

But that would be in the future. In the autumn of 1857 the inspectors knew exactly the path they needed to take. They would soon realise, however, that because central government could not, or would not, provide a guiding hand, they would have to tread that path alone. To realise why that was, it is important to understand the political aspect of the police.

The Home Office

Although the Home Secretaries of the period 1856–74 were guided by certain accepted principles of police in society (for example, the police should not be armed), there 'is no evidence that any Home Secretary in the period had any policy as to the way the police should develop'.[73] Parris goes further, even calling the Home Secretaries 'indifferent to police matters', saying, for example, that the repeated recommendations of the inspectors in trying to eradicate the tiny borough forces 'were not even considered at ministerial level'.[74]

Even approaches by local police authorities rather than the inspectors did not alter this attitude. When Gloucester City, Flint Borough and Caernarfonshire County all sought advice from the Home Office over various matters, their queries were dismissed arbitrarily without even referral to the appropriate district inspector.

Perhaps if Sir George Grey had remained as Home Secretary things would have been different. After all, it was Grey who had provided the driving power to get the 1856 Act passed in the first place, which at least showed some interest in police matters. But Grey left the Home Office in February 1858, only four months after the first report of the Inspectors of Constabulary in October 1857. His replacement, Spencer Walpole, would only last for one year before handing over to his successor, Thomas Estcourt, who in his turn was destined to last for only three months.[75]

The Home Office was, in any case, not large enough for elaborate administrative machinery to deal with police matters,[76] and the number of staff engaged on police work remained small, which Jenifer Hart adds, 'no doubt limited its capacities for interference'.[77] All papers from the inspectors came into the Home Office and were minuted as to action by a clerk who sent them to a permanent under-secretary,[78] who was a civil servant. There is ample evidence to suggest that 'most decisions' were made by the permanent under-secretaries, with only a tiny proportion of police business ever reaching the desk of the Home Secretary in person.[79]

Permanent under-secretaries, who were unelected civil servants and not elected politicians, even had the power to sway the mind of the Home Secretary, as when the Home Secretary refused to allow Cheshire County to be armed, a decision made only after the direct interference of the permanent under-secretary.[80] The hard-pressed Home Secretaries all too often 'took little interest' and normally made decisions on recommendations from others, in other words, from the permanent under-secretaries.[81]

Central government, therefore, through its executive office of the Home Secretary, provided no lead or direction in which the police service should have been going. This 'easy-going' organisation of the Home Office at this time,[82] coupled with the strong conviction of the local governmental nature of the police, meant the Home Secretary and his under-secretaries rarely attempted to co-ordinate the inspectors' activities or policies.[83] Nor did they show any inclination to, because during this period, according to Jill Pellew, the idea of 'dispassionate central officials comparing and co-ordinating the work of the field workers was still embryonic'.[84]

The Inspectors of Constabulary, in the absence of any lead from central government, were left to decide their own actions – which is exactly what happened following their First Report in October 1857. The evidence upon which future policy was to be formulated was uncovered purely by the inspectors themselves after the first inspection, and it was on this evidence alone that William Cartwright could itemise the Inspectorate policy for the foreseeable future. And it was the following of this policy, right from the start, that influenced and determined the shape of the later Victorian police service.

From the beginning, William Cartwright was the *primus inter pares* of the inspectors. The most extensive comments in the annual report for 1857/58[85] came from Cartwright, who expounded upon all the six main policy points, whilst the contributions from Woodford and Willis were only minor reports, both seemingly playing second fiddle. In Cartwright's report, only the second to be published, it is clear from his prose that he was extremely enthusiastic and optimistic about the future, believing that it was only a matter of time (and a short time at that) before all the six major aims would be attended to.

Although he makes no specific comments on the inspectors' first aim (the elevation to efficiency of all forces), Cartwright indirectly refers to this topic by citing a tremendous occasion of inter-force co-operation. He describes the royal visit to Birmingham during that year, stating that 1,125 police constables were assembled from other forces at short notice, including 200 from the Metropolitan Police, for crowd control. This demonstration of co-operation between neighbouring forces, which served as an answer to the fourth of the efficiency questions asked of every force, satisfied Cartwright so obviously in his description of it that it was almost superfluous of him to add at the end 'all went well'.

In stressing the inefficiency of the small boroughs and urging them to consolidate with their surrounding counties, Cartwright refers to the 'immense advantage of consolidation, without which it is impossible to make this system as perfect as it should be'. To back up his argument, he quotes letters from the magistrates of fourteen consolidated boroughs, all expressing delight at the advantages of being policed by their surrounding county forces. However, Cartwright, at this time, was still naive enough in his expectations at this early stage of the Inspectorate to think that this question would be settled by the boroughs themselves.

In his comments on the pension question, Cartwright expresses his concern over the lack of schemes in the borough forces. 'I am strengthened in my suggestion,' he wrote, 'that a new Act of Parliament is necessary for the purpose of enabling boroughs to establish superannuation funds.' This was all Cartwright said on the pension question, no doubt believing those few words would be the spur for action to be taken.

Although not directly referring to the pay scales, Cartwright did bring attention to financial matters indirectly related – allowances. He recommended the rationalisation of allowances for the serving of summons and warrants, and for the travelling allowances of police officers attending at courts outside their divisions or forces.

Purpose-built police stations and the improvement needed in cells and lock-ups came next. 'When the great advantages of station houses are more practically demonstrated,' wrote Cartwright, 'everything will be done under this head which can reasonably be expected.' As with the other topics, Cartwright thought it sufficient for him to simply bring the Home Secretary's attention to the matter and not go into any descriptive lengths.

Similarly treated was the last policy point, that of civil administrative duties for the police. Cartwright merely reiterates the advantages of using policemen as relieving officers under the Poor Law, Weights and Measures Inspectors and Inspectors of Nuisances and Common Lodging Houses.

In the 1857/58 annual report, unlike the First Report, Woodford did allow himself to make a small general report. He drew attention to the fact that there were no superannuation schemes in the majority of his borough forces, and also commented on the numerous complex systems of bureaucracy employed, each force differing completely from its neighbour. He mused on the inefficiency and unsuitability of this, especially when papers were sent from one force to another, which hardly eased the way for the last four efficiency questions. Woodford advocated, therefore, a universal system of paperwork throughout the United Kingdom forces.

Perhaps he realised his naivety soon afterwards when reflecting on the structures of the police system he and his fellow inspectors were trying to build – that of individually controlled units, each autonomous and separate from each other. To create a universal system of paperwork would require an umbrella administrative power, almost tantamount to a national police ministry, which, at a time of minimal police interest from central government, would be next to impossible to achieve. Woodford perhaps realised this after publication and would never refer to it again. Even today, after 150-odd years, the only national paperwork system that has been achieved is by the Crown Prosecution Service, when it published the awesome *Manual of Guidance* for the preparation of crime files, and thus introduced the national MG forms.

Willis, in his report, stressed his recommendations for boroughs under 5,000 population to consolidate, and brought attention to the difficulties of the smaller borough forces in maintaining a pension scheme. Thus in his comments, Willis was supportive of Cartwright's main report in emphasising some of the main policy points (as indeed was Woodford).

At the end of the second inspection year, in the autumn of 1858, the Inspectorate policy was again clearly set out and the spirit of optimism distinctly discernible. The inspectors had no reason to be disillusioned. And, as if further to support their encouraging prognosis, in 1859 the County and Borough Police Act (22 and 23 Victoria, Chapter 32) was passed, which was a modifying Act of Parliament addressing itself to some of Cartwright's six minor points, but which, under Section 9, made borough police superannuation funds compulsory. This Act, and Section 9 in particular, was arguably a direct result of Cartwright's petitions in the 1857/58 annual report. The future did indeed look rosy.

The inspectors' annual reports for 1858/59[86] and 1859/60[87] seemed to continue in the same vein. Again, it was Cartwright who wrote the biggest report, with Woodford and Willis remaining in the background, although obviously supporting Cartwright by what comment they did make.

In Cartwright's general report in the 1859/60 annual report, perhaps we see the first dawning upon him that things were not to be that easy. 'Of the … inefficient small boroughs there is nothing satisfactory to report,' he wrote, 'and I completely relinquish all hope of seeing them placed upon a proper and

efficient system without the assistance of the legislature.' From this statement
it seems to be clear to Cartwright that leaving the small boroughs to decide
amongst themselves whether to consolidate or upgrade to efficiency was plainly
just not working. What was needed, if persuasion was useless, was coercion – an
Act of Parliament forcing inefficient boroughs into efficiency or consolidation.
However, Cartwright did not develop his idea further in the 1859/60 annual
report but left it at that, no doubt hoping that the Home Secretary would be
goaded into action.

There was no action from the Home Office. Since February 1859, only eighteen months before the publication of the 1859/60 annual report, there had been
two Home Secretaries. Thomas Estcourt had taken over after Walpole's year-
long stay in February 1859, only to be replaced himself by Sir George Lewis
just three months later. With such volatile fluctuation of Home Secretaries, perhaps it is no wonder that police matters, not regarded as the highest priority of
the Home Office at that time, should have been ignored. And in July 1861 the
Home Secretary changed again. Lewis was relieved of office to be replaced by
none other than Sir George Grey, the architect of the 1856 County and Borough
Police Act.[88]

With Grey back in the Home Office by July, Cartwright had three months
before the next annual report was due. In the annual report for 1860/61,[89]
Cartwright obviously felt at ease enough in his relations with Grey to recommend publicly that a coercive Act of Parliament should be passed, either to make
the inefficient borough forces consolidate or upgrade themselves into efficiency.
He wrote:

> Each inspection adds to my conviction that the small boroughs will neither voluntar-
> ily make their forces efficient, or consolidate with the counties. If it were the only
> object, to give these small boroughs the protection and security they require, it might
> be thought a question entirely for themselves to decide; but there is a deeper interest
> in their being made efficient as to the general working of the police force throughout
> the country, as these small boroughs, with inefficient forces, not only affect the net-
> work which should be effectively established from sea to sea, but are often the haunts
> of those who commit their depredations in adjoining districts, and are more difficult
> to be detected than those persons who are under the immediate supervision of com-
> municating forces.

This question was also emphasised by Willis in his report. Edward Willis' general
reports were increasing in length yearly and were becoming more apposite as his
general confidence gradually increased. No doubt he had thought himself the
junior of the first three inspectors, being the last to be appointed and being the
chief constable of a city police rather than a large county as Woodford had been.
Nevertheless, it is clear by the 1860/61 annual report that Willis was equal in

confidence to Woodford and would within a few years surpass him to become the unofficial second most influential inspector.

Although the 1859 Police Act had made borough superannuation schemes compulsory, the inspectors were finding that some borough Watch Committees were simply ignoring their legal obligations. 'There appears to be no desire on the part of the Authorities,' wrote Willis, 'to comply with the Act, or indeed to place the forces which are also otherwise in an inefficient state, in a more efficient condition.' He continues: 'With the exception of Faversham, no attempt has been made by any borough in the southern district hitherto reported as inefficient, to place the police establishments in a more satisfactory condition.' Willis concludes from this, in direct support of Cartwright, that only coercive legislation would correct the small boroughs' efficiency problems. All in all, the 1860/61 annual report showed a total of sixty-four inefficient forces in England and Wales (including the only inefficient county, Rutland, but this was to be its last year of inefficiency) and thirty-two boroughs not having superannuation funds.

From the optimistic prognosis of the late 1850s, by the early 1860s the inspectors were realising that it was not to be as plain sailing as they thought. And in the 1861/62 inspection, they met a hitherto unforeseen headache which further exacerbated their policy aims.

The national census had been taken in 1861, with the subsequent adjustment of population figures. This meant that the ratio of police officers per 1,000 population had to reassessed, with the resulting increase in police establishments needed to keep the Exchequer Grant. This, however, appears not to have caused too many problems, as the efficient forces readily complied and the inefficient forces ignored it anyway, as they had nothing to lose.

Nevertheless, in some instances, the 1861 census created problems. Cartwright singled out the case of Grantham Borough. The 1851 census figures, on which all the ratio figures had been calculated up until then, gave the population as over 5,000. But the 1861 figures counted 4,946, just 54 short of the magic 5,000, the cut-off point for the Exchequer Grant. So, from being an efficient borough receiving the Exchequer Grant one day, to a borough failing to qualify for the grant the next day, through no fault of its own, but still having its police force to pay for, Grantham Borough Police found itself in a quandary. Cartwright could only stand and stare and offer sympathy.

There were only two alternatives: either soldier on without the Exchequer Grant or consolidate with Lincolnshire. 'Consolidation,' wrote Cartwright in the 1861/62 annual report,[90] 'would, if tried, give satisfaction, but which I always find unpalatable to the authorities in the first place.' In the event, Grantham chose not to consolidate and soldiered on regardless (up to 1947, in fact, when it was forced by legislation to consolidate with Lincolnshire).

By the 1863/64 annual report,[91] it is clear that the flush of enthusiasm of the inspectors of the late 1850s had dissipated. Gone are Cartwright's comments on each of the six main aims. Instead he gives a terse general report which, for the first time, is of equal length to those of Woodford and Willis. The main contents of the three inspectors' reports is a list of the still inefficient forces in their areas, which, apart from Deal Borough Police becoming efficient, Flint Borough Police consolidating with Flintshire County Constabulary, and one new force being created, Reigate Borough Police, is still exactly the same as in the previous year's report.[92] Thus, in Cartwright's succinct crisp prose, 'little happened over the year'. The total of 59 inefficient forces (out of 223)[93] is still an incredible number even after eight years' work of the Inspectorate. It reflects the lack of interest in police matters by central government and by Parliament in general, and the fact that the inspectors' efficacy by only being an advisory body was limited without the backing of compulsory legislation.

In the period 1859 to 1874 (except one minor 1865 Act) no Act of Parliament was passed which affected the county and borough police forces of England and Wales.[94] Also, from 1856 to 1880, only ten questions about the rural police were asked in Parliament, with just one reference to provincial policemen during this time.[95]

Is it therefore any wonder that the inspectors became dispirited, as they realised that central government was giving them no support? And to add to this sense of disillusionment, so clear in the 1863/64 annual report, Cartwright also brings attention to the county pension funds.

Although all counties had funds (under the Police Act 1840, Section 11), the inadequacy of some of these funds was worrying to Cartwright. He suggested that the fees for summons and warrants be used to augment the pension fund rather than being deposited for use in the general police fund; to have to report that all was not well with the county pension funds, as well as still having some backsliders amongst the boroughs on this question, must have added to Cartwright's feeling of frustrated impotence.

The annual reports for 1864/65,[96] 1865/66[97] and 1866/67[98] are similarly unenthusiastic. The usual topics are referred to with the usual comments: consolidation of the small boroughs is urged or compulsive legislation; the now (urgent) need for examination of the superannuation schemes for all forces, county and borough; and the need for higher pay scales to stop the drift away from the police service.

The Police Superannuation Act (28 and 29 Victoria, Chapter 35) had been passed in 1865, but this only concerned the pension rights of borough chief constables and gave the authorities power to award a lump sum in lieu of a pension for constables under 60 in certain medical circumstances. This Act had no influence over the real question of superannuation, and was so minor that none of the inspectors made any more than a passing reference to it in any of their reports.

It is significant, however, that the Home Secretary of the time was Sir George Grey, who possibly had a hand in producing a ray of light over the pay question.

In March 1866 the Home Office implemented new rates of pay and this was commented upon favourably by both Cartwright and Willis in the 1865/66 annual report.

The sixth policy point also gets a favourable mention in the 1864/65 annual report. Cartwright expresses satisfaction over the matter of extra duties of police officers. He especially singles out a Poor Law relief system adopted in the Wickham Market Union, with the local constables of the Suffolk County Constabulary being appointed assistant relieving officers. The success of this sixth policy aim was probably not because of any concerted pressure by the Inspectors of Constabulary, but more because of the local authorities' budget-conscious appreciation that the local constabulary was already in existence and available twenty-four hours a day, and therefore they did not need the expense of employing anybody else.

Woodford retired in 1867 and Cartwright in 1868; they were replaced by William Elgee and Charles Cobbe. Elgee had formerly been the chief constable of Lancashire County and Charles Cobbe of the West Riding of Yorkshire, so, together with Edward Willis, the inspectors all had police experience. It would have been hoped that two new inspectors coming into the Inspectorate would revitalise it in some way, but this did not seem to be the case. In fact, it was quite the reverse. Cobbe, in the annual report for 1869/70,[99] concludes his personal summary with: 'The men are generally very healthy, well conducted, respectable and intelligent. They appear to be well supervised, and their duties seem well arranged, and well attended to.' This in itself is not noteworthy, until it is realised that this statement is reproduced, word for word, comma for comma, in the next three of his annual reports. This seems to show a certain lack of original thought – or perhaps, interest?

Even Willis and Elgee seemed to revert to stereotyped reports by this time. The annual reports from 1869/70 to 1872/73[100] are virtually the same, merely giving police responses to licensed premises, pedlars, vagrants, ticket of leave men and tables of crime figures. The complacency and apathy of these reports is noticeable, and must reflect the dispirited, demoralised state of the three inspectors at this time.

The period 1856–74 was not the most productive time for the Inspectors of Constabulary. Starting off with the high ideals of achieving the six main aims (which never varied, despite changes of inspectors), it was realised over this period that the accomplishment of all these would be impossible. The Inspectorate was an advisory body and, without the legal powers of coercion, was powerless against police authorities who would not yield to persuasion. By 1874, therefore, four of the six main aims were still unfulfilled.

By 1874, there were still 52 borough forces inefficient, out of a total of 223. Of these 52, 31 had populations under 5,000, and 19 of them with populations over 5,000 were 'chronically inefficient'.[101] Perhaps the reason why these boroughs were impervious to the urgings of the inspectors is because of their constitution. The politically elected Watch Committees were not so heavily accountable to the Home Secretary, as regards to regulations, pay, allowances, minimum standards of recruits and choice of chief constable, as were the county constabularies. Without coercive powers the Inspectorate was impotent, so to achieve what they had done by 1874 was no mean feat. In the First Report of 1856/57, 128 forces were inefficient, and in 1874 there were 52.

On the pension question, many of the boroughs, and even the counties, had superannuation funds which were far from adequate, and despite constant urgings, by 1874 things were dire, with no prospect of getting any better.

On the question of a standard national pay scale, it was the boroughs, yet again, which were the bugbear. The Home Secretary had no power over the Watch Committees of the boroughs on this score. 'This lack of control is curious,' writes Jenifer Hart, 'when one remembers that the Exchequer was reimbursing local police authorities one quarter ... of their expenditure on pay.'[102] So, on this question, no progress had been made.

It was on the last two policy aims that the inspectors could at least look back with a small degree of pleasure. By the mid-1860s, any second-rate accommodation had been dealt with by the force itself, as it strove to make itself more comfortable. On the question of giving policemen more civil social legislation to do, by 1874 this was a complete success, as the local authorities already had policemen there to do the jobs and therefore had no need to spend money on employing additional people.

So 'successful' was this that in some boroughs the police seemingly came to be the major social agency in the town. For instance, in Godalming Borough in 1880, the chief constable, as well as being the Billet Master and Chief of the Borough Fire Brigade, was also Inspector of Nuisances, of Common Lodging Houses, of Explosives, of the Petroleum Acts, of the Dairy and Cowsheds Act and of the Food and Drugs Act.[103] In Guildford Borough, in 1909, the chief constable was the Inspector of the Contagious Diseases Act, the 1907 Butter and Margarine Act, the Hackney Carriage Act, the Food and Drugs Act, the Petroleum and Explosives Acts and Inspector of Common Lodging Houses.[104]

So seriously did some borough chief constables take on the mantle of being the main social welfare providing agency that it led to the phenomenon of boys' clubs, welfare schemes and benevolent societies, all being established and run by the local police. It is not known how many of these there were, as little research has been done on the subject, but these are the ones that are known at the present:

Birmingham Police Aided Association for Clothing Poor Children
Blackpool Borough Police Poor Children's Clothing Fund
Burnley Police Youth Club
Cambridge City Police Fund for Assisting the Poor and Needy

Great Grimsby Police Boot Fund
Hyde Police Lads' Club
Hull Police Boys' Club
Northampton Borough Police Good Samaritan Society
Norwich Police Lads' Club
Oxford Police-Aided Association (for clothing for poor children)
Preston Borough Police Holiday Homes for Poor Children
Shrewsbury Borough Police 'Boots for Bairns' Scheme

The organisation of boys' clubs is perhaps understandable, as by diverting the energies of bored youths into more acceptable channels, the possibility of them turning to crime is lessened. But for the police to see themselves as the main providers of shoes and clothes is part of the Victorian philanthropic movement of the late nineteenth century, before the British Welfare State got into its stride. Cynics would say, however, that it was a way of currying favour with the working class, with whom the police had to deal with daily.

By 1874, the police service of England and Wales was still in a highly disconnected state. Eighteen years' work by the Inspectorate of Constabulary had achieved only partial success, and the optimism of the 1850s had given way to disillusionment and disenchantment by the early 1870s. Lack of action and support by central government had heightened the Inspectorate's sense of isolation. Nine Home Secretaries in eighteen years[105] had seemed to provide no stable, continuous police policy during the period, and, judging by their reports, the Inspectorate, seeing no end to the gloom, viewed the second half of the 1870s with pessimism.

Things, however, were about to change.

SEVEN

1874–90

This miraculous change was brought about by the accession of a new Home Secretary. Richard Assheton Cross was appointed on Saturday 21 February 1874 by Benjamin Disraeli, following the General Election which gave his Conservative Party its first unhindered taste of power after its brief skirmish in 1868.[1] The appointment of the previously unnoticed Cross was a complete surprise. 'Disraeli made his sensational choice, Richard Cross,' writes Robert Blake, 'a completely new man who had never held office before … he possessed deep knowledge of local government, and turned out to be a great Home Secretary.'[2] Blake continues that when Disraeli entered office in 1874, he was content to leave British colonial policy to his Secretary of State for the Colonies, Lord Carnarvon, and was also content to hand over the responsibility of social reform to his Home Secretary, Richard Cross,[3] a statement backed up by Cross himself in his autobiography.[4]

So in 1874, the British police service was placed into the hands of the completely new and untried Richard Cross as Home Secretary, and in effect he played 'a large part in shaping the principles of the social reforms which are perhaps the greatest achievement of the ministry of 1874–1880'.[5]

Amongst those greatest achievements are police reforms, because one of the first pieces of legislation passed by the Disraeli government was the Police (Expenses) Act 1874 (37 and 38 Victoria, Chapter 58), which received the Royal Assent on Friday 7 August 1874, only five months or so after the start of the ministry. This Act, which according to Critchley 'is the starting point of the final cycle of police reforms',[6] increased the Exchequer Grant from 25 per cent to 50 per cent of pay and clothing, and is one of the first Acts of Parliament introduced by the Disraeli government in the new spirit of 'collectivism'.[7]

Collectivism is the phase of extensive state intervention that replaced utilitarianism from the late 1860s onwards, and 'became accepted as the working creed of English politics. It assumed that each person had certain claims on society to ensure him adequate conditions and opportunities to fulfil himself. Whereas the individualist assumed each person the better judge of his own affairs, the collec-tivist assumed the state to be.'[8]

The state, therefore, through the new Home Secretary, was finally looking to extend influence over its police forces, both borough and county, and the Police (Expenses) Act 1874 was the start. Quick to sense this new spirit of reform from the Home Office, the Inspectors of Constabulary, in the 1873/74 annual report, took the opportunity to emphasise again what they thought needed reforming; in other words, their six policy aims.

The parliamentary under-secretary at the Home Office was Sir Henry Selwin-Ibbetson, who, for some reason, was also favourably disposed towards the police, in contrast to his predecessors.[9] It was Selwin-Ibbetson who, influenced by the 1873/74 annual report of the inspectors, in January 1875 could approach the Home Secretary urging him to do something about the dire straits which the police superannuation funds were then in.

The direct result of this was the Select Committee 'to enquire into the Police Superannuation Funds in the Counties and Boroughs of England and Wales', estab-lished by Cross on Thursday 18 March 1875, with Selwin-Ibbetson as chairman. Included on the committee was Fairfax Cartwright, the Member of Parliament for South Northamptonshire and none other than the son of William Cartwright, the very first Inspector of Constabulary. Fairfax Cartwright, who had been agitating for police superannuation reform for some time, had obviously been influenced by his father, who no doubt saw that Fairfax, as an MP, had far greater opportunities to badger Home Secretaries in the House than he had as a non-member.

Numerous witnesses gave evidence, from the Inspectors of Constabulary and chief constables of counties and boroughs, right down to constables, as well as medical doctors, financial experts and local politicians. The committee took two years to publish its report, which it did in April 1877 as the Select Committee on Police Superannuation Funds.[10]

There were several suggestions in the report, but the main one was the recom-mendation that policemen should have the legal right to a pension after fulfilling certain conditions, instead of the pension being at the discretion of the Police Authority as was the custom at that time, with the right to appeal if a pension was withheld. This, the supreme point of the 1877 report, was exactly what the inspectors had been campaigning for since 1856, twenty-one long years before. With the ammunition of the report, the inspectors expected a bill to go before Parliament sooner rather than later, and in the 1876/77 annual report, Edward Willis said exactly that.[11]

The inspectors were equally hopeful of more reform under this pro-police Home Secretary when in the same year that the Superannuation Report was published, the Municipal Corporations (New Charters) Act was passed. This Act was the first to lay down compulsory powers over police matters rather than advisory, as had previously been the case.

32 York City Police in 1881. Note that some helmets (for reasons unknown) have badges on and some do not, and note also the long service chevron worn on the right cuff, one chevron for every five years.

In effect, the 1877 Act dictated that from hereon in, no newly created borough would have police powers unless it had a population of over 20,000. So although it stopped short at actually banning any existing forces of boroughs below 20,000 people, it at least prevented the creation of any more. Therefore, even though technically not facilitating the achievement of the second policy aim, it was at least a step in the right direction.

Meanwhile, the inspectors' continued battering at the Watch Committees of the small borough forces was making some small progress. By 1875, the number of inefficient forces had been reduced to thirty-eight, down from fifty-two in 1870, and eighty boroughs had consented to be policed by their surrounding counties by 1876. Things were slowly improving.

But they were stopped dead in 1880. In April, the Conservative government of Disraeli was ousted in favour of the Liberal Gladstone and this meant a change of Home Secretary. Replacing Richard Cross was Sir William Harcourt, who was out of an entirely different mould and would set back police reform by a good ten years.[12] Naturally, Sir Henry Selwin-Ibbetson went too, being replaced with Sir Matthew Ridley as parliamentary under-secretary. It was Sir Matthew Ridley who could order that any paperwork sent to police authorities from the Home Office 'should be absolutely free from any taint of dictation or direction'.[13]

This was a direct reversal of the spirit of collectivism and of the opinions of Cross and Selwin-Ibbetson, but it echoed the opinions of the Home Secretary himself, who 'delighted to pour scorn on any suggestion that Whitehall knew best'.[14] Harcourt was definitely anti-Inspectorate of Constabulary, and made little attempt to conceal his disdain of the inspectors and their work. 'Nothing can be more ridiculous,' he wrote, on learning that one of the tests of efficiency of a police force was a ration of policemen per population; 'it is time that a little practical common-sense should be brought to bear on these matters'.[15]

With such antagonism from the Home Office, there is little wonder that the Inspectors of Constabulary once more became dispirited and considered themselves unwanted. The annual reports from 1880 onwards reflect this feeling all too well: they are lacklustre, stilted and stereotyped. The Inspectorate slipped back into the pre-1874 depths of despair. Little did they know, however, that help was appearing on the horizon; very soon they would achieve all their policy aims in one fell swoop – and from an entirely unforeseen direction.

The fourteen months between June 1885 and August 1886 were unsettled months for Britain. Gladstone's Liberals were ejected in June 1885, being replaced with Lord Salisbury's Conservatives, who lasted for eight months. In turn they were ousted by Gladstone's Liberals; and seven months later, Lord Salisbury's Conservatives, having had enough of all this governmental ping-pong, managed to get themselves elected with such a majority that they would survive the full six years. Henry Matthews (later Lord Llandaff) was appointed Home Secretary in August 1886.[16]

The third Reform Act, which had been passed in 1884, together with the accompanying Redistribution Act of 1885, was the culmination of years of drive towards democracy in Britain. In effect, these two Acts gave the vote 'to working men in the countryside … and [made] institutional changes that undermined the political power of the landed aristocracy'.[17] Now, the Conservative government was set to pass the Local Government Act of 1888, which 'was no more than an inevitable sequel to the Reform Act of 1884'.[18] It was to be this Act of 1888, making 'changes in local government inevitable',[19] which would be the answer to the last thirty years of prayers by the Inspectors of Constabulary.

The 1888 Local Government Act, although keeping the judicial powers of the county magistrates, now placed county administration into the hands of politically elected, newly formed county councils. The reform of local government, therefore, was the primary concern of this Act. But the police were controlled by local government, so the police question had to be included in the debates, meaning Parliament was then faced with the question 'who controls the police?' Was it to remain with the local gentry – the bench of magistrates in Quarter Sessions? Or was it to be in the hands of the new county councils, with their (inexperienced) elected politicians of all social classes? Tempers were heated in Parliament when this question was decided.[20] It became obvious that both sides were entrenched;

on the one hand were those who saw the management of the police as a judicial matter (the magistrates); on the other, there were those who saw it as an administrative affair (the county councils).

Compromise had to be reached. The proposal that control of the police should be divided between the magistrates and the county councils met with hostility from both sides. Yet the proposal was adopted; it had to be, because there was no other solution. The control of county police forces, therefore, passed into the hands of a committee consisting of equal numbers of magistrates and local politicians; this body, under Section 9 of the Act, was henceforth known as the Standing Joint Committee.

All the heated debate seemed to concern the counties, and probably provided a smokescreen, as the boroughs hardly rated a mention and their Watch Committees remained untouched. So the provision of the Act to abolish police forces in boroughs with less than 10,000 population was accepted by Parliament 'without a murmur of protest'.[21]

It must have been with incredulity that the Inspectors of Constabulary looked at this Act, which in one fell swoop achieved what they had failed to do in thirty years. As a result of this Act, virtually overnight all the tiny borough police forces were swept away, and in 1889 the total number of police forces in England and Wales was reduced by forty-two, to 183.

The figure of forty-eight forces amalgamated in 1889, as given by Critchley in 1967,[22] and repeated in every police history book since, is wrong. The following are the forty-two borough police forces which amalgamated with their surrounding counties in 1889, together with their final manpower:

	Final strength
Abingdon Borough	6
Arundel	3
Basingstoke	8
Bideford	6
Blandford	3
Brecon	6
Bridgnorth	2
Buckingham	4
Chard	2
Chichester	9
Daventry	2
Deal	9
Dorchester	8
Dunstable	3
Falmouth	4
Faversham	9

Godalming (second formation)	3
Haverfordwest	6
Helston	1
Hertford	9
Hythe	3
Leominster	8
Lichfield	8
Ludlow	5
Maidenhead	11
Maldon	5
Newport, Isle of Wight	10
Penryn	2
Pontefract	8
Richmond (North Riding)	4
Romney Marsh Liberty	?
Rye	3
St Ives (Cornwall)	1
Sandwich	2
Southwold	1
Stamford	10
Stratford-on-Avon	8
Sudbury	6
Tenby	3
Tenterden	4
Torrington	2
Wisbech	11[23]

Some of these borough men, who were physically fit, were taken into the county forces that had taken over, but there were many who were pensioned off; and there were some chief constables who obtained appointments as senior officers in the absorbing county force or in completely fresh forces. For instance, John William Lawson, the last chief constable of Stamford Borough, became the second chief constable of Peterborough City Police; and Philip Stephen Clay, chief constable of Brecon Borough, was immediately appointed as chief constable of Southampton Borough Police, stopping there for three years until becoming chief constable of Nottingham Borough Police, a position he held until 1912.[24]

The inspectors' annual report of 1888/89 was a complete contrast to those of the previous years.[25] Gone are the lists of inefficient small boroughs, as each inspector (now Charles Cobbe for the Midland Region, Charles Legge for the Northern Region and William Elgee for the Southern Region) comments favourably on the effects of the 1888 Local Government Act. Every single police force in the land was now efficient – except one.

The 'wooden spoon' prize for the very last police force in England and Wales to remain inefficient went to Congleton Borough Police, under Chief Constable Jonathan Hall. However, within that very year even this 'chronically inefficient' borough would be deemed acceptable, because in the 1889/90 annual report it is listed as efficient.[26]

It was with sighs of relief that the inspectors finally achieved their first two policy aims. But there was still a significant issue outstanding: the pension. All the inspectors in their 1888/89 annual report expressed concern over the pensions question, and the Conservative government duly took note.

A bill concerning police superannuation was introduced into Parliament. It went through virtually unopposed[27] and was passed on Tuesday 5 August 1890, becoming known as the Police Act 1890 (53 and 54 Victoria, Chapter 45). The supreme achievement of the Act was that it gave a decent pension as of right to policemen retiring after twenty-five years who fulfilled certain conditions. This was the culmination of thirty-four years of work by the Inspectors of Constabulary. The dire pension situation had been highlighted by Cartwright in 1856, and now in 1890 it had been rectified. When the Police bill went into Parliament, it was accompanied by a document entitled 'Memorandum in explanation of the Police Bill 1890',[28] which succinctly summed up the convoluted history of the fight for police pensions. And a fascinating story it is.

What would the reaction be today if all the fines imposed for drunkenness and assaults on police went towards police pensions? But that was indeed the case before pension rights were settled by the 1890 Police Act.

The borough police forces mainly date from 1835, after the passing of the Municipal Corporations Act; but the 1835 Act did not provide for the establishment of a pension fund. All Section 82 of the Act provided for was 'compensation for injury received on duty' or 'on being worn out in the service'. No scale of amounts was prescribed and these awards were only made at the discretion of the Watch Committee.

A year after the 'permissive' County Police Act 1839 came the legislation which provided for part of the fines imposed on drunks and for assaults on police to go towards police pensions. Remaining in force for fifty years, the County Police Act 1840 made pension schemes compulsory for all county forces. As well as the fines from drunks and assaults, 2½ per cent was deducted from wages. The fund was further enhanced by paying in the stoppages of pay during sickness, the fines levied on policemen for misconduct, the proceeds from the sale of old uniforms and, finally, up to 50 per cent of the rewards given to the police for convictions (in the days when police officers could accept reward money).

In 1872 a bonus was added. Up to half of the fines collected from offences under the 1872 Licensing Act could be added to the fund as well. Could this be one of the reasons for the Victorian police's preoccupation with public houses and working-class drunkenness?

Pensions under the County Police Act 1840 amounted to half pay for officers with between fifteen and twenty years' service, and two-thirds of pay for those with more than twenty years' service. To qualify, an officer had to be over 60 years old. Only medical pensions were payable to anyone under the age of 60, and then only for an injury received on duty.

The main stumbling block of the 1840 Act was that the pensions were given only at the discretion of the county magistrates, who were then the Police Authority. Therefore, some men could make thirty years' worth or more of contributions and still not receive a pension at the end of it, because the magistrates could withhold it for any reason they thought fit. It was this that rankled with the newly formed Inspectorate of Constabulary in 1856, and it was one of its major policy aims to abolish this arrangement.

With county force pensions apparently settled, that still left the borough forces with no pension scheme. An attempt was made by the Police Act 1849 to remedy this. It failed because it was not made compulsory, and the complicated regulations and seemingly large pay-outs made it unpopular with the parsimonious town councils. Consequently, only a few boroughs set up funds under this Act.

Income for the fund came from misconduct fines, proceeds from the sale of old uniforms, all the money paid to the police for the service of summons and warrants, and deductions of 1/36 of weekly pay. This provided pensions of half pay for service after fifteen years; half pay plus one-third of half pay for service between fifteen and twenty years; two-thirds of full pay for twenty years; and full pay plus one-third pension for over twenty years.

The pension was adjusted according to how many years the pensioner had served in each rank. No person under 50 could receive benefit, except on medical certificate. But, as in the counties, a pension was only given at the discretion of the Watch Committee, the borough Police Authority.

Few boroughs ever took up the 1849 Police Act pension scheme, so for ten years, men in most borough forces had no pension to look forward to. This was deplored by the newly arrived Inspectors of Constabulary in 1856. Probably as a direct result, the Police Act 1859 was passed. It scrapped the complicated 1849 Act and made borough pension funds compulsory using the same formula as the one in use in the counties, but with the addition of extra income from the service of summons and warrants.

Borough chief constables came under the same pension scheme as the rest of their force, but the county chief constables were treated differently, as indeed they were for almost every aspect of Victorian police administration. The county chiefs did not contribute to their pension schemes, but on retirement, for which they had to be over 60, the Quarter Sessions granted them an annual fixed sum not exceeding the yearly total for a top rate constable. This came from the county rate fund and not the police pension fund.

33 Chief Constable Benjamin Goldsmith and three PCs of Tenterden Borough Police, one of
the small borough forces affected by the Local Government Act of 1888. Tenterden Borough
Police was absorbed into the Kent County Constabulary.

There was a small amendment to the police pension scheme by the Police
Superannuation Act 1865. This applied to counties and boroughs, and gave power
to grant a temporary annuity to any officer under the age of 60 who was incapable of duty, until he either retired permanently or returned to work.

But there was disquiet among the police, and this was promulgated by the
Inspectors of Constabulary. Their main criticisms were: there was no provision for
orphans where no widow was left; the age of 60 was discriminatory against men
who joined young – an officer joining at 20 had to serve for forty years to receive
the same pension as a man who joined at 30 and served for thirty years; officers
changing forces could only carry half their accrued pension from the old force
to the new force, and only if going to a higher rank, and even then only on the
recommendation of the chief constable; and pensions were still only given at the
discretion of the Police Authority, for which there was no appeal against adverse
decisions.

During this time the Metropolitan Police had its own superannuation arrangements, which were not much different from those of the counties or boroughs.
These arrangements were consolidated in 1862, but as with their provincial colleagues, even the Metropolitan Police had no right to an automatic pension.

The social as well as political conditions of mid-Victorian Britain, where police
matters were never very high on successive Home Secretaries' agendas – coupled

with the rapidly declining influence of the Inspectors of Constabulary – ensured that nothing was done on this subject.

The breakthrough came in 1874. In that year, Benjamin Disraeli started his first real stint as Prime Minister, and gave the job of Home Secretary to the politically unknown Richard Cross. Cross, a political live wire, and arguably the best Home Secretary of Victorian Britain, saw the discontent within the police service and in 1875 established the Select Committee on Police Superannuation Funds to look at the whole question of police pensions, both provincial and Metropolitan.

The committee's report, published in 1877, recommended that a pension of three-fifths of salary should automatically be given after twenty-five years without reference to the Police Authority. It said that officers should have the option of continuing for another three years to earn a two-thirds pension. Chief constables were included in the proposals, there was provision for widows' and orphans' pensions and there would be full pension rights on transfer between forces. The report also said that there should be an appeal system against dismissal as there was evidence that some police authorities had sacked men on the point of retirement for trifling offences to avoid paying them their pensions.

The report recommended that the 2½ per cent deduction from pay should continue, but fines imposed for drunkenness would no longer be paid into the fund, although the fund would still receive fines for assaults on police.

Controversy was caused, however, by one of the committee's recommendations, and it was this which became the main obstacle to a decent police pension Act for the next thirteen years.

The committee decided against a national pension fund, favouring local funds instead, and it recommended that any shortfall in the police pension fund was to be made good out of the local rates. Not surprisingly, this produced an explosion of opposition from the local authorities. Four attempts within three years were made to get legislation passed based on the 1877 report. All failed because the local authorities saw no reason to top up police pensions out of their rates.

It was not until 1888 that the difficulty was resolved. The 1888 Local Government Act took control of the county police out of the hands of the magistrates and placed it with the Standing Joint Committee, half magistrates and half county councillors from the newly formed county councils. These county councils gave a different financial authority to the county, providing the opportunity for another attempt at police pension reform.

A bill was proposed based on the 1877 report, but with one important difference. This time, central government instead of the local authority would top up the police pension with an Exchequer Grant. This promptly removed most opposition, and police pensions were thus unified and reformed by the great Police Act 1890, passed in August of that year. Although there were adjustments for the Metropolitan Police, the Act gave the service a universal pension scheme that was awarded automatically instead of at the discretion of the Police Authority.

Modifications have been made over the years, but the scheme of 1890 is almost the same as the one in use today. Widows' pension rights would be consolidated by the Police (Pensions) Act 1918.

Compulsory retirement at 55 years of age for constables and sergeants, 60 for inspectors and superintendents, and 65 for senior officer ranks, with the option of extending service by up to five years, was introduced by the Police Pensions Act 1921 (11 and 12 George V, Chapter 31), followed by the Police Pension Act 1926, which raised contributions to 5 per cent of pay.

A barrage of legislation was inevitable during the war years, but all this was consolidated by the Police Pensions Act 1948, which provided the power to introduce regulations for the administration of pension funds. This arrangement lasted until 1987, when advances in line with contemporary thinking and economics were introduced. For example, policewomen then had to pay an 11 per cent contribution, the same as their male colleagues, to provide for a widower's pension.

Today, the pension scheme is administered under the National Police Pension Scheme, which was introduced in April 2006. All officers now pay a 9½ per cent contribution for a pension of half the final salary plus a fixed lump sum, part of which can be commuted.

This is a fair and just reward for services rendered. But it did not come about overnight; it was only achieved as the result of hard-fought campaigns over a period of more than 170 years of tortuous development. Consequently, in 1890, the police service of England and Wales looked settled. No police force, either county or borough, was considered inefficient, and although one or two would have their knuckles rapped severely (for example, Colchester Borough over the state of its police station in 1892[29] and Boston Borough over its management in 1900[30]), between 1890 and 1919, no Exchequer Grant was ever withheld from any Police Authority.[31]

Yet not everything in the garden was rosy. Since the Municipal Corporations Act of 1877, newly created boroughs of less than 20,000 population were precluded from keeping police forces; but the Act had allowed boroughs already in existence of less than 20,000 population to keep their existing forces, and the Local Government Act had only eradicated the forces of boroughs under 10,000 population. So in 1890 there were still twenty-nine small forces serving populations between 10,000 and 20,000, with twenty-seven forces having less than twenty men, including one county, Rutland.[32] Nevertheless, they were all run efficiently, and problems caused by the size of these forces, or lack of it, would not surface for a few years yet.

Although a standard national police pay was never achieved in the nineteenth century, the variation in the rates of pay between different forces was looked upon with tolerance. The lowest starting wage in 1901 appears to be 18s 10d per week for constables of Oxfordshire and Wiltshire counties. The highest starting wage for constables was 26s 10d per week in Barrow-in-Furness Borough.

34 The Bacup Borough Police in 1938. The chief constable, Ernest Sturt, is wearing the Sam Browne Belt in the front row. Included are four members of the Bacup Borough Police Fire Brigade wearing their brass firemen's helmets. Like all the other Borough Police Fire Brigades, it was nationalised in 1940 to form the National Fire Service.

After twenty-five years' service, a constable of Wiltshire County (the lowest payers of all) received 23s 8d, and those in the highest paid, Blackburn and Leicester Boroughs, received 34s per week.[33] This discrepancy was reflected in the different skills needed for each force. A rural constable in central Wales would certainly face less aggravation than a constable in Barrow-in-Furness Borough on a Saturday evening, and was paid accordingly. In the absence of any national negotiating machinery, discrepancies like these could be expected, and it would become a crucial factor in the next twenty years or so. Nevertheless, police pay at the turn of the twentieth century was at least adequate in comparison to national wages.[34]

The sixth aim of the Inspectors of Constabulary, the appointing of police officers to civil administrative positions, was the first aim to be achieved fully. So successful was it that the police themselves by the late nineteenth century were baulking at such an extra workload, and chief constables and high-ranking officers had come to see these duties as detracting from the reason for which they became policemen in the first place.[35]

From the turn of the twentieth century, the police did gradually come to do less of this work, as the local authorities appointed non-police officers in their stead. Even so, the practice continued until well into the twentieth century and it was to be one of the aims of the Inspectorate of Constabulary to abolish it. But it was not until 1953, when the 'Report of the Committee on Police Extraneous

Duties' was published, that the performing by police officers of civil administrative duties was abolished completely.[36]

The most important extraneous duty that had been introduced, and one which would remain until the Second World War, was the establishment of the borough police fire brigades. Although the earliest police fire brigade is reputed to be the Liverpool Police Fire Brigade, started in 1837,[37] it was not until the 1880s that the majority of chief constables of large boroughs, backed by their Watch Committees, started to set up fire brigades, managed and manned by borough policemen. This was assisted by the Police Act 1893 (56 Victoria, Chapter 10), which gave official sanction to borough policemen acting as firemen, and preserved their pensions and welfare rights as policemen should they be injured on duty when fighting fires.

These borough police fire brigades persisted until well into the twentieth century, but it was rapidly becoming apparent that the two disciplines did not mix. There were several instances when a fire brigade was needed but the policemen required to man it were engaged elsewhere.

In 1936 a committee was established under the chairmanship of Arthur Balfour, 1st Lord Riverdale, to look at this whole matter. The result was the Fire Brigade Act 1938, which recommended that fire brigades be established entirely independent of the police.

The annual report of the Inspectors of Constabulary for 1938/39 gives the names and strengths of the borough police fire brigades on the eve of the Second World War. There are sixty-five of them:

Ashton-under-Lyne (6 full time personnel/23 part time); Bacup (1/12); Barnsley (0/20); Barrow-in-Furness (1/12); Bradford (0/10); Bristol (85/0); Blackburn (13/19); Burnley (11/0); Cambridge (8/5); Canterbury (0/1); Cardiff (43/35); Carlisle (5/15); Carmarthen (0/16); Chesterfield (11/7); Dewsbury (2/11); Doncaster (0/11); Dover (2/0); Dudley (1/18); Gateshead (8/18); Glossop (1/13); Gravesend (2/8); Great Yarmouth (4/11); Hereford (0/10); Huddersfield (21/13); Hyde (0/27); Kendal (0/23); Kingston-upon-Hull (40/0); Lancaster (0/4); Leamington (0/13); Leeds (68/24); Lincoln (5/19); Liverpool (169/78); Manchester (200/0); Merthyr Tydfil (2/84); Neath (1/0); Newark (0/5); Newcastle-upon-Tyne (46/28); Northampton (3/0); Norwich (6/154); Nottingham (82/0); Oldham (44/4); Penzance (0/8); Plymouth (0/27); Portsmouth (17/5); Rochdale (22/8); Rotherham (16/7); Saint Helens (1/26); Salford (38/0); Scarborough (0/16); Sheffield (66/0); Shrewsbury (0/50); Southport (1/20); South Shields (4/15); Stalybridge (4/7); Stockport (18/4); Sunderland (16/24); Swansea (11/26); Tynemouth (1/8); Wakefield (3/10); Wallasey (15/1); Walsall (0/18); Wigan (4/15); Wolverhampton (3/21); Worcester (1/15); York (3/26).

Therefore, there were 1,135 full-time borough police firemen and 1,108 part-time borough police firemen.[38]

The outbreak of the Second World War threw tremendous strains on the borough police fire brigades, which could not cope with the twin duties of policing and fire fighting. As a result, in 1941, the Fire Brigade Act of 1938 was implemented, and all fire brigades, both police and non-police, were nationalised into the National Fire Service, a new body entirely independent of any police involvement.

After the war, the Fire Service Act of 1947 abolished police fire brigades, decreeing that policemen were no longer to be employed as firemen. The Act gave the responsibility of the fire brigades to the local authority, the county councils, where it remains.

The year 1890 could be described as the *annus mirabilis* of the police service, although it is doubtful whether anyone noticed at the time. Of the Inspectors of Constabulary who started it all off in 1856, only Willis of the original three was still alive to see it. It was as though he was holding on to see if his work would ever come to fruition, as he died in February 1891, aged 85, just six months after the passing of the 1890 Police Act.[39]

EIGHT

1890–1914

With the police service now seemingly settled, having secured a decent pension system, a tolerable pay structure and no inefficient forces, everything looked rosy. The police service was set for a contented future, which is probably why the Home Office completely ignored it again, and why all welfare matters now came from individuals and not from central government, who, thinking that the service had a decent wage and pension, wondered what more it could possibly want. And so the Home Office was content to leave police matters to local government – there was no political leadership or, indeed, police policy emanating from the Home Secretary, which is why two individuals did what they did. In the period 1890 to 1914 two private individuals stand out as giants in police welfare matters. One is Catherine Gurney and the other is John Kempster.

Catherine Gurney, Police Benefactress

The lone policeman was taken aback when the lady offered him a religious tract.

'Why, do you think a policeman has a soul?' he asked.

'Why, of course he has,' she replied.

'Well, you're the first person who's ever thought so!'

It was this chance meeting on a Sunday in London in 1883 that convinced Catherine Gurney what her life's work should be. Catherine had always been grateful for the protection of the policemen she met on her lonely night-time walks on the way to her Bible class in Wandsworth, but now she felt guided to devote the rest of her life to the welfare – physical and spiritual – of British police officers.

Catherine Gurney was born on 19 June 1848 into a well-to-do, middle-class home. Her father was a shorthand writer at the House of Commons and also Treasurer of the Religious Tract Society. So Catherine and her sisters grew up in a household of high intellectual pursuits and firm Christian principles.

35 Catherine Gurney, founder of
the Christian Police Association, two
police convalescent homes and two
police orphanages.

Young ladies of this class and background were educated privately, and were
never sent out to earn a living. So it is no wonder that ladies with time on their
hands turned to philanthropic and charitable works to occupy themselves.

Catherine was no exception. She started a Bible class for the poor working men of Wandsworth, near to her home in London. It was while walking to
Wimbledon Common that she met the policeman who was to change her life.

Catherine founded the Christian Police Association (CPA) in 1883 at
Resington Lodge, Kensington, where her family had moved after the death of
her father. Catherine found that there were Christian men in the Metropolitan
and other police forces who needed, and would welcome, a link with other
like-minded men in their isolated job, a job that set them apart from the rest of
society.

The CPA caught on rapidly. Branches were opened all over the country
and a magazine, *On and Off Duty*, was started. The aims and teachings of the
Association were based on the Bible, and Scripture Union tracts were used in a
Bible Reading Union. The Association grew so quickly, with its meetings, garden
parties, parade services and concerts, that Resington Lodge could not cope. New
headquarters were desperately needed.

The Police Institute was opened in 1889 in Adelphi Terrace in the Strand and this was to become the base for Catherine Gurney's work. Other institutes were opened in Leeds, Cardiff and Sheffield, all catering to the physical and spiritual needs of police officers.

It was whilst visiting the wives and families of sick and injured officers that Catherine's next mission became clear to her. She was surprised at the sudden return from a convalescent home, after only a couple of days, of a young officer for whom she had secured a place for two or three weeks. The young man was extremely tired and agitated, and explained that although the home was wonderful, he had found it impossible to sleep because in the next bed was a violent criminal he had arrested only a short time previously.

That was when Catherine recognised the need for a convalescent home solely for police officers. She talked it over with Sir Edward Bradford, then Commissioner of the Metropolitan Police. With the help of two friends, Mary Griffin and Mary Bell, a suitable house was found in Hove.

The Police Convalescent Home was opened in March 1890 and in its first year had 102 visitors. But it soon became clear that a larger building was needed. The ladies managed to raise more than £8,000. This included the promise by a London builder, Mr Willett, to build a house at cost price and a £3,000 donation from a Mr Henry Whiting of London, who was dining with Sir Edward Bradford when the new Police Convalescent Home was mentioned.

It was opened in July 1893 in Portland Road, Hove. During the first year, 457 officers from the southern forces stayed there. The home remained at Portland Road until November 1966, when it moved to larger premises on the Kingsway Sea Front, still in Hove. Eventually, even Kingsway became too small, and in June 1988 HRH the Queen Mother opened the present Police Convalescent Home at Flint House in Goring-on-Thames, although it is now known as the Police Rehabilitation Centre.

Catherine's thoughts turned next to police orphans – she had been touched by the sight of a policeman's five children in a county workhouse. With the success of the convalescent home at Hove, several small houses were rented in and around the town to provide welfare and accommodation for children. For five years, happy homes were provided for them, but larger premises were again needed.

Miss Bell's generosity once more provided a home, this time at Redhill in Surrey, to where the orphanage was moved in 1901. By this time it was called the Southern Provincial Police School, and over the years was enlarged many times. Just after the Second World War, however, it closed, as other bodies of the Welfare State were taking over the same work.

The school was sold and the Gurney Fund was established out of the proceeds, which paid allowances to orphans of police officers from the southern forces. Funds came from voluntary monthly contributions from serving officers.

36 Catherine Gurney, with staff and inmates at the Police Convalescent Home at Hove, 1908.

Meanwhile, the CPA was still growing and branches sprang up all over the world. Catherine visited all the overseas branches on a world tour, returning in 1893. Once home, she set about providing a convalescent home and orphanage for the north. The homes at Hove and Redhill could only cope with the southern forces, so Catherine felt two more homes must be established in the north.

One day, whilst walking in Harrogate, Catherine met PC Chappell of the West Riding of Yorkshire Constabulary. She asked him if he knew of suitable premises and he directed her to an empty building which had been a boys' school, St George's, near to the Otley Road. This was ideal, but the asking price was £12,000. Catherine's offer of £9,500 was refused.

Soon afterwards, when staying with friends in Bolton, Catherine spent the whole night in prayer. She recalled later: 'I felt the question must be fully faced and thought out. It was about 3.30 a.m., when I finally decided in prayer to make another bid for the house.'

Next morning, she sent a telegram to the owners offering £10,000 with the words: 'As for an orphanage, hope it may be accepted.' One day later she received her reply: 'As for an orphanage will agree, subject to legal advice.'

The inevitable fundraising followed. The purchase price was obtained by personal visits and through friends, and in January 1898 St George's, with its 12 acres of grounds, opened its doors.

From the start, St George's housed both the Northern Police Convalescent Home and the Northern Police Orphanage, with accommodation for thirty adults and thirty children. But within months it was obvious that there would not be enough room for both. It was decided the orphanage should stay at St George's and a new convalescent home should be built on part of the estate. Yet again, more fundraising had to follow, but by this time Catherine was an old hand at it. The new building, St Andrew's, opened in May 1903.

St George's and St Andrew's continued side by side, both being enlarged continually. In 1956, however, St George's stopped being an orphanage for the same reasons as the Southern Provincial Police School at Redhill. The St George's Fund was established to pay allowances to orphans of police officers of the northern forces.

The Northern Police Convalescent Home at St Andrew's, Harlow Moor Road, Harrogate, still thrives, although under its new name of the Police Treatment Centres. Its patron is HRH Prince Andrew, Duke of York, who in 1989 opened the new wing that is named after him.

Catherine Gurney continued working for all her institutions throughout her life, and in 1919 she was created an Officer of the Order of the British Empire, receiving her insignia from the king. By this time her health was failing and she suffered a long illness, worn out by her incessant labours. After weeks of unconsciousness, she died on 11 August 1930 at Hove. She was 82, and she wished to be buried in Harrogate. Her funeral at the Harlow Moor cemetery, Harrogate, was attended by two Inspectors of Constabulary, four chief constables, senior officers representing the Chief Constables' Association and representatives from New Scotland Yard, the Police Federation and several county and borough police forces.

The debt the police service owes to Catherine Gurney is immense. The inscription on a basket of red roses at her funeral summed everything up. It read simply: 'A Beloved Lady'.[1]

John Kempster, Founder of *Police Review*

What made John Kempster become interested in police matters is not known, but in 1892 he was granted an interview with Sir Edward Bradford, Commissioner of the Metropolitan Police. Kempster wanted to discuss the possibility of a police magazine. Bradford dismissed the idea perfunctorily, saying that:

> he was perfectly satisfied with things as they were … teaching was amply provided; promotion was perfectly impartial; the authorities had ample means of communication with the men; and every man in the force, down to the latest recruit knew that he could, without the slightest risk, see the Commissioner himself and communicate any real grievance without the certainty of redress.[2]

Kempster knew what complete rubbish that was simply by talking to Metropolitan constables who told him exactly the opposite. Undoubtedly it was the same in the provincial borough and county forces. The result was *Police Review and Parade Gossip*, first published in January 1893.

'It was started by me,' said Kempster to the Select Committee on Weekly Rest Days in 1909, 'because in communication with some Metropolitan constables, I discovered that they had many difficulties, but that no individual constable dared to make a complaint. I saw that they needed a paper that would ventilate their troubles, advocate their interests and assist their better education.'[3]

And ventilate troubles was certainly what John Kempster did. Until his death on 13 December 1916, the *Police Review* instituted many campaigns to redress anomalies and sometimes downright bloody-mindedness by some police authorities. The contribution of John Kempster to police officers' welfare has not been made enough of by police historians, but it was significant.

The PC Cant case in 1893 is an example of this. A subscription was opened to pay the court costs of PC Cant appealing against a decision not to count his pension contributions on transfer from another force. He won, and established a legal precedent. There was also the 'Great Boot Case' of 1894, where the Metropolitan Police were supplied with boots that made them 'lame and punished'. Kempster got the practice of issued boots stopped, and the men received a boot allowance instead so that they could buy their own boots that actually fitted them.

Similarly, he campaigned for, and achieved, a lighter-weight summer uniform, instead of the men having to wear the sweltering winter-weight uniform all the year round – this in the days before 'shirt sleeve order' of shirts with epaulettes (not introduced until well into the 1950s). Also, the Police and Citizens' Association was formed in 1894 primarily to provide educational courses for policemen, but it also concerned itself with welfare matters. This lasted until 1921, when it was wound up, since the Police Federation and the National Association of Retired Police Officers (NARPO) made it no longer necessary.

In 1894, under the heading 'Policemen for police appointments', the *Police Review* criticised the Kent Standing Joint Committee for appointing an army officer straight to chief constable. Major Henry Edwards, with no police experience whatsoever, was appointed chief constable in August 1894. The fact that he was the son-in-law of the chairman of the Kent County Council also rankled. In the event, although Henry Edwards was appointed chief constable, he died of a heart attack after only six months in office, but his successor, Lieutenant-Colonel Henry Wade, was also an army officer with no police experience.

This had been a practice which had bedevilled the police service ever since the early days of the 'new police', but mercifully would be stopped by the Police Regulations of 1920 – although attempts to circumvent them would be made in 1925 in Cumberland and Westmorland, and as late as 1940 in Bedfordshire. Imagine the spluttering indignation and the resentment of Members of

Parliament if an army officer was appointed straight to the office of Prime Minister over their heads, without first being elected to Parliament or having the least bit of knowledge of how a government is run. And what would have happened had a police superintendent been appointed straight to captain of a Royal Navy warship or to colonel of a regiment of the army, over the heads of the incumbent officers?

The *Police Review* also campaigned on numerous occasions against penny-pinching police authorities who tried to diddle policemen out of their rightful pensions by using the lamest of excuses. PC Austin of Brighton Borough Police appealed against the decision of Brighton Watch Committee to award only a twenty-year pension, even though he had contributed for twenty-eight years. Eight years of the pension was docked for alleged misconduct. PC Austin lost his appeal on a technicality, but the resulting furore caused the passing of the Police Superannuation Act 1906 (6 Edward VI, Chapter 7) and the Police Superannuation Act 1908 (8 Edward VI, Chapter 5), which stopped these iniquitous practices.[4]

Kempster was involved in many cases such as this, but his most noteworthy achievement was to agitate for the police to get one day off in seven. Previously, the police had no day off at all: it was a continuous seven-day-a-week job. It was perhaps a measure of the indifference of successive Home Secretaries that this matter had never been raised by them before. Other trades and occupations had been accommodated, for example, since 1874: factory workers had their hours regulated to fifty-six a week (ten hours Monday to Friday and six on Saturday, with Saturday afternoon and Sunday off – and, since 1870, bank holidays as well).[5] There were no such luxuries for the police, who still had to perform the grinding continuous duty of seven days a week, fifty-two weeks a year.

Inspired by a campaign which had been waged since 1900 by Kempster, James (later 1st Baron) Remnant, MP for Holborn, introduced a bill into Parliament in 1908 to provide one day's rest in seven for the police. This bill was allowed to lapse on the establishment of the 1908 Select Committee to look at the question.

Numerous witnesses were called to the Select Committee, including Kempster himself, who said:

I thought it my duty as editor of the *Police Review* as directly as possible to ascertain the feelings of the men on the subject of your Inquiry, and I therefore inserted in one week's issue some printed questions, with the result that I received replies from 2,583 constables of various ranks, in addition to numerous letters addressed separately to the editor.[6]

The result was the Police (Weekly Rest Day) Act 1910 (10 Edward VII and 1 George V, Chapter 13). This Act was actually steered through Parliament by the new Home Secretary, Winston Churchill, who was in the position for twenty months between February 1910 and October 1911.[7]

Incidentally, as well as the Weekly Rest Day Act, Churchill's time as Home Secretary included one of the most traumatic experiences that the British police service had suffered. On Friday 16 December 1910, after hearing noises coming from the premises of H.W. Harris, a jeweller's shop at 11 Exchange Buildings, Houndsditch, in the City of London, five unarmed City of London policemen arrived at the scene at 11.30 p.m.

Sergeant Robert Bentley, after being refused entrance by a man who spoke no English, opened the door and was immediately gunned down in a hail of bullets. Sergeant William Bryant, who was with him, was also hit and collapsed seriously wounded. Sergeant Charles Tucker rushed up and died instantly, shot in the heart. PC Ernest Woodhams, standing a few feet away, was also shot. He collapsed with serious wounds to his legs.

PC Walter Choat, who had been posted to keep watch at the end of the street, on hearing the shooting ran to the scene and grabbed one of the murderers, a man called George Gardstein, who was the leader of the gang. Another of the gang, seeing Gardstein captured while trying to shoot Choat, fired eight shots in rapid succession, hitting both men. Choat died instantly and Gardstein was later found dead in nearby Grove Street.

The gang members, who were Latvian and politically motivated, were burgling the jeweller's to provide funds for their movement. A national hunt for the gang followed, including its supposed leader, Peter 'the Painter' Piatkow. Finally, on Tuesday 3 January 1911, the gang was located in a house in Sidney Street, Stepney, which is in the Metropolitan Police area.

The infamous 'Siege of Sidney Street' lasted for about fifteen hours, and ended with the gang members in the house being shot dead and the house set on fire. The only bodies found were those of two men called Svars and Josef, but Peter the Painter had disappeared and was never found.

Winston Churchill, as Home Secretary, had arrived to view the scene just before noon and gave orders for a battery of the Royal Horse Artillery to be summoned, although what use Churchill thought cannon would be against three men in a terraced house can only now be goggled at. For a politician to think he knew better than the police commander at the scene, and to give overriding operational orders to the police, was extremely rare, and thankfully remains so to this day.[8]

Also at the siege was a certain PC Arthur Hogg, Metropolitan Police, who had been in the force for all of three weeks. He was destined to be the last survivor. He retired in 1935 and died in Derby in August 1980.[9]

All five of the City of London policemen involved in the original incident were awarded a new decoration, the King's Police Medal, which had only been established less than two years previously. Sergeant Bryant and PC Woodhams, the two survivors of the original incident, and the next of kin of the three murdered officers received their medals from King George V at Buckingham Palace.

The King's Police Medal had been instituted in July 1909 as a direct result of the Tottenham Anarchists Outrage, on Saturday 23 January 1909. Two Latvian immigrants, Jacob Lepidus and Paul Hefeld, had been waiting for a wages delivery in Tottenham High Road in north London. Armed with automatic pistols and plenty of ammunition, when the van containing the wages arrived, they grabbed the wages bag and shot at the driver and anybody else who tried to stop them. The shots brought out police officers from the police station just over the road, who began a 6½-mile chase through north London. During the chase, over 400 shots were fired, resulting in twenty-five people being wounded, but more seriously caused the deaths of PC William Tyler, one of the chasing officers, and a 10-year-old boy, Ralph Joscelyne, who was running for cover from the hail of bullets.

After a long chase, involving trams, milk floats, horse-drawn vans and petrol-driven vehicles, Hefeld shot himself when cornered near to Chingford Brook and died three weeks later in hospital, completely refusing to speak. Lepidus barricaded himself into a house, but committed suicide as PC Charles Eagles, DC Charles Dixon and PC John Cater, despite being fired at, were breaking in to apprehend him.

Public outrage was immense, especially over the shooting of an innocent 10-year-old. Public opinion also wanted due recognition to be given to Eagles, Dixon and Cater. It was found, however, that no decoration existed to do that. The Albert Medal, instituted in 1867, was for saving life, at sea or on land, but there was no decoration to award civilian gallantry, especially by the police.[10]

Sir Edward Henry, the Metropolitan Police Commissioner, pressed Herbert Gladstone, the Home Secretary, for this to be rectified. The result was the King's Police Medal, instituted on Wednesday 7 July 1909. The decoration was given either for acts of gallantry or for meritorious service.

37 Thomas Leadbetter, chief constable of Denbighshire County Constabulary 1878–1911. He was one of the twenty recipients in the very first list for the award of the King's Police Medal for Meritorious Service in November 1909. His KPM (with original ribbon without centre stripe) is nearest his left arm. A central silver stripe was added in 1916 to form the ribbon in use today, and the order of wearing is also different.

The first awards for gallantry were made, quite properly, to Eagles, Dixon and Cater of the Metropolitan Police, who were listed as recipients on page 8243 of the *London Gazette* of Tuesday 9 November 1909. Nine other awards of the KPM for Gallantry were listed, including Inspector Walter Moore of the Great Yarmouth Borough Police, Sergeant William Barron of the Elgin Constabulary and PC John Walsh of the Dublin Metropolitan Police, all acknowledged for the arrest of armed criminals.

The first awards for meritorious service appeared in the same issue of the *London Gazette*. Sir Edward Henry received the award, as did six English and Scottish chief constables, and thirteen high-ranking officers of English, Scottish and Irish police forces.

Over the years, the King's/Queen's Police Medal has undergone changes. The award for gallantry is now only given posthumously and the award for merito- rious service is now extended to all ranks instead of just the higher echelons, as was the practice when the medal was established. The very first constable to be awarded the decoration for meritorious service rather than gallantry was PC Charles Bates of the Northamptonshire County Constabulary in 1926.

Coincidentally, a few years earlier, it had fallen to the Northamptonshire County Constabulary to usher in another 'first' – it had become the very first police force in the entire world to use a motorcar to catch a fleeing criminal. The frenetic car chase is now standard fare for television and film cop shows; however, the original one was a more sedate affair.

The arrival of Barnum and Bailey's Circus in Northampton for the Easter holiday weekend in April 1899 caused enthusiastic ripples through the town. The advance publicity had whipped up a frenzy of excitement, and it was to be expected that someone's criminal mind would take advantage.

True enough, a printer, Frederick John Phillips, decided to put his professional talents to use and printed some spurious Barnum and Bailey 'Free Tickets'. On Thursday 27 April, just a few days before the circus was due, Phillips visited three shops in what were then small villages on the very outskirts of Northampton. Each shop was kept by a woman, no doubt chosen deliberately, and in each one Philips gave the same line of patter.

Posing as an advance publicity manager for Barnum and Bailey, Phillips asked whether he could put up a poster in the shop window, in return for which the lady shopkeeper would receive some free tickets for the 3-shilling seats. When the gullible ladies agreed, Phillips dished out his forged tickets, saying that he would bring the poster in the next day, and oh, incidentally, it was customary to give a small sum for the poster now.

Amazingly, all three women fell for this. Harriet Scott of Far Cotton gave him sixpence; Agnes Cotton of Duston gave him 1 shilling, and Jane Botterill of Dallington gave him another sixpence. With the money in his pocket, Philips was soon on his way out of the district.

It was Jane Botterill who, realising that she had been duped, alerted Sergeant Hector Donald Macleod of the Northamptonshire County Constabulary. On hearing that the fleeing criminal had been seen going towards Weedon, Sergeant Macleod contacted Jack Harrison in Northampton. Harrison was the proud owner of a newfangled Benz motorcar and, commandeered by Macleod, the two were soon driving out on the Weedon road.

They caught up with Phillips between Harpole and Flore. Despite the usual protestations, which Macleod had heard before, Phillips was arrested and brought back to Northampton. In reporting the chase, *Autocar* magazine wondered dryly whether at any time during the chase the speed limit had been broken, which in 1899 was an exhilarating 12mph.

In October 1906 the chief constable of Birmingham City Police, Sir Charles Rafter, wrote to Lord Alverstone, the Lord Chief Justice, on a matter which, totally surprisingly given the police involvement with the law, had not been settled for over fifty years, and one in which even the learned judges had very differing opinions. Rafter, in asking Lord Alverstone for advice, said that on the same circuit, and within a few months of each other, one judge had severely rebuked one of his constables for having cautioned a prisoner, while another had severely rebuked one of his constables for not having cautioned a prisoner. Who was right?[11]

38 Sergeant Hector Macleod (photographed when a PC), Northamptonshire County Constabulary, who was the first police officer in the world to capture a fleeing criminal by using a motorcar, in April 1899.

39 PC Charles Rowland of the Devonshire County Constabulary, wearing the 'slouch hat'. In the jingoism surrounding the victory of the Boer War, some police forces adopted the South African-style slouch hat in honour of the British army in South Africa. The fashion only lasted a few months during 1900 and 1901 before the realisation came that this type of headgear was entirely unsuitable for the British climate.

40 There was no official pattern for the uniform of a chief constable. Consequently, each force had carte blanche to design its own, resulting in many wonderful extravaganzas, especially on the sleeves. This is David Turner, chief constable of Barnsley Borough Police 1896–98 and Oldham Borough Police 1898–1917, in the magnificent uniform of the chief constable of Oldham. The medal is the commemorative police medal of the coronation of King George V in 1911.

The result was the Judges' Rules. Taking six years to come to fruition, the Judges of the King's Bench formulated the Judges' Rules for the guidance of the police and judiciary in dealing with criminal matters. Previously, various forms of the caution had been used, from 'Be careful, it will be used against you on your trial if you are committed by the magistrates' to 'You need not say anything unless you like, whatever you say will be used against you', and all the variations in between.[12]

The Judges' Rules introduced the now familiar caution of 'You are not obliged to say anything unless you wish to do so, but what you do say will be put into writing and may be given in evidence' when a person is first arrested. Note the use of the word 'may' and note also that there is no 'against you' at the end. The rules also introduced procedures for taking written statements, and so on.

The Judges' Rules lasted until 1964, when they were slightly amended, but the Police and Criminal Evidence Act of 1984 (Chapter 60) introduced totally new criminal guidelines, including the new caution: 'You do not have to say anything, but it may harm your defence if you do not mention when questioned something which you later rely on in court. Anything you do say may be given in evidence.' Notice again that it is 'may', not 'will'.

Overnight, therefore, legions of policemen and policewomen had to forget the Judges' Rules caution, which had been drummed into them since the first day of training school, and replace it with the PACE caution. Some got it wrong, as did

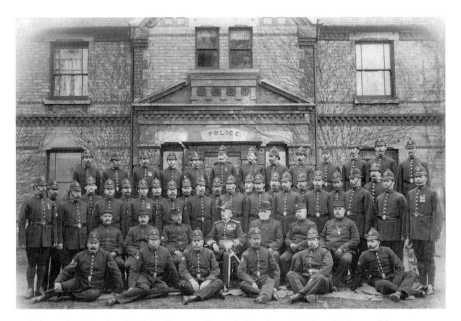

41 The entire Huntingdonshire County Constabulary in 1908, taken in front of the county headquarters at Godmanchester. The chief constable, Alan Chichester, is seated in the centre, in the Huntingdonshire version of the chief constable's uniform.

42 Thomas Orde Hastings Lees, chief constable of the Isle of Wight Constabulary, 1890–99, wearing the fairly restrained Isle of Wight pattern of chief constable's uniform. The medal is the 1897 Diamond Jubilee Medal given to him personally by Queen Victoria at Osborne House for his handling of the island's jubilee celebrations.

43 James Carter, wearing the monochromatic but still impressive uniform of the chief constable of Windsor Borough Police, 1907–39.

44 The son of James Carter, Cyril Carter was the last chief constable of York City Police 1954–68, before it was amalgamated with the North and East Ridings of Yorkshire to form the York and North East Yorkshire Police in 1968. By this time, the chief constables' uniforms were the same as for every other rank, with rank badges on epaulettes, but with the addition of collar braid.

many screenwriters for television and films, some of whom had only just learned that British police officers gave the Judges' Rules caution and not the American 'Miranda' caution ('You have the right to remain silent …').

The Police (Weekly Rest Day) Act of 1910 gave policemen exactly that – one day off in seven. However, the 1908 Select Committee had also touched on the second great grievance of the early twentieth-century police service – the right to confer and the lack of suitable channels to address grievances to the authorities.

Surprisingly, the two Inspectors of Constabulary had not been called to give evidence to the Select Committee. This was an indication of the indifference of the Home Office to police matters. In 1907 one of the three Inspectors of Constabulary, Charles Legge, had died whilst holding office, and the Home Secretary, Herbert Gladstone, had declined to replace him. Thus, from 1907 until the magic year of 1919 there were only two Inspectors of Constabulary, an arbitrary resolution that would have dire consequences for the police, although it would ultimately lead to far better things.

This complacency and lack of any police policy, or indeed interest, from the Home Office was highlighted when the senior Home Office official at the Select Committee was asked what the Home Office view of a weekly day off for the police was. He admitted that there was no view and conceded that nobody had ever attempted to find out what the rank-and-file policemen thought either.[13]

The only system in place at that time for the rank-and-file policemen to communicate their feelings to the hierarchy was through the annual reports of the Inspectors of Constabulary. Yet the inspectors had been reduced to two, and were demoralised, so it is doubtful that their reports were even read, let alone acted upon. In any case, the Inspectorate did not oversee the Metropolitan Police, so could not pass on any grievance from that quarter.

It is clear to us, looking back, that in the few years prior to the Great War the police service of Britain was in a mess due to the lack of proper police policy, leadership and management, coupled with a discontented service. Although the Police Weekly Rest Day had applied a sticking plaster, it had not operated on the broken bones underneath.

In the early years of the twentieth century, the police were called upon more and more, especially in matters of civil unrest. The years just before the Great War saw unprecedented industrial action, especially from the coal miners of the country. In 1902 a six-month strike erupted in Denaby in the West Riding of Yorkshire, when miners withdrew their labour over a 5-shilling-per-week allowance for the inhalation of coal dust.

Serious rioting took place in Tonypandy in November 1910, where, on the insistence of the Home Secretary Winston Churchill, the army was called in under the command of a certain Nevil Macready. In South Wales, in 1911, miners struck when their employers attempted to reduce wages. Rioting and looting were particularly heavy and violent, especially in Llanelli, where railway wagons

**An extra copper is always handy
if you are a bit short !**

45 Always a butt for humour,
policemen have starred in
many humorous postcards.
This one is early Edwardian.

were filled with either petrol or gunpowder and exploded, resulting in loss of life.
In all these disturbances the police were in the middle, reviled by the strikers, and
praised and reviled in turns by the employers. Political motives ascribed to the
police in these disputes are misplaced. In the middle of a riot, the principal object
is to restore order, stop damage to property and protect lives – the policeman's as
much as anybody else's.

Stopping damage was paramount, as by the Riot Damages Act of 1886 (49 and
50 Victoria, Chapter 38), the police had to pay for any damage caused by a riot.
The theory was that the police were there to stop riots, but if one occurred then
the police had to pay for it as a 'punishment' for neglect of duty in the first place.
An indication, perhaps, of the late Victorian view of its police service.

NINE

1914–19

The Great War saw many new duties placed on the shoulders of the police: checking on enemy 'aliens' and arresting where necessary; ensuring compliance with new wartime regulations, such as lighting and licensing; guarding vulnerable points from expected air attacks (Zeppelin raids) and dealing with the aftermath when they occurred. In fact, one PC gained everlasting fame after one such raid.

PC 354 Charles Smith of the Essex County Constabulary was forever afterwards known as 'Zep' Smith for his arrest of the captain and crew of Zeppelin L33 after it crashed near the village of Little Wigborough, Essex, on Sunday 24 September 1916. He was immediately promoted to sergeant for 'his coolness and judgement'. Zep Smith survived the war and died in April 1977, aged 94.[1]

Instances like that aside, the Great War was not a great war for the British police. Recruiting was stopped for the duration and the shortage of manpower caused by this was further exacerbated when policemen were allowed to join the armed forces. In fact, there is evidence to show that the men picked for release by some chief officers were those most involved with the infant National Union of Police and Prison Officers (NUPPO), of which much more will be said. This did not help morale any more than the suspension of the weekly rest day, thus putting the police back to continuous duty. This was ominous, although it is doubtful whether anybody realised it then. Ironically, it was to be these new pinching constrictions imposed on the police during the Great War which would provoke reactions that would clear away all the iniquities of the old Victorian police system and provide the foundations for the police service we have today.

The start of this revolution, for revolution it was, can be attributed to, ironically enough given its previous indifference, the Home Office itself. For the very first time, the country was faced with a war right on its doorstep. The past wars of the British Empire had taken place far away in Africa, Egypt, India, China and the like. To be faced with a catastrophic war in Europe, just a few miles away across the Channel, and having to suffer the consequential life-taking Zeppelin raids on cities, brought wartime conditions very much to the Home Front. The Home Office was thus forced to supply some sort of leadership to the police service of the country in an attempt to co-ordinate police response to all this unique mayhem. The result was the very first Central Conference of Chief Constables in 1918. Although chief constables' associations had been in existence since 1858 for the counties, and 1896 for the boroughs, the Central Conference was the first time that the Home Office was also involved.[2]

The country had been divided into eight provincial police districts, with each district having its own conference, but district delegates went to the first Central Conference held in March 1918. Although held fairly late in the war, it was a start – chief constables and the Home Office were actually talking to each other.

However, that was at the top level. Down below in the rank and file things were very different. The suspension of the weekly rest day was unimpressive to policemen, but the real grouse was the 'right to confer', or the lack of it. Having no union, unlike other trades which had powerful unions that were listened to by their employers, the rank-and-file police officers were impotent in the face of authority. And the genesis of the unpleasantness to come can be found in the shenanigans of a certain individual called John Syme.[3]

Born in 1873 in Scotland, John Syme joined the Metropolitan Police in 1894. A strict teetotal Presbyterian, he did not join in the carousing of his colleagues, but stopped to study in single men's lodgings. As a result, he was in demand for his knowledge of the regulations when his colleagues needed help, and thus retained a certain amount of popularity and quickly gained promotion.

In 1909 he was promoted to inspector at Gerald Road police station in Westminster, and this is where the trouble begins. His defence of two of his officers (PC Lowder and PC Osbourne) in a complicated case involving a refused charge led to clashes of personality between Syme and Sub-Divisional Inspector Reed and Chief Inspector Sherrington. Everything was blown out of all proportion and each twist and turn added more and more venom against Syme. In response, Syme voiced his opinion of Reed and Sherrington alleging corruption and misuse of power. Since he did not 'shut up' when told to, he was transferred to another station in the suburbs and was eventually dismissed in June 1910. He then devoted the rest of his life to proving that his dismissal was unjust by continual agitation and threats against all figures of authority in the Metropolitan Police.

Determined to stop the official injustice in the Metropolitan Police, in October 1913 Syme published an advertisement in the *Police Review* announcing the formation of the Metropolitan Police Union, with head offices in a private house in Westminster. The Metropolitan Police Commissioner, Edward Henry, immediately sent a circular to all ranks saying that any police union was unlawful and any Metropolitan Police officer joining it would be dismissed. Nevertheless, the union was formed, with members joining in secret. Then, in an attempt to widen its membership, the union changed its name to the National Union of Police and Prison Officers, NUPPO.

Although Syme was in prison (for the second time) for publishing libellous pamphlets against Henry and the Metropolitan Police, NUPPO continued to grow. Since the authorities had other things on their mind, NUPPO was ignored, but the intolerable conditions suffered by the police due to the Great War still festered on.

During the war, the cost of living doubled; police wages did not. It was with envy that the policeman looked at the wages, supplemented by overtime, of the factory and munitions workers; and police wages were further reduced by 1 shilling per day for every day taken off because of illness. The times were ripe for the malcontents to stir up trouble. And stir it up they did.

The explosion came in August 1918. PC Tommy Thiel of the Metropolitan Police had been an active member of NUPPO and had been energetically recruiting from some of the provincial forces. He had been very fruitful in Manchester, where he had signed up 400 recruits. Unfortunately, one of those 400 had shown all the NUPPO correspondence to the chief constable of Manchester City Police, Robert (later Sir) Peacock, who promptly sent a complaint to the superintendent at Hammersmith police station, where PC Thiel was stationed, complaining that a member of the Metropolitan Police was undermining the loyalty of the Manchester City Police.

Thiel was summoned in front of the commissioner on Monday 25 August 1918 and dismissed. NUPPO now had its martyr, and on Thursday 28 August an ultimatum was sent to the Metropolitan Police. It demanded an increase in the War Bonus of 66 per cent, to £1 weekly, to be made permanent and pensionable; an extra War Bonus of 12½ per cent of wages; complete recognition of NUPPO; and reinstatement of PC Thiel. If not complied with, NUPPO would take strike action at midnight that day. This would only apply to the Metropolitan Police, as no provincial force was involved.

However, this was August, and Whitehall was closed for the holidays. Nothing decisive was done by the deputies left in charge and thus the inevitable happened. At midnight, the night-shift men returned to their stations and by midday on Friday 29 August, 6,000 men out of 18,000 in total had declared themselves on strike.

As Sir George Cave, the Home Secretary, was away on holiday, Lloyd-George, the Prime Minister, instructed General Smuts to act as Deputy Home Secretary. Although his political service had been mainly in his native South Africa, Jan Smuts had been commissioned into the British army in 1916 and was seconded as a member of the British War Cabinet. Smuts, however, seemed incapable of comprehending the seriousness of the moment and adamantly refused to see the strikers' leaders, as he said they were not recognised representatives of the men. This was a huge mistake.

By midnight on Friday 29 August 1918, almost the entire Metropolitan Police had come out on strike, only the far-flung suburbs having men reporting for duty. The next day, Saturday, the City of London Police also came out on strike; after all, although they were a totally different police force, they were suffering the same privations. London was therefore almost totally without police cover, and a frightened Lloyd-George ordered in the army to guard key government buildings. His nail-biting disquiet, however, was misplaced. Except for one tiny shop in the East End, no looting or rioting took place, which perhaps is a tribute to the good people of London.

Lloyd-George was a politician first and foremost, and he knew that he had to act fast, no matter what it took. He ordered his Home Secretary to come back from holiday, and next day, they both met the strikers in Downing Street. Lloyd-George promptly reinstated PC Thiel and promised an immediate pay increase; also, although a police union could not be recognised in wartime, he promised that as soon as hostilities had ceased, the police union question would be looked at. The strike ended immediately. As good as his word, the pay increase was announced and membership of NUPPO was to be tolerated provided it did not interfere with discipline or call for strike action.

Lloyd-George knew when he was in a corner and knew he had to acquiesce. Had he or his deputies taken a hard line, things would have turned extremely ugly. A large city such as London, the capital of the Empire, was impossible to contemplate without police cover. However, there had to be a scapegoat, and in this instance it was the Metropolitan Police commissioner, Sir Edward Henry, who was 'eased' out of office within the day. Sir George Cave, the Home Secretary, also offered to resign, but Lloyd-George, knowing that no one else wanted the job at that time, refused Cave's offer.

Lloyd-George and Cave were politicians, and politicians can do things differently when not over a barrel. The strikers' delegates thought that by saying that NUPPO could not be recognised in wartime, Lloyd-George implied that it would be recognised in peacetime. Lloyd-George and Cave, however, had no such intention, and a police union, affiliated to the Trades' Union Congress with the right to strike, was never their intention.

As Edward Henry left the Metropolitan Police, his replacement was Sir Nevil Macready, another army officer with no police experience. It was Macready who had commanded the troops during the mayhem in Tonypandy in 1910. Opinion of Macready as Commissioner of the Metropolitan Police is polarised.[4] On the one hand, he was placed there by Lloyd-George to provide firm discipline, especially to NUPPO, which, emboldened by its supposed new status, was effectively challenging him on control of the discipline within the Metropolitan Police. Meetings between the two ended abruptly when Macready found that NUPPO had written to the Home Secretary over his head, accusing him of duplicity.

On the other hand, Macready introduced reforms and innovations into the Metropolitan Police which had never been achieved before and were badly needed. So on the whole, his term at Scotland Yard is looked upon with approval. He left in 1920 to return to the army.

Nevertheless, he had to contend with what would become the death throes of NUPPO, although neither then knew it. When the Great War ended in November 1918, NUPPO, remembering Lloyd-George's 'promises', started agitating for formal recognition. Lloyd-George refused point-blank, and thus sowed the seeds of the next police strike. Although he had other things on his mind, such as the Versailles Conference and the aftermath of four years of total war, he knew that trouble would still be forthcoming if he stood by and did nothing; in any case, he could not face another police strike.

Desborough Report

Fearful of facing peacetime with a discontented police service, the 'Committee to enquire into the state of the police service of England, Scotland and Wales' was hastily appointed in March 1919. It consisted of five politicians and one army officer, all under the chairmanship of William Henry Grenfell.

Born into the Victorian privileged classes, Willy Grenfell was to pull the British police service out of the Stone Age and into the twentieth century. Better known as Lord Desborough, he was the 'action man' of his day, and his life could almost have been plucked out of the pages of the *Boys' Own* comics.

Willy Grenfell was born in London on 30 October 1855. His father owned 12,000 acres of Buckinghamshire land and his great-grandfather was the Earl of Harewood. Educated at Harrow, the young William played for the cricket 1st XI of 1873–74, before going on to Balliol College, Oxford, where he graduated in 1879. A natural sportsman, Grenfell's sporting activities throughout the whole of his long life of ninety years have to be seen to be believed. Whilst at Oxford, he gained 'Blues' for athletics and for rowing, taking part in two University Boat Races, and he was the 'stroke' for the Oxford Eight that rowed across the English Channel in 1878. He was President of the Oxford University Athletics Club and the Oxford University Boating Club, and on top of all this was Master of the University Draghounds. He won the Thames Punting Championship in three successive years; he sculled from London to Oxford on the Thames in twenty-two hours non-stop; he swam across Niagara Falls twice; he climbed the Matterhorn by three different routes and on one occasion climbed five different Alpine peaks in eight days; he went big game hunting in the Rockies, India and Africa, and deep-sea fishing off the coast of Florida; he was President of the Amateur Fencing Association; and in 1908 was President of the London Olympic Games. He also kept a team of bays and was President of the Coaching

46 William Grenfell, 1st Lord Desborough.

Club and Four-in-Hand Club; and at various times he was President of the Marylebone Cricket Club and the All England Lawn Tennis Association at Wimbledon.

Though not a regular soldier, he saw active service when the *Daily Telegraph* sent him as a special correspondent to cover the Suakin Campaign of 1888 in Egypt. The *Boys' Own* flavour of this extraordinary man's life was typified when, during the Suakin Campaign, he apparently found himself totally alone, facing a charging mass of screaming tribesmen, armed with nothing more lethal than a rolled umbrella!

Nevertheless, coming from 'the ruling classes' of his time, it was decreed in the stars that Grenfell would enter politics, which he did in 1880, as Member of Parliament for Salisbury. He was returned in the General Election of 1885 and became personal private secretary to the Chancellor of the Exchequer. He lost his seat in 1886 when his party, under the leadership of William Gladstone, was ousted from government.

During his time away from Parliament he concerned himself with local politics, and at some stage or another filled almost every local government and local justice office that was open to him in Buckinghamshire and Berkshire. It was estimated that at one time he was serving on no less than 115 committees. He was elected back to Parliament in 1892, this time for Hereford City, but because of a squabble over the Home Rule bill, Grenfell resigned his seat soon afterwards. He was next elected to Parliament in 1900, when he became the Conservative Member for High Wycombe in Buckinghamshire.

In 1905 he was raised to the peerage as Baron Desborough of Taplow (Desborough being an old name for a part of Buckinghamshire), and in 1908 he was awarded the KCVO.[5] Lord Desborough was regarded as the Superman of his day, and a man who could get things done. It is little wonder, therefore, when the government wanted fast action in 1919, that it was Lord Desborough who was chosen to lead the committee to look at the structure of the police service.

The committee held 34 sittings and heard 148 witnesses, including police officers of various English, Welsh and Scottish forces, and of every rank from Inspector of Constabulary down to police constable. The most urgent matters were attended to first: pay, pensions and representation. In taking evidence on pay, Desborough heard some appalling tales.[6]

He found that the average pay of a police constable was less than a Newcastle City Corporation road sweeper and less than a Birmingham City Corporation dustman. He found that one constable from an English county force could only dress his wife and children in rags and, because he had to buy his own uniform, could only afford to do so out of profits made from selling vegetables grown on his allotment. Numerous other instances of the same kind emphasised that the pay and morale of the British police service had sunk to a very low point indeed.

In finding out the minimum necessary weekly income for a cross-section of police officers in different circumstances, Desborough subjected their weekly household budgets to fine scrutiny, even down to how much jam and how many Oxo cubes each family needed per week. Comparisons between their minimum required income and their actual wages were startling. A married Metropolitan police constable with two children needed £3 13s 0d per week and received £3 12s 1d, which was 11d or 1.25 per cent short. A married constable with four children in an English county force needed £3 18s 3d and received £3 2s 9d, which was 15s 6d or 20 per cent short. But, most horrendous of all, a married constable in a Scottish county force needed £3 9s 5d and actually received only £2 3s, an astonishing weekly shortfall of £1 6s 5d or 38 per cent.

The completed Desborough Report was published in two parts. The second part appeared in January 1920 and addressed the administration of the police. The first part, the most urgent, dealing with pay, pensions and representation, was rushed through by July 1919.

Of the sixteen recommendations in the first part, the most important were those concerning pay and representation. Desborough recommended an immediate pay rise of 33 per cent, backdated to 1 April 1919. On the question of representation, he stated that 'it is essential that means be provided … to enable the police, as well as the Police Authorities, to submit their views through their chosen representatives to the Central Authority with regard to any changes of pay or other matters affecting the service as a whole'. The direct result of this recommendation was the establishment of the Police Federation and the Police Council.

So desperate was the government to avoid confrontation with the police service that it had no real choice but to put the Desborough Report into action with minimum delay. The Police bill was introduced into Parliament on 8 July 1919, and subsequently the Police Act 1919 received the Royal Assent on 17 August 1919, just six weeks after the publication of the first part of the Desborough Report.

The Act accepted all the recommendations of Desborough in their entirety, including the establishment of the new Police Federation, which was to kill off once and for all the renegade and unofficial National Union of Police and Prison Officers, NUPPO, which had just called another national police strike.

On the face of it, it is hard to fathom the motives of the policemen who came out on this police strike. Although it was the fourth strike in police history, it was actually the first provincial strike, as the first three strikes were purely Metropolitan Police affairs.[7]

The first strike was in November 1872, occurring after the dismissal of PC Henry Goodchild, the would-be secretary of a pay-negotiating committee, when the men of D, P, T and E Divisions of the Metropolitan Police refused to go on duty. The strike did achieve limited success in improved pay scales, but the underlying grievance of not having any negotiating machinery festered on.

A complete refusal to set up any sort of negotiating committee was the direct cause of the second police strike. In July 1890, 130 men of E Division, Metropolitan Police, refused to go on night duty. Thirty-nine of the strikers were dismissed, and a few days later staged a 'riot' outside Bow Street police station, which was broken up by a troop of lifeguards. No real progress was made by this strike.

The third strike of August 1918 resulted, as we have seen, in the Desborough Committee, and just one year later the recommendations in the Desborough Report were well known, delivering more or less what had been asked for over the past forty-six years. However, the police bill going through Parliament at that time contained the clause which sought to make it illegal to belong to any union other than the proposed Police Federation. This was such a direct challenge that hotheads in the NUPPO heartlands were set to fight it.

After PC Thiel's sorties, the Merseyside forces had their fair share of NUPPO members. Consequently, on 1 August 1919, 955 men of Liverpool City Police, 114 of the Birkenhead Borough Police, 63 in the Bootle Borough Police and 1 man of the Wallasey Borough Police, together with 119 men of Birmingham City Police, 1,056 men of the Metropolitan Police and 57 men of the City of London Police, all refused to go on duty.

Liverpool was the worst affected. So bad was the situation – with three days of riots resulting in loss of life – that the army, complete with tanks, was sent on to the streets to stop looting. A day later, they were joined by the battleship HMS *Valiant* and the destroyer HMS *Venomous*, both sent up the River Mersey to guard Pierhead.

The strike, however, quickly melted away, as did NUPPO itself, when it emerged that a large proportion of the NUPPO executive had never come out on strike to support their members. Being satisfied with Desborough's recommendations, 97 per cent of the country's policemen ignored the strike. But of the 2,365 policemen that did not, every one of them was subsequently dismissed and, despite appealing, none was ever reinstated.

The Desborough second report appeared in January 1920, after nine more sittings of the committee. It concerned itself with police administration, including the establishment of a department of the Home Office purely for the police, and the recommendation that in the future the Exchequer Grant be extended to include half of all the annual police costs, instead of just half of the pay and pensions as previously. This last proposal made the annual police costs of the government rise from the annual £7 million paid in 1914 to the £18 million in 1920.

The complete list of all the Desborough recommendations would be tedious to describe. But at a stroke, in just six short months of 1919, the committee, under Willy Grenfell, Lord Desborough, achieved such a complete transformation of the British police service that sometimes the 1920s and 1930s have been called 'the golden age of policing'. It is sad, therefore, to find that the contentment Lord Desborough brought to the police was not reflected fully in his own life. Despite all his sporting achievements and his privileged background, he was not immune to the tragedies of life. Two of his sons were killed in the mincing machine of the Great War and the remaining son died, unmarried, in a car crash in 1926. However, his elder daughter became Lady Salmond, the wife of the marshal of the Royal Air Force, Sir John Salmond, and his younger daughter became Viscountess Gage.

William Henry Grenfell, 1st Baron Desborough of Taplow, died on 9 January 1945 at his house at Panshanger, Hertfordshire. He was 90 years old.

As influential as the Desborough Report was, perhaps it was not quite so influential as the other noteworthy outcome of the Great War – 'lady policemen'.[8] Perhaps the pioneer of women police (in Britain, at least) was Constance Antonina Boyle, invariably known as Nina Boyle. Although influenced by the Suffragettes, Nina Boyle and Edith Watson belonged to the breakaway group, the Women's Freedom League, where their main preoccupation was not votes for women, but for equal treatment by the law and in the law courts.

By 1914, Edith Watson had been observing the law courts for two years in the cases where women and children appeared, either as the accused (especially prostitutes) or as injured parties. She found grossly biased judgements and sentences. For example, a woman received nine months' hard labour for soliciting, but no offence existed (or exists) for men who use prostitutes. Her constant agitation for reform, demands to the Home Office and physical obstruction inside the courts led to several arrests.

With the declaration of what would become the Great War, fate took the lead, and it was decided to abstain from legal disruption and instead help the women and children caught up by the upheavals of war. Nina Boyle thus advertised for ladies to act as women volunteer police. She offered her recruits to serve as special constables, but was turned down because the Home Office wanted 20,000 *men* to serve as specials, not women. Nevertheless, she continued recruiting, but soon learned of another lady doing exactly the same thing.

Margaret Damer-Dawson was from the affluent middle class and had become incensed at what was known as the 'White Slave Trade' – the procuring of women for prostitution overseas. Margaret Damer-Dawson and Nina Boyle combined their talents to form the Women Police Volunteers (WPV), with Damer-Dawson as commandant and Boyle as deputy. Thanks to her social background, Damer-Dawson convinced the Commissioner of the Metropolitan Police, Sir Edward Henry, to allow the WPV to train and patrol the streets of London as volunteers.

Probably the first woman to appear in the WPV uniform was the remarkable Edith Watson in September 1914. She was from a working-class London family, but had educated herself to such an extent that she was not overawed by the likes of Damer-Dawson, her social opposite.

Damer-Dawson's brother-in-law was a captain at the large military camp in Grantham, and consequently an invitation was sent to the WPV to help to control the huge increase in women of 'notorious bad character' who had flocked to the camp. Two ladies were sent to Grantham, but unfortunately, this was to cause many problems.

At an army camp in Cardiff, the commanding officer, using his powers under the emergency Defence of the Realm Act, had actually imposed a curfew on women during the hours of 7 p.m. and 8 a.m., and as such had already tried five women, found them guilty and given them three months' imprisonment each. This so encouraged the commanding officer at Grantham that he tried the same thing, but went a step further; he allowed the two WPV ladies, Mary Allen and Ellen Harburn, to accompany military police patrols and gave the power of entry into suspected women's homes.

This appalled Nina Boyle, who created such a furore that the curfew was declared illegal and stopped. It was possibly this which led her into confrontation with Margaret Damer-Dawson, with the inevitable internal squabbles, and resulted in Boyle's resignation, along with that of Edith Watson and Eva Christie. This split caused the organisation to change its name to the Women's Police Service (WPS) in February 1915.

Although there were other volunteer women police groups, such as the National Union of Women Workers and the Bristol Training School for women patrols and women police, it was to be the WPS that would provide the basis for policewomen in provincial forces. At the end of the Great War, many of the 500 or so WPS who had served at the army camps and munitions factories were

47 The standard pattern of policewomen's uniforms during the Great War and into the 1920s. This lady is from an unknown force.

recruited into the provincial borough and county forces, and within a few years would be fully fledged, attested police constables with all the same legal powers as their male colleagues.

Margaret Damer-Dawson died in 1919 and Mary Allen took over as commandant. However, soon the provincial forces were recruiting directly for themselves, without going through the WPS, which therefore gradually faded away. Although being renamed the Women's Auxiliary Service, it ceased to exist in 1940, having never recovered from the taint of Mary Allen's expressed admiration for Hitler and Mussolini during the late 1930s.

In the Metropolitan Police, on the other hand, Sir Edward Henry, aided by Mrs Louise Creighton (widow of Mandell Creighton, Bishop of London, 1897–1901), who was the force behind the National Union of Women Workers, set up his own Women Special Police Patrols in 1916. These were completely separate from the WPS and patrolled mainly in Hyde Park, where acts of public indecency where a continual nuisance. Thus in London, there was a confusing rivalry between the WPS and the Special Police Patrols.

48 The policewomen's section of the Birmingham City Police in the 1930s. By this time, policewomen had become fully integrated and attested members of the service, with the same powers as their male colleagues, although the uniforms were still based on the male designs. Properly designed feminine uniforms came along much later.

With Sir Edward Henry's precipitate 'resignation' after the 1918 police strike, Sir Nevil Macready, the new commissioner, who had no truck with the WPS because of alleged high-handedness with women the WPS came into contact with, carried the idea of the Special Police Patrols to its logical conclusion. In December 1918, 100 women were recruited and, under the guidance of Mrs Sofia Stanley, trained to be fully empowered police constables, taking up regular duties in February 1919. These were the first Metropolitan policewomen.[9]

Thus, the Metropolitan Police and the provincial forces arrived at the employment of women as police constables in slightly different ways, but with the same end result. We can look back on the achievements of the pioneer heroines: Nina Boyle, Edith Watson, Margaret Damer-Dawson, Mary Allen, Ellen Harburn, Edith Smith (who replaced Mary Allen at Grantham, but had been given full powers of arrest by the Grantham Borough Police, thus making her the first 'official' policewoman in the country), Louise Creighton, Dorothy Peto (of the Bristol Training School), Sofia Stanley and Lilian Wyles (the first policewoman to become a detective constable – in the Metropolitan Police).

We can also look at the heroines of today. Read the two books by Norman Lucas: *WPC 'Courage'. The heroism of women of the British Police Forces*, and its sequel, *Heroines in Blue. Stories of Courage by women of the British Police Forces*. You will be amazed.

TEN

1919–39

It cannot be emphasised too much what a complete pivotal point the Desborough Committee was. Lord Desborough's deep understanding not only of the police function, but of the police system in Britain, brought the service out of the dark ages into the light of modernism. His report covered everything, even the old chestnut of a national police force.[1]

He had considered that option again but had rejected it, saying that 'the preservation of law and order in this country is primarily the function of the proper local authorities'.[2] However, he did emphasise that 'under the present system, lack of uniformity has developed to an undesirable degree'.[3] His proposed solution was to introduce a 'greater measure of centralisation and standardisation of conditions of service'.[4] Desborough's careful comparison of the duties of police officers from large city forces and rural forces shows his remarkable understanding at work.[5] His conclusion, therefore, was that 'the duties of policemen are fundamentally the same in character throughout the forces within our terms of reference … and do not justify the wide differences in pay, pensions and housing conditions'.

Thus, his overlying recommendation was that the police service of Britain would be far better served by a greater degree of uniformity and standardisation of pay and conditions, housing and pension schemes. The government, frightened of anymore confrontation with the police and fearful of entering post-war peacetime with a discontented police service, accepted Desborough's recommendations in full, with no provisos.

As such, a brand new consultative system was quickly put into place. At the Home Office, F Division was established, which gave for the first time a department directly responsible for the police, and through which the Home Secretary could get more involved by being able to regulate police pay and conditions, in total contrast to the indifference of the previous ninety years.

This dedicated Home Office department was the first part of the new machinery assembled on the recommendation of Desborough, for the channels of communications deemed necessary between top and bottom. The second and third parts were also hastily assembled.

The Police Federation was established in 1919 for the 'purpose of enabling members of the police forces in England and Wales to consider and to bring to the notice of police authorities and the Secretary of State, all matters affecting their welfare and efficiency, other than questions of discipline and promotion affecting individuals'.[6] At long last, for the first time in ninety years, the Police Federation gave the police what they had been agitating for – the right to confer; a representative, negotiating body.

But in granting this, constraints were placed upon it. The right of the police to take strike action was specifically withdrawn, and it was made a criminal offence for any police officer to strike or for anyone to induce him to do so. Thus it was called the Police *Federation* rather than a police *union* for precisely this reason.

The constitution of the Police Federation is worth attention as a skilful act of administration, stemming directly from the recommendations of Lord Desborough. His knowledge of human nature was awesome. He knew that discussion would be inhibited if all ranks of the police met together in one large committee, as policemen would be afraid of speaking out in criticism of a colleague of a higher rank, fearing later personal, spiteful reprisals. So in each force, three separate branch boards were established for the three ranks of constable, sergeant and inspector/chief inspector. However, the three must come together at some point, so each force had an amalgam of the three rank committees, called a Joint Branch Board.

Each rank had a central committee, elected at that rank's yearly central conference. The three central committees then sat as a single joint central committee, and it was this joint central committee that was given access to the reigning Home Secretary. Thus, even the smallest voice of the lowliest probationary constable could be heard nationally.[7]

Implementation of this exciting new development was rapid, and the first central conferences were held at Central Hall, Westminster, in mid-November 1919, only four months after the passing of the Police Act 1919. The three ranks met in separate halls, and their first task was to elect chairmen and then their central committees. Eventually, James Farley of the Metropolitan Police was elected for the constables; Alfred Thomas of Bristol City Police for the sergeants; and Chief Inspector Thomas Faulkner, Metropolitan Police, for the inspectors. As soon as each rank's central committee was chosen, the first joint central committee was held. The first chairman was PC Farley, and he was destined to hold this office periodically for the next eighteen years.

Surprisingly enough, no official report of this momentous occasion was published, but the *Police Review* printed substantial articles from officers who had attended. Many topics were discussed, including the lack of an appeal system for officers dismissed from their forces. This was to bear fruit eight years later when the Police (Appeals) Act 1927 (17 and 18 George V, Chapter 19) was passed, which gave policemen exactly that. This was added to in 1943 by the Police (Appeals) Act (6 and 7 George VI, Chapter 8), when the right of appeal was extended to those officers who, though not dismissed, had been punished by a reduction in rank or pay.

Over the years and up to the present time, the Police Federation has fought many battles. Some have been lost, but some have been won, and considering the Police Federation does not possess the ultimate industrial weapon of withdrawal of labour, this means that their negotiating skills must be applauded. Anyway, as the *Police Review* said in 1919, 'the Police Federation is now a well-established fact, and it has come to stay'.[8]

The third part of the representative machinery of the Desborough Report was the Police Council. Meeting for the first time on Tuesday 6 July 1920 at the Home Office, the chairman was the Home Secretary, Edward Shortt. The council consisted of representatives of every body concerned with the policing of the country, from the Home Office to the local authorities to the policemen themselves, of all ranks and many forces.

The Police Council was an advisory and not an executive body, and only met periodically (only seven times in the first ten years to 1930), but it was generally agreed that the first task was to get to grips with Desborough's demands for standardisation and uniformity. So the first council looked at such things as conditions of service, educational requirements for entry, rank structure, rules for promotion, annual leave periods, and so on. The results of all this, after four days of intense brainstorming, were the Police Regulations of 1920.

The Police Regulations – ninety of them, as mapped out by the Police Council – also came into use quickly, by October 1920, and covered every facet of police conduct and administration:

Regulations 1–6: dealt with ranks, areas and strengths of forces

Regulations 7–11: qualifications for appointment

Regulations 12–26: all aspects of discipline by unifying the police disciplinary code (remembered by generations of police officers by the mnemonic DISOBEDIENCE LAC – Discreditable conduct, Insubordination, Soliciting drink, Obtaining favours, Betraying confidences, and so on)

Regulations 27–32: qualifications for promotion

Regulations 33–40: hours of duty

Regulations 41–43: annual leave

Regulations 44–46: personal records

Regulations 47–86: scales of pay, clothing, equipment, and so on

Regulations 87–90: legality and promulgation of the regulations.

The chief constables were not lagging behind, either. Seeing the establishment of the Police Federation, which provided representation for the ranks up to chief inspector, the chief constables also decided to act. The County Chief Constables' Association and the Chief Constables' Association (for the boroughs) continued on with the Chief Constables' Conferences which had started during the war. Eventually, all these bodies were to unite in 1948 to form ACPO – the Association of Chief Police Officers. ACPO still thrives and now represents all provincial police officers of assistant chief constable upwards, as well as the senior ranks of the Metropolitan and City of London Police.

Not to be left out, in 1920 the superintendents formed a system of district conferences, ostensibly to elect representatives to sit on the Police Council. This eventually grew into the Police Superintendents' Association, formed along its present lines in 1952.

By late 1920, after just fourteen incredible months, the police service had overturned ninety years of governmental apathy, thus proving it could be done when needs be. This consultative structure had been set up from scratch and was entirely new. But what of the existing police representative body, the Inspectorate of Constabulary?

Desborough had deemed the Inspectorate as essential, inspecting, as it did, every force, every year. What better way to check up on these new developments? Therefore, he recommended 'that the number of Inspectors should be increased to three, *at least* [my italics], in order to enable them to carry out the requisite inspection work, and to have time to consult with and advise the Home Office on current questions of police administration'.[9]

But the County and Borough Police Act of 1856 had stipulated the number as three, so in order to increase the number of inspectors, a new Act of Parliament would have to be passed. In the event, however, the government did nothing.

This appeared not to worry the inspectors (Sir Leonard Dunning and Llewellyn Atcherley) at that moment, and the inspectors' reports of 1919/20[10] and 1920/21[11] see the inspectors looking forward with optimism to a new 'golden age'. As if to emphasise this regeneration, the 1920/21 report appeared in a new format – quarto, instead of the foolscap of the previous sixty-four years.

The 1919/20 report, being the last of an era, is the last to mention individual forces by name. Banbury Borough was criticised for not maintaining discipline; Colchester Borough, Gravesend Borough, Maidstone Borough, Swansea Borough and Ramsgate Borough were all 'warned' over lack of manpower; and Truro City was censured over not paying rent allowance and only 50 per cent of the new Desborough pay scales. Sir Leonard Dunning added that the Truro City Watch Committee had fully expected to be amalgamated with Cornwall County, hence their parsimony. So for the year 1919/20, Truro City was the only force found inefficient, with the Exchequer Grant being withheld; this was the first force reported inefficient since Congleton Borough in 1890. In fact, Truro City did amalgamate with Cornwall County the following year.[12]

In the annual report for 1919/20, Dunning welcomed the new representative machinery in the shapes of the Police Federation and the Police Council, and also stated that for the first time the City of London Police (but still not the Metropolitan Police) would now be inspected yearly and, if found efficient within the terms of reference, would also receive the Exchequer Grant, which it had never done before. After the 1919/20 report, although cases of concern are referred to, no force is ever mentioned by name, as it was made clear that separate reports on each force were to go directly to the Home Secretary via the new Home Office Police Department.

The function of the Inspectorate had undergone subtle changes after the Police Act of 1919. Due to the establishment of the Police Department at the Home Office, the questions of pay, allowances and pensions had been taken out of their hands. The establishment of the Police Federation, representing the voice of all ranks up to chief inspector, had meant that any grievances went straight to the Home Office, thus bypassing them as well. Similarly, the Police Council, representing all facets of police administration and chaired by the Home Secretary himself, made the possibility of the Inspectorate acting as a conduit of opinion from grass roots to central government totally unrealistic.

Thus, in the 1919/20 annual report, Sir Leonard Dunning set out his perception of the new functions of the Inspectorate, and the new criteria for force inspections:

    i   ensuring sufficient manpower
    ii ensuring discipline has been maintained
    iii ensuring the force has been efficiently managed
    iv ensuring that the police service as a whole has been fully and properly
        administered

Dunning also referred to the new Police Regulations. These had come into effect on Friday 1 October 1920.[13] 'These Regulations,' said Dunning in the 1919/20 report, 'introduce nothing new – but seek to make it uniform.'[14] He added: 'They were adopting that uniformity which Desborough had recommended, rather than police nationalisation which Desborough had rejected.'

The Police Regulations, however, contrary to Dunning's opinion, did introduce something new. It stopped a practice which had concerned many police officers, especially of superintendent rank, for many a long year.

Ever since the county forces had begun, the tendency was to appoint chief constables straight to their office, thus ignoring experienced superintendents who had risen through the ranks. The vast majority of these chief constables were military or naval officers, whose previous knowledge of police administration and of policemen themselves (who are a unique breed at the best of times, as, by the very nature of their job, they have to be) was absolutely nil. Yet these men were chosen in preference to experienced men. Human nature being what it is, there were probably some members of the force who looked upon such men with stoic sufferance.

The Police Regulations attempted to stop all that. From now on, under Regulation 9, chief constables would only be promoted from inside the service. At least, that was the theory. Regulation 9 also included a get-out clause saying that a person with no previous police experience may be appointed if he 'possesses some exceptional quality … which specially fits him for the post, or there is no candidate from the police service who is considered sufficiently well qualified'. This loophole, however, was to be applied only at the Home Secretary's discretion, and not all Home Secretaries were the same.

In 1925 Lieutenant-Colonel Alfred Bartlett was chosen by the Cumberland and Westmorland Standing Joint Committee as chief constable. Although he had spent the previous four years 'studying police duties in the office of the Oxfordshire Chief Constable', Bartlett's career had been purely in the army with no police experience whatsoever. The Home Secretary, Sir William Joynson-Hicks, refused to sanction the appointment.[15]

However, in 1929 John Chaytor, a lieutenant-colonel in the South Staffordshire Regiment, having no previous police experience, was chosen to be the chief constable of the North Riding of Yorkshire County Constabulary. No objection was made by the (new) Home Secretary, John Clynes, and Chaytor remained in office for the next twenty-nine years.[16]

But yet again, in 1940, Lieutenant Commander Richard Coleridge, son of Lord and Lady Coleridge, who had been invalided out of the Royal Navy, was chosen by the Bedfordshire Standing Joint Committee as chief constable. Sir John Anderson, the Home Secretary, refused the appointment. After much discussion between Anderson and Bedfordshire, including questions in the House by the parliamentary spokesman for the Police Federation, Mr Valentine McEntee, the Home Secretary won and Coleridge was ousted as chief constable.[17]

In July 1940, when faced with the illness of Chief Constable William Lucas, the Monmouthshire Standing Joint Committee appointed Sir Talbot Chetwynd, Bart, as acting chief constable instead of the deputy chief constable, William Spendlove. Chetwynd had spent all his life in the army, retiring in 1930, although in 1939 he was the commandant of the Monmouthshire Special Constabulary.

The excuse of the Monmouthshire Standing Joint Committee to appoint Chetwynd rather than Spendlove (which they should not have done, as the loophole in Regulation 9 quite obviously did not apply in this case) was because they did not want to disrupt the management of the force by moving the DCC from his division to headquarters. Chetwynd's appointment lasted only three months, before sense prevailed and William Lucas returned as chief constable, serving until 1950. The thoughts of William Spendlove are not recorded as, no doubt, no one was interested.[18]

This leads on to a related subject, which indicates a trend for growing Home Office control over the police, or at least the police authorities, which were supposedly independently local. By the late 1930s, the Home Secretary was taking it upon himself not to sanction any chief constable's appointment if he thought the candidate was insufficiently experienced, even if he was a police officer. For example, in 1944 Sidney Ballance, the deputy chief constable of Wolverhampton Borough Police, had been chosen by the Wolverhampton Watch Committee to succeed Mr Edwin Tilley as chief constable. Herbert Morrison, the Home Secretary, refused to sanction the appointment, saying that the new chief constable must come from another force.[19]

Similarly, in 1944 in Macclesfield, in 1947 in Salford and in 1958 in Gateshead, the promotion of the deputy chief constable to chief constable was blocked by the Home Secretary. In all four of these cases, the deputy concerned had joined the force as a PC, had been promoted through the ranks and had served in no other force, and it was the Home Secretary's contention that this situation was bad for the police force as a whole.

However, at least two appointments managed to slip the net. Arthur Cust, joining St Helens Borough as a PC in 1913, served in no other force apart from war service and was promoted through the ranks – he was appointed as chief constable in 1939, a position he held until 1946. Willis Clarke did exactly the same, but this time in a county constabulary, Derbyshire. Joining as a PC in 1910, he had two years' war service, rejoined Derbyshire in 1916, became a sergeant in 1918, an inspector in 1921, superintendent in 1926, assistant chief constable in 1941 and chief constable in 1951, before dying whilst holding office in 1952.[20]

In both these cases the Home Secretary did nothing, and there may be more instances where he also chose not to act. Nevertheless, the policy of the appointment of chief constables, as laid down by Regulation 9 of the Police Regulations, was always to be fraught with polemic and would not be solved until examined by the Willink Committee in 1960. Their findings would subsequently be included in the great Police Act of 1964. Today, to be appointed a chief constable, a candidate must have served in a different force in one of the ACPO ranks of assistant chief constable upwards or equivalent rank in the Metropolitan Police.

This leads quite logically to the whole subject of chief constables. It is worth stopping for a moment to reflect on this remarkable breed of men and now women.

Chief Constables

There are problems with the definition of the term 'chief constable' because in the early days, some chief officers of provincial borough forces were called 'super-intendent'. However, in the counties, the term 'chief constable' has always been used to designate the chief officer, and indeed is specifically mentioned as such in Section 4 of the County Police Act 1839.

But the term is harder to track down in the boroughs. Right up until the late 1890s, some borough and city forces were still referring to their chief officer as 'head constable' (Liverpool, for instance), but the Police Regulations of 1920 addressed this, so it is fairly accurate to say that by the start of the 1920s every chief officer was called the chief constable.

To confuse matters, the Metropolitan Police also used the rank chief consta-ble, which was introduced in 1886, to refer to the rank between superintendent and assistant commissioner. A chief constable of the Metropolitan Police was in charge of one of the four districts into which the Metropolitan Police had been divided. In 1889 it was decided to create the appointment of a chief constable for the Criminal Investigation Department; and in 1923 a chief constable of the Traffic Division.

The rank was abolished in 1946, when that of commander was established in its stead. This also eradicated the confusion of a provincial chief constable being the chief officer of his force, whilst the Metropolitan chief constable was several steps down in his.[21]

Only recently, with the publication of *The British Police: Police Forces and Chief Officers 1829–2000* by Martin Stallion and David Wall, has a list of chief constables been available to the public.[22] Pioneering though this work is, it only gives a list of names, it does not give biographies. But a study of this breed we call chief constables yields fascination in the sheer variety of backgrounds, stories and per-sonalities of these men – and since 1995, with the ground-breaking appointment of Pauline Clare to Lancashire, women as well.

There have been many gallant chief constables. Some were awarded medals for bravery whilst actually holding the post. Keith Webster, for instance, whilst chief constable of Gravesend Borough Police, was awarded the King's Police Medal for Gallantry in 1938 for the attempted rescue of children from a burning building.[23] Others earned decorations before they became chief constables. In 1941 John Gott (Northamptonshire 1960–72), then an inspector in the Metropolitan Police, was awarded the George Medal for rescuing people from a damaged building during the Blitz.[24] And others earned their decorations in other walks of life.

In 1888 Pulteney Malcolm (Cheshire 1910–34), a young lieutenant in the Gurkha Rifles, was awarded the Albert Medal for attempting to save the life of a comrade who had fallen over a cliff in India.[25] There is also an instance of the son (Second Lieutenant Alfred Victor Smith) of a chief constable (William Smith,

49 Frederick Lemon, chief
constable of Leeds City Police
1919–23 and Nottinghamshire
County 1923–49, was holding
office at the same time as his
son, (Sir) Richard Lemon, chief
constable of the East Riding
of Yorkshire County 1939–42,
Hampshire County 1942–62 and
Kent County 1962–74.

St Albans City 1901–05; Burnley Borough 1905–24) being awarded the Victoria
Cross during the Great War.[26]

Two chief constables have been murdered on duty and others have suffered violent deaths. William Campling, whilst chief constable of Saffron Walden Borough,
was shot in the back and legs, and died from his injuries in November 1849.
Henry Solomon (Brighton Borough 1838–44) was murdered by a man called
John Lawrence who hit him over the head with a poker when being questioned
about a theft.

On a foggy night in November 1945, the car of the Cambridgeshire chief constable, William Edwards, hit a dimly lit tank convoy near Cambridge. Mr Edwards
and the county Special Constabulary commandant, Captain Reginald Nicholson,
both received fatal injuries.

Furthermore, wartime conditions contributed to the death of Herbert Allen
(Southampton Borough 1940–41), who was injured in a road traffic accident
during an air raid in Southampton. He never recovered and died as a result –
the only chief constable ever to have been killed as a direct result of enemy
action!

There have been several sporting chief constables. Cecil Moriarty (Birmingham
City 1935–41) was capped for Rugby Union by Ireland; Charles Charsley
(Coventry City 1899–1919) was goalkeeper for England on several occasions; and
John Hanlon (Leamington Spa Borough 1938–39) sprinted for the British team at
the 1928 Olympic Games in Amsterdam.

50 Frank Ward always boasted of being the youngest ever chief constable when he was appointed to Lancaster Borough in 1884 in his twenty-sixth year, although this has yet to be verified.

51 Richard Lemon became chief constable of the East Riding of Yorkshire in 1939 when he was definitely 26 years old. Knighted in the New Year Honours List of 1970, this photograph of Sir Richard and his family was taken outside Buckingham Palace, after he received his accolade from HM the Queen.

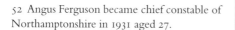

52 Angus Ferguson became chief constable of Northamptonshire in 1931 aged 27.

Some officers have stood out in other ways. Michael Whitty (Liverpool City 1836–44) is the only chief constable to have achieved an entry in the *Dictionary of National Biography*. A journalist and author of immense powers, Whitty eventually became the owner and editor of the *Liverpool Journal* in 1855.

Other chief constables came from distinguished parentage. In the cases of Evelyn Scudamore-Stanhope (Herefordshire 1895–1923) and George Anson (Staffordshire 1888–1929), their fathers were both earls, of Chesterfield and Lichfield respectively. Charles Walsh (Radnorshire 1900–09) was the son of Lord Ormathwaite, who incidentally was also the chairman of Radnorshire Police Authority. Cries of nepotism were heard when Walsh was elected, especially when it was found that he was probably medically unfit for the job because of his wooden leg.

As with other professions, sons often followed in their fathers' footsteps. Frank Williamson (Carlisle City 1961–63; Cumbria 1963–67; Inspector of Constabulary 1967–72) was the son of John Williamson of Northampton Borough Police. Richard Sydney Eddy even followed his father into the same job. He took over from Richard Eddy in Barnstaple Borough in 1905.

Some sons held office at the same time as their fathers. Donald Ross became chief constable of Argyllshire in 1927, while his father, Roderick Ross, was still chief constable of Edinburgh City. The Oswald Coles, Junior and Senior, were chief constables of Worcester City (1923–29) and Oxford City (1897–1924). Frederick Lemon (Leeds City 1919–23; Nottinghamshire 1923–49) was the father of Richard (later Sir) Lemon (East Riding of Yorkshire 1939–42; Hampshire 1942–62; Kent 1962–74).

James Watson (Peterborough City 1909–15; Preston Borough 1915–37) was the brother of John Watson (Congleton Borough 1902–08; Devonport Borough 1908–14; Bristol City 1914–30). Dawson Mayne (Shropshire 1840–59) was brother to Richard Mayne, Commissioner of the Metropolitan Police from 1829–68; but were Otway Mayne (Buckinghamshire 1897–1928) and Jasper Mayne (East Suffolk 1899–1933) from the same family?

Sir Francis Peel (Bath City 1931–33; Essex 1933–62) is a direct descendant of Sir Robert Peel. Sir Robert's influence must have been so strong that his valet, John Stevens, joined the police and finished up as chief constable of Newcastle upon Tyne City, 1836–54. The Peel influence can also be glimpsed when two of the original 'Peelers', joining in 1829, became chief constables: William Brown (Sunderland Borough 1837–55) and Alfred List (East Lothian 1832–40; Midlothian 1840–77).

Does the ability to run a police force only come after years of experience or are some men born with it? Some men have become heads of police forces when extremely young and others have been older or have continued in the job until a great age. Although Frank Ward always boasted of being the youngest man ever to become a chief constable, being elected to Lancaster Borough in 1884 in

53 James Kellie-MacCallum, chief
constable of Northamptonshire
1881–1931. Although not the longest
serving chief constable of all time,
he was definitely the oldest when he
retired, aged 86.

his twenty-sixth year, his claim is probably disputed by William Sylvester, who
became the chief constable of Rochdale Borough in 1863, giving his date of birth
as 27 September 1843. Ward also reckoned himself the youngest man ever to have
joined the police when he was sworn in as a constable in the Leeds City Police at
the age of 16 years 4 months.

   Those stories need to be checked, but there is no disputing the fact that Sir
John Dunne became chief constable of Norwich City in his twenty-sixth year in
1851; Richard Lemon became chief constable of the East Riding of Yorkshire at
the age of 26 in 1939; Angus Ferguson at the age of 27 to Northamptonshire in
1931; and John Jackson at the same age to Oldham Borough in 1849.

   At the other end of the scale, Charles Stretten was 85 when he retired from
Cambridgeshire in 1915, but James Kellie-MacCallum was one year older when
he retired in 1931, after a fifty-year tenure in Northamptonshire. Although Kellie-
MacCallum holds the record for being the oldest chief constable of all time, his
fifty-year service in just the one force, incredible though it is, is still beaten by
George List, who was chief constable of East Lothian from 1840 to 1893, and
before that chief constable of Musselburgh Burgh from 1835. Also, Sir John
Dunne was a chief constable for fifty-one years, but in three forces: Norwich,
Newcastle-upon-Tyne and Cumberland and Westmorland.

Northamptonshire, incidentally, holds the record for the shortest-serving chief constable. Charles Pearson, the then chief constable of Caernarfonshire, was elected by the magistrates to be the new chief constable of Northamptonshire in October 1875, at a morning sitting of Quarter Sessions. On being appointed, Pearson walked from the sessions building to look at the force headquarters, which at that time also contained the chief constable's accommodation. Not liking what he saw and not thinking it big enough for his large family, he marched straight back into Quarter Sessions and demanded new living quarters. The magistrates made two attempts at compromise, but Pearson turned both of them down. Not getting what he wanted, he promptly resigned. He had been chief constable of Northamptonshire for all of three hours!

Although George List is the longest serving chief constable of all time, he doesn't come top of the list for total police service:

	Service in years	Years as chief constable
Richard Jones, Merionethshire	60	39
Charles Stretten, Cambridgeshire	59	27
William Gordon, Dumfriesshire	58	40
George List, Musselburgh/East Lothian	58	58
Picton Phillipps, Carmarthenshire	57	32
James Christie, Greenock	56	42

54 Charles Pearson, the 'three-hour' chief constable.

Alfred Richardson, Newcastle/Halifax	55	43
Edward Holmes, Leicestershire	53	39
Thomas Blackburn, Tynemouth	53	26
James Olive	53	--★
Alfred Arnold, Rochester	52	28
John Scott, Perth	52	20
Thomas Smith, Hamilton	52	16
Sir John Dunne, Norwich/Newcastle etc.	51	51
James Lowden, Ayr	51?	48
George Sinclair, Accrington	51	25
James Kellie-MacCallum, Northamptonshire	50	50
George Butler, Barnsley	50	41
Robert Davies, Hove/Portsmouth	50	35
William Phillipps, Carmarthenshire	50	33
Robert Birnie, Montrose/Angus	50	30
John Jackson, Sheffield/Oldham	49	49
Thomas Bell, Bootle	49	23
George Staunton, East Suffolk	49	9
Edward Parker, Birkenhead	48	10
Henry Hastings, Surrey	48	48
John Jones, Dumfriesshire	48	48
William Chadwick, Stalybridge	48	37
Frederick Mardlin, Northampton	48	36
William Nott-Bower, Leeds/Liverpool, etc.	47	47
Charles Fox, Oxford	47	32

★ James Olive was never a chief constable of a provincial force, having spent all his service in the Metropolitan Police.

The first name on the list, Richard Jones, served in every rank in just the one force. He joined Merionethshire in 1890 as a constable and, after promotion through every rank, took over from his father, Thomas Jones, as chief constable in 1911, himself then serving in that rank until 1950.

A similar story is told by the fifth name on the list, Picton Phillipps. He joined Carmarthenshire as a constable in 1883 (where his father, William Phillipps, also on the list, was chief constable), was promoted through the ranks and was chief constable between 1908 and 1940. Since his father is also on the list with a total of fifty years' service, all of them also with Carmarthenshire, father and son between them clocked up 107 years' total police service, sixty-five of them being as chief constable.

A total service of fifty years plus in this modern day and age now seems totally senseless and unacceptable. Indeed, lengthy stints of services were stopped by the Police Pension Regulations 1921, which laid down compulsory retirement ages.

Not on the list, having served an aggregate of a mere twenty-three years as chief constable, is Sir Percy Sillitoe. But those twenty-three years were with five different forces: Chesterfield, East Riding of Yorkshire, Sheffield, Glasgow and Kent, which is the record for the most chief constableships to any one man. After that, Sir Percy spent another seven years as Director of MI5.

The award for the most meteoric rise through the ranks must surely go to Rowland Parker. Joining the Salford City Police as a constable in 1923, he was appointed to be the chief constable of Stalybridge Borough in February 1924, less than one year later. On the opposite side of the coin, the Canterbury City Watch Committee demoted its chief constable to sergeant (see Chapter 5 for the story of Benjamin Carlton).

Finally, there must be something remarkable in the way Oldham treats its policemen. In its 120-year history, no less than thirteen chief constables started out as constables in the Oldham Borough Police: John Wyse (Boston), Edwin Winch (Truro and Norwich), Henry Kenyon (Penzance), James Clegg and Alfred Appleyard (Margate), Albert Winterbottom (Hartlepool), James Watson (Peterborough and Preston), George Rowbotham (Stockport), Herbert Hilton (Carmarthen), George Hardy (Wigan), John Casburn (Grantham), Edward Saggerson (Middlesbrough) and Arthur Mayall of Oldham Borough itself.

Similarly, Grimsby Borough Police produced eight men who were constables in that force and who later became chief constables: Charles Griffin (Brighton), Albert Scott (Luton), James McConnach (Newark), William Forster (Newcastle-under-Lyme), John Campbell (Dudley), John Huxtable (Clitheroe), Frederick Pearce (Bridgwater) and Charles Tarttelin of Grimsby itself.[27]

In the golden glow of 1919 and 1920, proper democratic machinery was established for the first time for all ranks of the police. Never again would strike action take place, and never again would it ever be contemplated. However, in those heady days of 1919, there began an unprecedented series of episodes which are not universally known about. The British government, following a request from the Greek government, sent out the first of two police missions to Greece in order to organise the Greek Police. In charge of the first mission was Sir Frederick Halliday, who had spent thirty years in the Indian Police and the previous three in charge of an internment camp in Islington. His second-in-command was Chief Inspector Harold Hawkyard of the Metropolitan Police, who returned in 1925 to be promoted to superintendent.

Halliday retired as Chief of the Mission in 1929, to be replaced by Jacynth Coke, chief constable of the West Riding of Yorkshire. Having achieved its object, the mission returned in 1931, and Coke became chief constable of West Suffolk.

A second police mission (which this time included the prison service as well) was sent in 1945, under the care of Sir Charles Wickham, who had just retired after twenty-three years as chief constable of the Royal Ulster Constabulary. This mission, comprising forty-five police and prison officers, lasted until 1952, when it returned.[28] These two missions are understandable in the light of the chaos into which Greece was thrown during the two world wars; to establish a functioning police force was paramount on both occasions.

For one government to request another government to organise its domestic, civil police meant that the British police model must have been looked upon with a certain amount of favour. Further exportation of the British police idea was to be accomplished by the British Colonial Police and the five United Kingdom Police Units, but they were to British-owned/controlled territories. For an independent foreign government to ask for assistance was, and is, unprecedented.

The early 1920s in Great Britain were notable for the amount of unrest that took place, both social and industrial. Adverse reactions after the Great War were understandable as the government fought economic pressures, whilst the general public wanted the 'land fit for heroes' far quicker than it was being delivered.

The government, now believing the police to be on their side after Desborough, looked to the service to maintain order, which they did. The Emergency Powers Act 1920 gave chief constables the right to call upon other forces for up to 10 per cent of overall strength in a mutual aid scheme. This worked well enough and the police contained any embryonic revolutions stirred up by industrial and political activists. Not even the 'Geddes Axe' of a 5 per cent cut in manpower in 1922, following the diktat of the Committee for National Expenditure under Sir Eric Geddes, made much difference. Accusations of 'police brutality' and heavy handedness (which are always made in stressful situations involving the police) were dismissed.[29]

The General Strike of 1926 was no different. Starting on Tuesday 4 May 1926, the strike itself only lasted until Wednesday 12 May. However, the miners carried on until November. During this period, the mutual aid scheme was used extensively and, because of that, the police contained all unrest at the collieries without any recourse to the military.

The police, not being affiliated to the TUC, were not obliged to follow the TUC diktat to strike, and this attracted public appreciation – something the police do not get much of, but is very welcome when it comes. The government must have secretly blessed Lloyd-George's far-sightedness of 1919 in forming the Police Federation and not the Police Union. The fact that the police could not strike and had thus protected the nation from anarchy caused an outpouring of thankfulness from a grateful public. The National Police Fund was launched by *The Times*, and in a few weeks had amassed over £200,000. The fund was used for welfare purposes for the police and their dependants.[30]

55 A good example of the mutual aid system working during the General Strike of 1926.
Three forces are represented here: Leeds City Police are in the centre (with belts) flanked by
Northampton Borough Police (to the left, with silver buttons) and Northamptonshire County.

As with life in general, this esteem was not to last. Public opinion was as fickle
then as it is now, and the next tantrum came just two years later. In Hyde Park
in April 1928, a plain-clothes patrol of PC Alexander McLean and PC George
Badger saw a couple sitting on a park bench. The man was 58-year-old Sir Leo
Chiozza Money, a former MP and well-connected financial journalist, friend of
Lloyd-George and definitely of the 'establishment'. The young lady was Irene
Savidge, a 22-year-old factory worker. Human nature being what human nature
is, the police officers noticed where the couples' hands were and promptly
arrested both of them for gross indecency in a public place. Money apparently
tried to pull social rank and demanded that he be let go, but to no benefit – he
was still arrested.

Cynics say that in a court of law, the person with the most money wins.
Chiozza Money hired a whole stable of lawyers, and at the Magistrates' Court
he was acquitted. Irene Savidge was thus also acquitted, although the magistrates had declined to listen to her testimony. The case was dismissed with costs
against the Metropolitan Police, with the magistrates severely criticising the
arresting officers.

Scotland Yard, incensed by this obvious case of pulling social rank, agitated to
get the case reheard. Fearful of unfavourable publicity, Chiozza Money turned to
his friends in Parliament to get the two officers arrested for perjury. The Home
Secretary ordered Scotland Yard to conduct an inquiry, and this is where the
alleged police chicanery begins.

Irene Savidge was fetched out of work and interviewed at Scotland Yard by Detective Inspector Collins and Detective Sergeant Clarke, who were both male officers. Detective Inspector Lilian Wyles was ordered out of the interview room and Irene Savidge was grilled by the two men with no other woman or legal representation present. Apparently, the questions were a bit risqué, with Collins at one point asking the colour of Irene Savidge's underwear.

Not surprisingly, Irene Savidge complained, and this was whipped up by Chiozza Money as a smokescreen to cover his dalliance with an unmarried girl thirty-six years his junior on a public park bench. All this bedlam eventually resulted in a Royal Commission to report on police powers and procedures. The commission was chaired by Lord Lea of Fareham and published its report in March 1929.[31] Nothing of lasting consequence came of it, apart from a few remarks that female interviewees needed to have other females present.

The commission was soon forgotten, as no fundamental breaches of police procedure had occurred – all that had happened was a couple of high-handed policemen using misjudged, crass and inept interview techniques which they thought they could get away with. In any case, the whole furore had only been caused by the pomposity of one man trying to prove his social superiority by browbeating the police. Had he kept his mouth shut, pleaded guilty and paid his fine, the whole affair would have blown over within days, hardly noticed.

Life has a sense of humour, though. Four years later, Leo Chiozza Money was fined £3 with 5 guineas costs when he pleaded guilty to the sexual pestering of a spinster lady on a train between Dorking and Esher.[32]

Although not achieving fruition until 1948, the idea of a national police college to train higher-ranking police officers dates its origin to 1930. The idea seems to be the concept of the Home Secretary, John Clynes, who the *Dictionary of National Biography* calls 'of sound judgement and unobtrusively influential'. Although he was prevented by illness from attending, his idea was first mooted at the Police Council meeting in March 1930.[33]

The Police Council established a subcommittee 'to consider and report upon the scheme for the establishment of a Police College', under the chairmanship of the Assistant Under-Secretary of State at the Home Office, Mr (later Sir) Arthur Dixon. The committee included a smattering of chief constables and an Inspector of Constabulary, Sir Llewellyn Atcherley.

The Dixon Committee reported in August 1930,[34] but a couple of months previously Dixon had explained his plan to the Chief Constables' Conference in Cardiff and had received a lukewarm response. The chief constables thought they had too much on their plates at that time, what with manpower shortages causing an increasing workload, increasing crime, increasing traffic problems and so on. The Dixon Scheme was shelved. And there it would have stayed – until 'Boom' came along.

'Boom' was Lord Trenchard, so nicknamed because of his habit of bellowing orders at people. He had been appointed as Commissioner of the Metropolitan Police in 1931, reluctantly if we believe the rumours, and had only agreed to take the position for three years, although had stopped on for an extra year by personal request of King George V.[35] Having no police experience whatsoever (his whole life thus far had been in the Royal Air Force), he was placed in charge of the largest force of police officers in the land. Again, if we believe the rumours, this was deliberate in order to instil discipline in a force where mutinous talk was circulating. The government, faced with the worst economic slump for many a year, had instigated a 10 per cent cut in wages for the whole of the public sector. The branch boards of the Police Federation voiced growing dissatisfaction, and Boom was given the job of sorting it all out.

Opinions are divided on the efficacy of his reforms, but amongst these were his two 'babies': the Hendon Police College and short-term contracts. The short-term contract was a proposition that police officers could sign on for a ten-year service in the Metropolitan Police and then retire with a gratuity. This showed Trenchard's complete lack of understanding of the job of a police constable. After ten years' service, a policeman is just reaching his peak of usefulness and experience. The short-term contract meant he would then depart, probably to another force, which would snap him up and benefit from a fully trained, experienced officer gained at no cost to themselves.

The second of Lord Trenchard's schemes was the Hendon Police College. Trenchard had been appalled to realise that of his 800 senior officers, he would only consider eleven of them to be 'educated'.[36] The rank-and-file policemen were still from the working classes and few had advanced beyond the rank of superintendent, which is probably what caused the contempt Trenchard felt for the rank-and-file policeman that he was never to lose. Trenchard wanted 'officer material' and realised that such men would not be attracted to the possibility of pounding the beat for ten years or so before they could even take the first step of promotion to sergeant.

Taking notice of the Dixon Scheme, Trenchard thought that the Metropolitan Police was big enough to set up a college of its own. Entrance to the college would be through one of two routes. Either a serving constable could be admitted after a competitive examination, or, the one which would cause the most aggravation, well-educated young men from the public schools, colleges and universities could enter directly, lured into the scheme by the promise of immediate appointment to the newly created rank of junior station inspector, thus skipping walking the beat as a PC.

It was this last category that irritated and inflamed the PCs of the Metropolitan Police. By reason of their more privileged background giving them a better education, within two years (the length of the course) a young boy with absolutely no experience of policing (or possibly of life in general) could be giving operational orders to a PC of twenty-five years' experience. Disdain for the scheme was enhanced when it was learnt that students were expected to include in their kit dinner jackets, dress shirts and patent leather evening shoes. However, the scheme went ahead and the first course was started at Hendon in north London on 31 May 1934, consisting of twenty serving officers and twelve direct entrants.[37]

No research has been done on the Trenchard Police College Scheme to find out how successful, or otherwise, it was. But what is known is that at least eleven later chief constables were graduates of the Scheme, and there undoubtedly were more: James Archer-Burton (Hastings, North Riding of Yorkshire); Ranulph Bacon (Dumbartonshire, deputy commissioner, Metropolitan Police); Nicholas Bebbington (Cambridge Borough, HM Inspector of Constabulary); John Blenkin (East Riding of Yorkshire); Robert Bolton (Northamptonshire); Peter Brodie (Stirling and Clackmannan, Warwickshire, HM Inspector of Constabulary, assistant commissioner, Metropolitan Police); Edward Dodd (Birmingham City, HM Chief Inspector of Constabulary); John Gott (Northamptonshire); John Nightingale (Essex); Joseph Simpson (Northumberland, Surrey, commissioner, Metropolitan Police); John Skittery (Plymouth City).

The Police College Scheme was not liked, however, either by the Metropolitan PCs or the provincial chief constables who were observing it. When Sir Philip Game took over from Lord Trenchard in 1936, the assistant commissioner was Sir George Abbiss, who was only the second senior officer of the Metropolitan Police to have risen from the ranks after joining as a PC in 1905 (the first was Sir James Olive, deputy commissioner 1922–25, who joined as a PC in 1872). Abbiss knew the rank-and-file feelings of resentment over the Scheme and persuaded Game to phase it out gradually. Game, more in tune with his force than Trenchard, obliged, and by the start of the Second World War, the Trenchard Scheme was completely extinct. Nevertheless, the idea of a national police college was still simmering in the background, but it would be another nine years before it finally arrived in its full glory, and in a more universally acceptable format by not including the ingredient of direct officer entry.

By 1921, the Inspectorate of Constabulary had had two years of close observation of the police in its new vitality, and two years of observing a society which was changing rapidly after war deprivations. In the annual report of 1920/21, Sir Leonard Dunning put his finger on two matters which were concerning him greatly, and which he believed would, if not addressed, have a detrimental effect on the efficiency of the police.

Dunning listed as his main concern the rise in crime levels, which he attributed to the lack of sufficient manpower, exacerbated by increasing traffic responsibilities and the number of extraneous duties having to be performed by the police. His second concern was the vexing question of the smaller borough forces.

In the 1920/21 report, Dunning quotes from the crime statistics. Some 33,866 crimes were known to the police in 1881, whilst in 1921 this number had risen to 85,173 crimes – an average increase of 1,280 per year. Taking into consideration the increase in population, this is still an enormous number, and Dunning thought, 'it is worth while to consider how far this is due to [the police] having to perform other duties'.[38] Every annual report of the Inspectorate between the wars mentions crime, with every inspector looking upon the yearly increase with resignation. They were powerless to do anything and knew it.

The 'Geddes Axe', with its desire for a 5 per cent cut in manpower, was actually achieved not by making officers redundant, but by not filling the natural vacancies that occurred. However, it was always the inspectors' aim to get the actual manpower of the police matching the agreed establishment. Figures of the number of vacancies, published in the Inspectorate's reports every year, show that after the initial responses to Geddes had worn off, parity was never achieved. In the seventeen years between 1923 and 1939, the yearly average number of vacancies in the police forces of England and Wales was 1,152, representing an average of 3.1 per cent understrength.[39]

In the Inspectorate's annual reports, constant mention was made of traffic regulation between the wars, from the 1920/21 report where Dunning said 'traffic control is an expensive duty',[40] to the 1937/38 report where Frank Brook said that traffic patrols 'have added considerably to the responsibility and work of the chief constables and other officers involved in this particular duty'.[41]

The rise of the motorcar was inexorable. Athelstan Popkess, writing in 1946,[42] gives the number of motor vehicles in 1904 as 17,810 and in 1946 as 2,386,500, a rise of 13,300 per cent over forty-two years, or an average increase of 56,400 motor vehicles per year. And this traffic needed regulating, with the police being the obvious, or indeed the only, body available. Dunning could see that the increase of policemen to look after traffic regulation would take policemen away from street patrol and thus the prevention of crime, which, after all, he writes, 'is the first duty of a police force'.[43]

'Traffic regulation,' said Dunning, 'hits the smaller force hardest: the little town which happens to be on a main road, especially if its streets, as they often are, unsuitable for constant and fast traffic, has to assign its men to traffic duty in greater proportion to its total strength, than is the case with the larger [forces].'[44] He gives the example of County Durham, quoting the county's public engineer, where self-propelled traffic had increased by 45 per cent to 92 per cent of all traffic between the years 1912 and 1920. Heavy motors had increased 22 per cent to 52 per cent of all traffic. The total weight of traffic had increased by 290 per cent over the same period. Mention was also made of some ways to deal with it, from traffic light systems to specialised motor patrol officers. The Road Traffic Act of 1930 was greeted with enthusiasm, introducing as it did the Highway Code a few years later, and giving chief constables the impetus to form dedicated traffic divisions.[45]

The traffic divisions were a new departure. Instead of all the PCs plodding the beat, some PCs were now given big flashy patrol cars to ride around in all day. The downside, of course, was that they had to police the roads, enforcing speed limits, ensuring motor vehicles were maintained in a safe condition according to the Motor Vehicle Construction and Use Regulations and dealing with road accidents where sometimes horrendous injuries and fatalities occurred. It is perhaps fair to say that traffic and the regulation of it was rapidly becoming the single most important job that the police had to do between the wars. Arguably, it remains so today, where perhaps the only contact some members of the public have with the police is through being stopped whilst driving a motor vehicle, mainly for exceeding the speed limit, which some drivers seem to regard as voluntary.

As such, logically and morally, if the police are to tell the public how to drive, then they must be better drivers themselves. The Metropolitan Police Driving School was established at Hendon in north London in 1934, and its civilian advisor was a well-known racing driver at the time, Mark Pepys, who was also the 6th Earl of Cottenham. Pepys worked out methods and techniques of driving, which resulted in the publication of his system in 1937 in a book called *Roadcraft*. The system of car control, as laid down in *Roadcraft*, is generally acknowledged to be the best there is, and is still being taught to this day. *Roadcraft* continues to be published, but has been added to by other experts over the years and is now a government publication of the HMSO. The Earl of Cottenham never lived to see the success of his system. He died in 1943 aged 40.[46]

In the annual report for 1921/22, Dunning touched on an issue which had its roots in the old six major policy aims of the Inspectors of Constabulary – the question of extraneous duties. These policy aims, it is to be remembered, formulated by William Cartwright nearly seventy years previously, encouraged the use of police officers in carrying these additional duties out because there was no other official body to do them. However, the realisation 'that the performance of local government administrative functions … [detracted] from their proper duties' had been voiced since long before the Great War. It was now time to rid the police service of them.

Dunning found it 'impossible to give a complete list of the miscellaneous duties which have been assigned to the provincial police', but some of these, he said, 'have been created by Parliament – those under the Diseases of Animals Acts … and the Finance Acts'. Each extraneous duty performed by a policeman 'must decrease his value for the prevention of crime'.[47]

Dunning quotes an extract from the annual report of 'a large city force' (which, no doubt, would be Liverpool City, of which he had been the chief constable from 1902 to 1912),[48] which detailed the extraneous duties performed 'by the man on the beat' and 'who is placed there to exercise that vigilance which will

56 A section of the Liverpool City Police between the wars, showing the large cockscomb helmets and armlets. Tough-looking men with a tough job to do, they had to force compliance of the law upon a city population, many of whom regarded obedience to it as optional.

go some way towards the prevention of crime'. He calculates that in performing these extraneous duties, 'the time lost to police duty proper was equal to the year's work of some 15 men'.[49]

Although the question of additional local government duties taking officers off the streets continued to concern the inspectors, this item was not given as much priority as that of taking officers off the streets to attend to traffic regulation. It remained burning in the background, but something serious would not be done about it until the Burrell Report, in 1953, abolished thirty-three extraneous duties that were no longer to be done by police officers.[50]

Dunning was adamant, however. All these factors added up. Extraneous duties and the extra calls upon time for traffic regulation all contributed to the increase in crime.

Dunning was also most vociferous on the question of the small borough forces, and the eradication of these was to be one of the main concerns of the Inspectorate up until the Second World War. Desborough had recommended that all non-county boroughs should have their police forces amalgamated with

57 Introduced in the 1930s, police pillars were situated in the suburbs of large cities to provide a means of quick communication to the policemen on the beat.

58 When the door was opened, it revealed a grill which covered a combined microphone and loudspeaker, which put the user in direct contact with the central police station.

the surrounding county, and that no future force be formed in boroughs under 100,000 population. Dunning agreed. 'There can be no doubt,' he wrote in the 1920/21 report, 'that wherever there is a border line, there is loss of efficiency, and it is no reflection on two forces, or on one or other of them, to say that if joined together, they would give more efficient service.'[51] The Inspectorate was thus looking to the government to introduce legislation to bring this about. However, things were not that straightforward.

The cities and boroughs that were affected had not taken Desborough's recommendations lying down. Protest meetings had been held by those local authorities whose forces were affected, which resulted in a deputation to the Home Secretary led by none other than Neville Chamberlain, at that time the MP for a Birmingham constituency and later to be the Prime Minister during the Munich Crisis of September 1938. This deputation probably had some effect as the Desborough Committee recommendations were not carried through – the government by that time had other things on its mind. Thus the question of the smaller borough forces lay unacted upon, and it was to be another ten years before it was looked at seriously again. In the meantime, however, the inspectors constantly drew attention to the idiocy of the small forces and demonstrated their determination to eradicate them by amalgamation with the surrounding counties.[52]

In the 1927/28 report,[53] for instance, Dunning gives the example of Tiverton Borough (total strength eleven: one chief constable, two sergeants and eight constables; population 9,172). 'The County of Devon and the Borough of Tiverton,' he said, 'discussed the merger of the latter with the County Police District, but failed to come to terms. This was unfortunate; little island police districts like Tiverton are anachronisms in these days of modern facilities of travel, fenced in as they are by boundaries of which nobody but the police take notice.'

Similar examples include: Reigate Borough in 1930/31[54] (total strength forty: one chief constable, two inspectors, seven sergeants, thirty constables; population 28,914); Congleton Borough in 1932/33[55] (total strength thirteen: one chief constable, two sergeants, ten constables; population 11,762); and Newark Borough (total strength twenty: one chief constable, three sergeants, sixteen constables; population 16,958).

Nevertheless, this question was not entirely ignored by the Home Office. In 1932 Sir Herbert Samuel, the Home Secretary, had established the Select Committee on Police Forces (Amalgamation).[56] This reported in 1934 to a new Home Secretary, Sir John Gilmour. Herbert Samuel had urged that all forces in non-county boroughs with a population under 75,000 be amalgamated with their surrounding counties, but the Select Committee eventually recommended the figure of 30,000. Thus, not really being what had been intimated, the Home Secretary, in the event, did nothing.

The question of the small borough forces, therefore, lingered on unresolved, and in 1939 the British police force entered the Second World War with 181 separate, autonomous police forces at 3.1 per cent understrength. But if the mainland British police forces were struggling at the start of the Second World War, forces based on the exported British police model were not. No apologies are made for including what follows below.

The British Colonial Police

The British have taken many useful things with them when they have gone out to colonise or administer other parts of the world, but history may well record that they took nothing which was to have a more profound and lasting influence than their particular conception of the police and its functions.

This was the opinion of Sir Charles Jeffries in his book, *The Colonial Police*.[57] Those heady days of empire have long since gone and the British Colonial Police is now largely a thing of the past. With the return of Hong Kong to the Chinese in 1999, only very few 'ex-pat' British policemen are now left serving out their time to pension in ex-colonies such as Bermuda and the Cayman Islands.

At its height, there were thirty-seven British Colonial Police forces around the globe, but these were only placed in British colonies, protectorates and trust territories (territories administered by Britain on behalf of the United Nations), whose affairs were handled by the old British Colonial Office. Canada, Australia, New Zealand, South Africa, Pakistan, India and Ceylon were sovereign states within the British Empire/Commonwealth and therefore administered themselves and their own policing. As such they had no need of the Colonial Police.

The colonies, whilst not independent sovereign states, nevertheless had their own government, laws, finances, civil service, judiciary and courts. But all came under the umbrella of the British government via the Colonial Office, whose aim was to steer these countries to responsible self-government, but within the British Commonwealth. When colonisation had taken place, the British had naturally taken their own judicial system with them. This was all very well, but the indigenous populations quite often did not understand these laws and looked upon them as alien, as indeed they were.

The colonial government, therefore, needed an organised police force to keep order and maintain the law. Obviously, not every colony was the same and the police force thus established in each colony was altered to suit the expedients of the different regions where necessary.

These colonial forces were different from British police forces in the fact that some of them were armed and were controlled by central government, not local government as in Britain. Therefore, colonial forces were related to but not identical to United Kingdom forces. Also, these early forces began by being organised along the lines of the Metropolitan Police, but this system did not prove adaptable to the colonies and a far greater influence on colonial policing was to be that of the (Royal) Irish Constabulary (RIC).

Organised along semi-military lines, the RIC policemen were armed, lived in military-style barracks and trained along military lines. The force was an agent of central government, especially in rural areas, where communications were poor or rudimentary and there was a greater risk of insurgency. Most importantly, the RIC operated a direct officer entry system where young men could be commissioned straight into the higher ranks. It was thus felt that the RIC was a far better model for colonial policing than the mainland British forces, which had quite different emphases of policing.

The policing of each colony generally (though not necessarily) fell into three chronological phases:

1 improvised arrangements for securing the basic essentials of law and order
2 the establishment of semi-military forces modelled on the RIC with a view to suppressing violent crime and outbreaks of public disorder

3 the trend to convert these semi-military forces into civilian police forces akin to
    British mainland forces, but still retaining some vestige of militarism

In the first two phases many, if not all, higher ranks were filled by European officers. The NCOs and rank and file were filled by locally recruited personnel, who
were not admitted as officers until the third phase.

Following on from the reorganisation of the Colonial Office in the 1930s after
the Fisher Report, it was recommended that a series of functional services be
established. Consequently, in 1936, all the existing police forces that had hitherto
been established in every colony then became part of a revamped and now unified service – the Colonial Police Service.

Undoubtedly, the 'father' of the Colonial Police was Sir Herbert Dowbiggin,
who had joined the Ceylon Police in 1901. He had become its chief officer in
1913 (that post being then known as inspector-general) and had made a series of
reforms and innovations.

In Ceylon, Dowbiggin set up a training school, a criminal investigation department, fingerprint and footprint (many people were barefoot) recognition systems,
a photographic branch, a Police Boys' Brigade (a type of rudimentary police cadet
system), boys' clubs (in an attempt to stave off delinquency) and a Police Savings
Association. Most of all, he gave the Ceylon Police a firmly based structure of
command and duties.

Due to his success in Ceylon, Dowbiggin was called upon to report on the
Cyprus Police in 1926, the Palestine Police in 1930 and the Northern Rhodesia
Police in 1937. So when the Colonial Office, and thus the Colonial Police, were
revamped in 1936, many of Dowbiggin's ideas were adopted.[58]

An 'officer class' of gazetted ranks (so named because each appointment was
published in the *London Gazette*, as was the custom in the armed forces) was
adopted. Thus a senior officer was commissioned into the service and not to any
individual colony. In effect, therefore, every senior officer (assistant superintendent and above) of any colony's police would now come from these gazetted ranks
and could serve in and be transferred between any Colonial Police force.

Standardised rates of pay, pensions and leave (including home leave) were introduced, with a fairly standard uniform of khaki shirt and shorts, black-peaked caps,
black socks and either black or khaki epaulettes. The term for the chief officer
would now become 'commissioner', although it remained inspector-general in
large countries (Nigeria, for instance, because it was so vast, had three area commissioners under one inspector-general).

Although each colony remained loyal to local expediencies, the new Colonial
Police Service introduced a universal *esprit de corps*, with officers feeling like they
were part of a whole disciplined service and not disparate groups. At the same
time, a separate Colonial Prison Service was introduced, which took away prison
administration from the police, for which they had been responsible before.

59 The British Colonial Police Training School at Kaduna, Nigeria, 1965. This clearly shows
that by this late stage of the British Colonial Police, only a handful of British nationals were
filling the senior officer positions, before being handed over to locally recruited personnel.

At this time, it was thought that an inspectorate, similar to the British Inspectors
of Constabulary, should be established. This idea would have been adopted at
that time, the late 1930s, but the Second World War intervened and it was not
until 1948 that the idea came to fruition. Mr William Johnson, then one of the
Inspectors of Constabulary, became the Police Advisor to the Colonial Office,
with Sir George Abbiss as his deputy.

During 1949 and 1950, Mr Johnson toured every colonial police force, advising
on police matters. In 1950 the title of the position was changed to Inspector-
General of Colonial Police. Mr Johnson returned to the Home Office in 1951,
and his position as Inspector-General was filled by Mr Walter Muller, who had
served under Dowbiggin in Ceylon and who remained until 1957, when the
appointment was no longer needed and abolished.

With colonies gradually gaining more freedom from the 1950s onwards, the
British Empire slowly came to be the British Commonwealth. After independence, each country established its own locally recruited and managed police force.
The British gazetted officers were therefore dismissed, but with financial compensation for loss of career; in some instances the British government took over
their pension commitment as well.

Thus, gradually, the British Colonial Police faded away. The last police force to
regularly take British police officers was the Royal Hong Kong Police, until its
return to China in 1999. Now that the Colonial Police has all but gone, a glance
through such books as *Police of the World* by Roy Ingleton or *The World's Police*

by James Cramer, and the excellent *At the End of the Line* by Georgina Sinclair, would show how many world police forces are still based upon the British model. Could that indicate, perhaps, that Sir Charles Jefferies was indeed right?

The British Colonial Police forces

The Caribbean and Atlantic

Bahamas

Barbados

Bermuda

British Guiana

British Honduras

Falkland Islands

Jamaica (with the Cayman Islands and the Turks and Caicos Islands)

Leeward Islands

Saint Helena (with Ascension Island and Tristan da Cunha

Trinidad and Tobago

Windward Islands (with Dominica, Saint Lucia, Saint Vincent, Grenada)

The Mediterranean

Cyprus

Gibraltar

Malta, GC

Near and Far East

Aden

Federation of Malaya

Hong Kong

North Borneo

Palestine

Sarawak (with Brunei)

Singapore

Africa

Gambia

Gold Coast

Kenya

Nigeria

Northern Rhodesia

Nyasaland

Sierra Leone

Somaliland

South African High Commission Territories (Basutoland, Bechuanaland

Protectorate, Swaziland)
Tanganyika
Uganda
Zanzibar

Indian and Pacific Oceans
Fiji (with Pitcairn and Tonga)
Mauritius
Seychelles
West Pacific High Commission Territories (British Solomon Islands, Gilbert and
Ellice Islands, New Hebrides)

ELEVEN

1939–45

Recruiting to the regular constabulary was suspended at the start of the Second World War as men were needed for more pressing problems elsewhere. But the police were already 3 per cent understrength, so the prospect of an immense increase in the workload did not sit comfortably.

This increase in the amount of work was caused by the umbrella legislation, the Emergency Powers (Defence) Act 1939 (2 and 3 George VI, Chapter 62), which came into force on 24 August 1939, ten days before the official start of the war. This was a skeleton Act, giving power to make regulations which 'appear to be necessary or expedient for securing the public safety, the defence of the realm, the maintenance of public order, the efficient prosecution of any war in which His Majesty may be engaged, and for maintaining supplies and services essential to the life of the community'.[1]

Under this Act, Regulations were made on 25 August, Amending Regulations on 1 September and further Amending Regulations on 23 November.[2] Therefore, between the start of August 1939 and the end of the year, over 2,000 Acts of Parliament, Regulations and Orders were passed, which dealt with all aspects of the emergency.

These Regulations put a vast amount of extra work upon the police forces of the country, from 'control of lights and sounds', in other words the blackout (Regulation 1682), to 'control of photography' (Regulation 1125) and everything else in between. All these Regulations and Acts required enforcement by the police, over and above the duties considered as 'normal'. Yet the police were still 3 per cent understrength.

This was ameliorated somewhat when the call-up of those policemen who were Army Reservists was postponed for three months in order to deal with all the extra work, as well as coping with any ensuing mayhem from the air raids which were expected right from the start of hostilities. In the event, of course, the air raids never materialised (during the so-called Phoney War), and by December 1939 the Reservists were being released.

60 Cyril Mason in the uniform of the Police Auxiliary Messenger Service, 1940.

This, of course, exacerbated the manpower shortage. The answer came in five separate ways, and the police during the Second World War were kept up to strength by four sources of 'manpower', plus another organisation of young men who did a valuable service.

The first was the Police Reserve, consisting of recently retired regular police officers who, for a small retaining fee, had contracted to return to the service in the event of war. The Special Constabulary in peacetime is a voluntary unpaid reinforcement to the regular constabulary, somewhat akin to the relationship between the regular and territorial army. These two bodies were already in existence, so they more or less instantly provided a pool of already trained and uniformed police officers.

The remaining three sources had to be instituted in 1939 when it became clear that war was inevitable. The Police War Reserve consisted of men over 30 years of age, who agreed to serve for the duration only and, although initially untrained (they were empirically trained 'on-the-job' by the remaining regular police officers), eventually came to carry out the full duties of the regular police.

In 1939 there were only 226 attested policewomen in the whole of England and Wales (including London),[3] so the Women's Auxiliary Police Corps (WAPC) was established in 1939 to provide more women to serve in the police. However, at the start, the WAPC only did the clerical and chauffeuring duties, but their case was backed by the Archbishop of Canterbury himself (Cosmo Lang), who pressed their cause to the Home Secretary.

This was successful because by 1942 the WAPC were 2,800 strong, and by 1945, 3,700 strong. The WAPC and regular policewomen came into their own when looking after the moral welfare of local girls in the vicinity of the army camps full of troops in the build-up to D-Day. Although the WAPC was disbanded at the end of the war, many of these ladies joined the police as attested regular policewomen.[4]

With all these extra personnel, and even when the 3,000 Army Reservists had gone, after December 1939 the police force of this country was bigger than it had ever been before – or since! In 1940 it was at 88,000, rising to its peak of 92,000 in 1942 – the pre-war strength had never gone above 60,000.[5]

There remained just one more source of manpower, recruited almost exclusively from the boroughs: the Police Auxiliary Messenger Service (PAMS). The anticipated air raids at the start of the war had been expected to obliterate telephone lines and other means of communications. The PAMS were young lads just out of school recruited to act as messenger boys when no other means of communication existed.

These young lads did great service on their bicycles when the bombs did start falling, and the PAMS remained until the end of the war. Since some of these young men then went on to join the regular constabulary and others were retained as boy clerks, they became a cheap source of manpower for the chief constables. And in the PAMS can quite clearly be seen the genesis of the later Police Cadet schemes.

By the Emergency Powers Act and the ensuing Defence Regulations (especially Regulation 39), the Home Secretary was given the powers to direct local chief constables. This, in effect, created a national police force, although the two wartime Home Secretaries, first Sir John Anderson and then Herbert Morrison, actually stopped short of such a drastic step. But the vestiges were there, and in some ways were actually taken up.

Being faced with the very real possibility of foreign troops treading the soil of Britain, the government had to make plans just in case communication with central government broke down – or indeed if there was no central government to communicate with. Taking notice of experience gained during the General Strike of 1926, the country was divided into twelve regions. Each region was placed into the hands of a Regional Civil Commissioner who had complete autonomy in his region if there was no central government, and thus each region was, in effect, a country within a country. The civil defence of each region was placed fairly and squarely into the hands of the regional commissioner, who had been chosen either from retired armed forces officers, such as General Sir Hugh Elles for the south-western region, or from the aristocracy, such as William Ormsby-Gore, 4th Lord Harlech, soldier, diplomat and politician, for the north-eastern region, and William Ward, 3rd Earl of Dudley, soldier and businessman, for the midland region.[6]

The regional commissioner needed to have control of the police forces within his region, so to each regional headquarters he assigned a police unit to liaise with the chief constables of those forces. Under the Defence Regulations, the Home Secretary was empowered to appoint further Inspectors of Constabulary, thus to each regional police unit was assigned an Assistant Inspector of Constabulary, complete with a staff officer. These police units acted as liaison officers between the regional commissioners, the chief constables of the region, the actual Inspectors of Constabulary and the Home Office itself.

No annual reports of the Inspectorate of Constabulary were made for the duration of the Second World War. However, a report was made up to 29 September 1945, and gave all the detail of the occurrences of the war years concerning the police and the regional commissioners.[7]

The Inspectors of Constabulary during the war years were Gordon Halland, Jacynth Coke, Sir Frank Brook and Sir Llewellyn Atcherley, who had retired in 1935 but was recalled for the duration of the war. In 1943 Halland was seconded to the Colonial Office and was replaced by Michael Egan, chief constable of Southport.

The 1945 report also lists the Acting Inspectors of Constabulary who were attached to the regional commissioners as: Captain G.E. Banwell, Colonel J. de Vere Bowles, Sir Charles Chitham, Sir Charles Banks Cunningham, Major G.W.R. Hearn, Mr F.C. Isemonger, Mr H.B.W.B. Lenthall, Captain R.N.G. Martin, Mr F.R. Parry, Colonel F.G. Peake, Captain T. Rawson, Mr J. Simpson, Sir Charles Stead and Mr M.I. Valentine.

An analysis of these names is interesting.[8] It can be seen that the Acting Inspectors during the Second World War had immense police experience, both home and colonial, and fully deserved their positions of responsibility during the war years. Godwin Edward Banwell had been in the Indian Police since 1920. He was appointed an Acting Inspector between 1941 and 1942, before becoming chief constable of the East Riding of Yorkshire, and subsequently of Cheshire.

John de Vere Bowles had an army background, including Provost Marshal, Commandant Corps of Military Police between 1931 and 1934.

Sir Charles Chitham had joined the Indian Police in 1906 and had been the inspector-general of police in the Central Provinces since 1931.

Sir Charles Banks Cunningham had also been in the Indian Police, since 1904, and was inspector-general of police of the Madras Presidency between 1930 and 1938.

George William Richard Hearn had been appointed the assistant chief constable of Staffordshire in 1935 after an army career. He was an Acting Inspector of Constabulary between 1940 and 1943 before returning to Staffordshire, where he was chief constable between 1951 and 1960.

Frederick Charles Isemonger had a background in the Indian Police, which he had joined in 1898. He was eventually the inspector-general of police for the North-West Frontier Province between 1925 and 1930. Following that he was chief of police of the British Municipal Council, Tientsin, from 1931–5.

Henry Benson Wyndham Ball Lenthall was a member of the Royal Ulster Constabulary, having previously been in the old Royal Irish Constabulary.

Francis Ralph Parry was a chief superintendent in the Lancashire County Constabulary, which he had joined in 1919.

Frederick Gerard Peake had an army background, but since 1921 had been the inspector-general of Gendarmerie, plus the Director of Public Security in Transjordon.

Thomas Rawson had joined the Carlisle City Police in 1909. Eventually he had become the chief constable of Hereford City from 1920 to 1927; of Swansea Borough from 1927 to 1931; and of Bradford City from 1931 to 1940, when he was appointed an Acting Inspector.

Joseph Simpson had a background in the Metropolitan Police, which he had joined in 1931, before graduating from the Trenchard Scheme. By 1937 he was the assistant chief constable of Lincolnshire, before being appointed an Acting Inspector in 1940. In 1943 he became the chief constable of Northumberland and of Surrey in 1946. In 1958 he became Commissioner of the Metropolitan Police, being knighted a year later. He was to die whilst holding office in 1968.

Charles Stead had joined the Indian Police in 1898, eventually becoming the inspector-general of police in the North-West Frontier Province in 1927, and the inspector-general of police in the Punjab a year later.

No biographical details can be found for either Captain R.N.G. Martin or Mr M.I. Valentine. However, although neither had been, or subsequently became, chief constables of British mainland forces,[9] judging by the backgrounds of the other Acting Inspectors, it must be assumed that these two gentlemen had similar experience, probably in the Indian or Colonial Police.

Tensions were apparent, as these regional police units probably led to a few ruffled feathers. It was made clear right from the outset that the regional commissioner was the boss, and if the crunch came, he would have jurisdiction over the chief constables, and as such had the power to give operational orders to the police. It did not help, either, when the chief constables learned that the regional commissioner also had the power to override the county Standing Joint Committees and borough Watch Committees, and remove or replace any chief constable who had lost the confidence of the regional commissioner himself.

61 Herbert Allen, chief constable of
Rochester City 1931–33; Huddersfield
Borough 1933–40; and Southampton City
1940–41. Herbert Allen died directly as the
result of injuries received in a car accident
during an air raid on Southampton, the only
chief constable to be killed by enemy action
during the Second World War.

62 William Edwards, chief constable of
Cambridgeshire County Constabulary
1941–45. On 15 November 1945 he was in a
police car being driven during the blackout
near Cambridge when he was involved in
a collision with a tank convoy. Reginald
Nicholson, the commandant of the county
Special Constabulary, was killed outright;
Superintendent Arnold, Detective Sergeant
Blows and Sergeant Dean also received
serious injuries, but survived. William
Edwards died ten days later from injuries
received in the crash.

63 Special Constable Brandon Moss,
Coventry City Police Special Constabulary.
For his rescue of trapped people from
bomb-damaged buildings during the
Coventry Blitz of November 1940, SC Moss
was the first British police officer to be
awarded the George Cross.

Thankfully, common sense prevailed, and no clash of authority ever came as all concerned worked towards the common aim. Even when the regional commissioner did exercise his powers in this direction, in the ordering of chief constables to send men to another force under the mutual aid scheme, no chief constable ever demurred. Several large cities under blitz conditions benefited from this, and during the whole of the war a total of 5,500 men from 103 separate forces were transposed under the mutual aid scheme.[10]

The Home Secretary was also given powers by the Emergency Regulations to merge forces compulsorily if he saw fit. During 1943 he did this to several forces, mainly the ones on the south coast and in the south of England, as it was thought that these areas were most likely to bear the brunt of any invasion. If Herbert Morrison had thoughts of continuing these powers to their logical conclusion, and merging all the forces of the country into a national police force, or at the very least into several large regional forces to match the areas of the regional commissioners, then those thoughts are sadly lost to us. The opportunity was clearly there at that time to create a national police force, but, in the event, was not taken. The conclusions we can draw from this are either that the Home Secretary did not want a national police force, or that he was too busy at that time to create one.

All the forcible amalgamations took place during 1943. The separate forces of East Sussex County, West Sussex County, Eastbourne Borough, Hastings and St Leonards Borough, Brighton Borough and Hove Borough were all amalgamated to form the Sussex Joint Police. Tiverton Borough was absorbed into Devonshire County and Penzance Borough likewise into Cornwall County. Salisbury City went into Wiltshire County; Guildford Borough and Reigate Borough went into Surrey County to form the Surrey Joint Police; and the Isle of Wight County and Winchester City were amalgamated into Hampshire County to form the Hampshire Joint Police. But the biggest shake-up of all came in Kent, when the borough forces of Dover, Folkestone, Gravesend, Ramsgate, Maidstone, Tunbridge Wells and Margate, plus the city forces of Canterbury and Rochester, all combined with Kent to form the Kent Constabulary.[11]

Thus, at a stroke, several of the small borough forces, so bemoaned about by the pre-war Inspectors of Constabulary, were eradicated. After the war, the Sussex forces promptly split back up again, and if larger forces or a national force was the aim after the war, a golden opportunity was lost. Again, the inference is that a national police force was never a considered proposition.

Although the Battle of Britain had stopped the invasion of troops, it did not stop the air raids. Many cities in Britain were subjected to the Blitz, which caused loss of life and severe damage to buildings, sometimes trapping people in the debris. As a result, many gallant acts of rescue were performed by the civilian population.

As the existing system of awards for gallantry by civilians was not considered adequate enough, in view of the many hundreds of stories being received of

'ordinary' citizens doing extraordinary things, in 1940 Winston Churchill set up
the Civil Defence Honours Committee with a view to establishing a 'new award
for gallantry'. The outcome was the establishment of the George Cross and the
George Medal on 23 September 1940.[12]

The George Cross would rank immediately after the Victoria Cross, and would
be awarded to civilians from all walks of life, but also to members of the armed
forces under certain circumstances. The George Medal was awarded far more
freely than the George Cross, but still required a high standard of gallantry.

The police forces of the cities subjected to the Blitz were doing great acts
of selfless gallantry daily. The first ten police officers cited as being awarded the
George Medal appeared in the *London Gazette* of 15 November 1940, all for
rescues from bomb-damaged buildings:

William Hack, PC, Metropolitan Police
Edward Jackson, PC, Metropolitan Police
Albert Parsons, War Reserve, Metropolitan Police
Edward Kerrison, PC, Metropolitan Police
Bernard Lees, PC, Metropolitan Police
William Gunn, PC, Metropolitan Police
Charles Nicholson, PC, Metropolitan Police
Ernest Rose, PC, Metropolitan Police
William Spain, PC, Folkestone Borough Police
Harold Young, Sergeant, Metropolitan Police

In total, throughout the whole of the Second World War, 124 awards of the George
Medal were made to officers of the British police forces. In contrast, because of
the more exacting standards required, just one George Cross was awarded to the
British police in the same period.[13]

On the night of 14 November 1940, the City of Coventry was subjected to
the most fearsome air raid. This resulted in the city centre being virtually obliter-
ated, along with its medieval cathedral. Special Constable Brandon Moss of the
Coventry City Police Special Constabulary spent seven hours tunnelling alone
into the debris of a bombed house to rescue three people. Despite falling beams,
leaking gas, unexploded bombs nearby and more falling bombs, he re-entered
the debris and rescued one more person still alive and recovered four bodies of
people killed in the raid.[14]

Special Constable Moss received his George Cross from King George VI at
Buckingham Palace. Such is the level of gallantry required for the award of the
George Cross that only eight more awards have been made to the British police
in the seventy years since the decoration's establishment. Seven have been to indi-
vidual police officers and one to a whole police force for collective gallantry.
No apologies whatsoever are given for listing these:

PC Kenneth Farrow, Cardiff City Police, 21 June 1948, for the rescue of a child from an enclosed water culvert.

DC Frederick Fairfax, Metropolitan Police, 2 November 1952, for the arrest of two burglars – the 'Craig and Bentley Case'.

PC Henry Stevens, Metropolitan Police, 29 March 1958, for the chase and arrest of a burglar, despite being shot and wounded.

PC Anthony Gledhill, Metropolitan Police, 25 August 1966, for the car chase and arrest of offenders despite being constantly shot at.

Superintendent Gerald Richardson (awarded posthumously) and PC Carl Walker, both Lancashire County Constabulary, 23 August 1971, for the chase of armed robbers through the streets of Blackpool, where Superintendent Richardson was fatally shot and PC Walker wounded.

Inspector James Beaton, Metropolitan Police, 20 March 1974, for the foiling of an attempted kidnap of HRH Princess Anne and Captain Mark Phillips, despite being shot and wounded.[15]

In April 2000 the Royal Ulster Constabulary was awarded the George Cross for collective courage in the face of immense political unrest. In the seventy-nine years of its history, 302 of its police officers have lost their lives in the course of their duties. In 2001 the Royal Ulster Constabulary was replaced by the Police Service of Northern Ireland.

Such was the intensity of the air-raid attacks on Britain that the police forces did not escape unscathed. During the Second World War, 285 British police officers lost their lives as a direct result of enemy action.[16]

As early as 1943, Herbert Morrison, the Home Secretary, was thinking of the end of the war. In his address to the Police Federation in December of that year[17] he mentioned the Civil Affairs Organisation, which had already been set up in the territories of former enemies now in the occupation of the Allies. He mentioned that the police were an integral part of this, and police officers would be needed to administer it. The object would not be to impose the British system of policing on to a conquered country, but to provide officers who were capable of organising local personnel so that the indigenous police system could be revitalised. Eventually, this concept was to flower as AMGOT (Allied Military Government of Occupied Territories), which would be part of the British Control Commission to Germany, established in 1946.

Herbert Morrison was also looking forwards to the policing of Britain after the war. As soon as it became apparent that invasion was unlikely and that the war could be won, Morrison established the Police Post-War Committee on 26 May 1944.[18] Its terms of reference were to report 'on the principles to be followed in the post-war police service'. Although the composition of the committee fluctuated for the three years of its existence, the committee always included the Inspectors of Constabulary, the Commissioners of the Metropolitan Police and

City of London Police, and never less than twenty chief constables of English, Welsh and Scottish forces, as well as senior officials at the Home Office.

Four reports were issued, all in 1947. The first dealt with the establishment of a police college for higher training[19] The second dealt with the beat system, police-women, prosecutions, recruitment and training.[20] The third dealt with police housing and buildings, and welfare concerns.[21] The fourth, in May 1947, dealt with the higher ranks and the Special Constabulary.[22]

Eventually, of course, the war ended. The police officers serving with the armed forces were now free to come home. But this was not all plain sailing.

A pre-war PC had been released into the army, where he had attained the rank of captain. Not wishing to return, he sent a letter to his chief constable resigning. The indignant chief constable replied asking why. The man wrote back saying that in the army he had become used to giving orders and commanding men, and thus knew that he was capable of something better than plodding the beat and having to take orders from a bunch of block-headed sergeants (or words to that effect). The chief constable wrote back saying that by the terms of the Police and Firemen (War Service) Act 1939, under which he had been released in the first place, he was legally obliged to return to his force, and so his request to resign was refused. There followed a long series of letters between the chief constable, the ex-PC and the Home Office exploring the legality of both sides.

Eventually, the chief constable had to accept the resignation, but he did so with bad grace. The ex-PC promptly joined the British Colonial Police and was sent to Kenya as an inspector.

The army had done wonders for other returning men as well. A chief constable of a midland county constabulary, with more army than police background, had always insisted on being addressed as 'Captain B—'. One story has it that a PC of his force, being welcomed back in 1946, was ushered into the chief's office where the chief constable was sitting at his desk writing. Without looking up, the chief snapped out a brusque 'I'm Captain B—', to which the PC replied, 'Oh, well in that case, I'm Major —', which had been his wartime rank. A major outranks a captain, so it should have been the chief constable standing up for the PC and not vice versa. After that, perhaps it was not surprising that the PC never got promoted.

TWELVE

1945–64

Despite all the privations facing the country after the Second World War, the police service was at least in the forefront of the minds of the government. Memories persisted of the horrors that had ensued in 1918 and 1919, only twenty-six years previously, and the government was not keen to repeat that.

Bearing in mind the work it had done during the war, the Inspectorate of Constabulary was the first to be legally remembered. As the Inspectorate had, in effect, been strengthened considerably during the war and had kept an eye on the police service during that time, it was in the best position to know the state of the service at the end of hostilities and could possibly be relied upon to be a future barometer of the police. Thus the Police (His Majesty's Inspectors of Constabulary) Act was passed on 7 March 1945, a good two months before VE Day, and seven months before the inspectors' report for 1945 had been written and published.[1]

In effect, the Act gave power to the Home Secretary to have any number of inspectors that he thought necessary, and was not tied to three as stipulated by the County and Borough Police Act of 1856. Also, under Section 1, the 1945 Act stipulated 'that one of that number [of Inspectors was] to be appointed as HM Chief Inspector of Constabulary'. Why this stipulation was never acted upon at that time (although it was to be later) or, indeed, why this Act should have been passed at all is not known. Certainly the Police Post-War Committee had not recommended it.

Even though all the inspectors sat on the Post-War Committee, not one of the reports mentions the Inspectorate, except perfunctorily. So although the committee had proposed important changes to the police service as a whole, no changes had been sought for the Inspectorate. As such, the genesis of the Police (His Majesty's Inspectors of Constabulary) Act in 1945 was not to be found in the Police Post-War Committee. Nevertheless, the Act was passed, with the main point of derestricting the number of inspectors. The Act, however, did not address the anomaly of the inspection year running from October to September, and this arrangement continued.

64 An annual inspection by the Inspector of Constabulary. Mr Frederick Tarry (HMI 1946–62) is inspecting Worcester City Police in 1947. The chief constable, Ernest Tinkler (1941-1955), is in the background accompanied by members of the Worcester City Watch Committee.

Henceforth, the number of inspectors was unlimited. However, it is under-standable if the inspectors gasped in ironic resignation at this point, because despite William Johnson being appointed as an inspector in 1945, both Llewellyn Atcherley and Jacynth Coke promptly retired after their wartime stints, putting the number of inspectors back to three. Yet all was not despondency, because in March 1945 history was made.

Barbara Denis de Vitré was an inspector in the Kent County Constabulary in charge of a section of twenty-three policewomen.[2] 'DeV', as she was known, had joined the Sheffield City Police in 1928 and in 1931 was sent to Cairo City Police to organise its Policewomen's Department. Returning to serve in Leicester City Police in 1931, she was promoted to sergeant in 1936 and was further promoted to inspector in 1944 on transfer to Kent.

DeV was the first woman on the Inspectorate staff, and was appointed as a staff officer with special responsibility for policewomen's issues. She was promoted to assistant inspector in 1948 but was a full inspector in all but name. She would die whilst holding office in 1960.

The annual report of the Inspectorate for the year ending September 1945 was the first to be published since 1939, and not only gave the review of the war years, but included the inspectors' concerns for the future – and it was becoming plain where the future problems would lie. Manpower and recruiting, and that perennial chestnut, the smaller borough forces, would be the worries from now on.[3]

During the war, the police service had received adequate manpower as it had been swollen by the four main sources of extra personnel: the Police Reserve, the War Reserve, the Special Constabulary and the Women's Auxiliary Police Corps. However, come peacetime, with everybody returning to normal, coupled with the demise of the regular police officers whose retirement had been postponed by the war, the strength of the police force plummeted. 'These factors will decrease the strength of the forces considerably,' said the inspectors, 'and it is estimated that 16,000 recruits are required to bring the police strength up to its normal pre-war establishment.' The recruiting of 'the right type of men' and then providing them with 'adequate training' was imperative.[4]

Optimism that these vacancies would be filled after the war can be seen in what happened next. During the Great War, the chief constables had divided England and Wales into eight provincial police districts, with each district holding its own Chief Constables' Conference. These districts had come to be accepted by the Home Office as the standard geographical divisions of the country. The Post-War Committee, taking notice of the figure of 16,000 recruits as envisaged by the Inspectors of Constabulary, decided that each district would need a police training centre to train recruits for the forces in its area, as well as to provide refresher courses for those men returning from the armed forces. Thus, the eight district training centres were established in 1945 and 1946:

Number 1 District Centre was at Bruche, near Warrington, and was opened on Monday 4 February 1946, for the forces of Cheshire, Cumberland and Westmorland, Lancashire, and all the city and borough forces contained in those counties, plus the Isle of Man Constabulary.

Number 2 District Centre was at Hawkshill, Easingwold, in the North Riding of Yorkshire, and opened on Monday 21 January 1946 for the forces of Durham, Northumberland, the North and East Ridings of Yorkshire, and all the cities and boroughs therein. Easingwold eventually closed and the Number 2 District Training Centre moved just up the road to Newby Wiske, near Northallerton.

Number 3 District Centre was at Forest Town, Mansfield, Nottinghamshire, which opened in November 1945. In October 1946 the Number 3 Centre was temporarily housed at Sutton-in-Ashfield, Nottinghamshire, before eventually finding a permanent home in May 1947 at Pannal Ash, Harrogate, which covered the forces of Derbyshire, Lincolnshire, Nottinghamshire and the West Riding of Yorkshire, plus all the cities and boroughs contained in them.

Number 4 District Centre was at Ryton-on-Dunsmore, Coventry, and was opened in June 1945. It covered the counties of Leicestershire, Northamptonshire, Rutland, Shropshire, Staffordshire, Warwickshire and Worcestershire, plus all the cities and boroughs.

Number 5 District Centre was at Eynsham Hall, Witney, Oxfordshire, and opened in 1945. It covered Bedfordshire, Buckinghamshire, Cambridgeshire, Isle of Ely, Essex, Hertfordshire, Huntingdonshire, Norfolk, Oxfordshire and East and West Suffolk, plus all the boroughs.

Number 6 District Centre was at Sandgate, Folkestone, Kent. It opened in 1945 for the forces of Berkshire, Hampshire, Kent, Surrey, East and West Sussex, and the boroughs.

Number 7 District Centre was at Chantemarle, Cattistock, Dorset. It opened in 1945 for the forces of Cornwall, Devonshire, Dorset, Gloucestershire, Somerset, Wiltshire and all the contained boroughs.

Number 8 District Centre was at Bryncethin, Bridgend, Glamorgan, and served all the Welsh forces, plus Herefordshire and Monmouthshire.

Number 9 District Centre was the Metropolitan Police, which had its own training centre at Hendon in north London.

All these training centres, because they were run by central government and not by the forces or districts, were called Common Police Services – in other words, shared by many forces. Other common services were put into place, mainly the forensic science laboratories, driving schools and detective training schools, which are all still in existence.

With all the training centres in place, the government then sat back expecting a deluge of recruits. That was to be wishful thinking. In the 1945/46 annual report of the Inspectors of Constabulary, the authorised establishment (the desired number of police officers) was given as 43,853, with the actual strength being 35,173, or nearly 20 per cent understrength.[5] The inspectors' 1946/47 annual report articulates the possible reasons for the lack of recruits, with unsatisfactory housing and higher wages in industry being two of the most important. This report also gives the deficiency in manpower of some forces, both county and borough. Derbyshire County, for instance, was 34 per cent below its authorised establishment, and Coventry City was 39 per cent below its authorised establishment.[6]

The situation was indeed serious and recruits had to be found. Thus recruiting missions were sent out to the various parts of the globe where British troops were still stationed.

The Police Recruiting Mission to the Middle East under the command of Thomas Lewis, chief constable of Carmarthenshire, went to Egypt and East Africa in July and August 1946, resulting in 600 recruits. The more ambitious Police World Tour between January and May 1946 went to India, Ceylon, China, Japan and Malaya, under the command of no less than three chief constables: Oswald Cole (Leicester City); Herbert Hunter (Staffordshire); and Arthur McIntosh (Dunbartonshire). All this resulted in just 500 recruits. A combined Police and Prison Mission to Palestine, resulting in the recruitment of over 1,000 men to the police and prison services, was held between January and February 1948 and contained two chief constables, Henry Studdy of the West Riding of Yorkshire and John Williamson of Northampton Borough. But this was a long way from the 16,000 needed.[7]

Due to this immense shortage of manpower, chief constables were looking again at the old system of beats and deciding there must be a better way of using what little manpower they did have. Many schemes were devised to make the most of the men available, and the best known, arguably, is the system that came to be known as the Aberdeen System.

Although this is considered to be the brainchild of James McConnach, chief constable of the Aberdeen City Police, who used it extensively, the system was, in fact, first worked in 1940 by Henry Diston, chief constable of Ashton-under-Lyne Borough Police.[8] The Aberdeen System was only suitable for large towns and cities, and consisted of groups of constables under the control of a sergeant being sent out in radio-controlled vehicles. They would go to one area of the city and flood that neighbourhood with policemen, thoroughly checking all property and people, and generally making their presence felt. After a specified period, maybe one hour, they would all return to the vehicle, go to another area and do the same thing there, eventually covering the whole city. They had complete flexibility and could return to any area at random times during their tour of duty, thereby keeping the criminals unsure of where and when they would encounter police officers.

This system was to be reported on by the later Oaksey Committee. But, because of the short amount of time that it had been in operation, the conclusion was indifferent, and although a similar scheme was tried in the West Riding of Yorkshire, it never really caught on and is not now in operation. However, the theory is sound and it is possibly time for it to be given another airing.

It was known as early as 1943 that victory in Europe would lead to Britain's involvement with the Allied Military Government of Occupied Territories (AMGOT), and that would probably mean policemen being seconded overseas. Inevitably this proved to be so, further exacerbating the shortage of manpower. Germany and Austria had been divided up into zones between the Allies, with each country being given one zone to administer. The British zone of Germany was in the north-west of the country and the British zone of Austria was in the south-east, in the Steiermark and Kartnen districts. British administration of these two zones would be performed by a Control Commission, part of which was a Public Safety Branch.

The German Public Safety Branch was placed under the direction of a British Inspector of Constabulary, Gordon Halland, who was given the rank of inspector-general. Halland had been an Inspector of Constabulary since 1938, and had previously seen service in the Indian Police before becoming the chief constable of Lincolnshire and then deputy assistant commissioner of the Metropolitan Police. The inspector-general of the British Austrian zone was John Nott-Bower,

65 Gordon Halland, chief constable of Lincolnshire 1931–34; deputy assistant commissioner of the Metropolitan Police 1934–38; and HM Inspector of Constabulary 1938–53. Gordon Halland was seconded as inspector-general of police in Ceylon, 1942–44, and was inspector-general of public safety in the British Control Commission in Germany 1945–50.

assistant commissioner of the Metropolitan Police, who had extensive experience in the Indian Police, and was the son of a former Commissioner of the City of London Police.

The Public Safety Branch had called for British police volunteers in late 1945 to form Special Police Corps, which were sent to Germany and Austria, not to inflict the British police model upon them, but to enable the German and Austrian police to get back on their feet by reorganisation and denazification, as well as by the administration of the civil courts.

Originally, the Special Police Corps was going to stop in Germany and Austria for seven years, but because of the tremendous progress made, by 1950 the Corps had been run down and was disbanded. Halland returned to the Inspectorate of Constabulary, retiring in 1953; Nott-Bower returned to become the Commissioner of the Metropolitan Police between 1953 and 1958. The seconded British police officers returned with tales of whole countries devastated by the megalomania of one man.[9]

Although the lack of police manpower would bedevil the service for many a long year from here on in, a glimmer of hope was espied in the other great concern of the pre-war Inspectorate of Constabulary: the small borough forces. Ever since William Cartwright had first articulated the problem in 1856, it had been one of the inspectors' policy aims to eradicate these.

Time and time again this had been intimated in successive inspectors' reports, but having no political power, the inspectors were reliant upon central government. Sometimes this worked, as in the 1888 Local Government Act; sometimes it did not, as in the interwar period when central government was occupied with other things. Nevertheless, central government was aware of the inspectors' feelings on the matter.

In early 1945 the mandatory wartime amalgamations of forces under the 1942 Defence Regulations were still in force, but the amalgamated police forces were unhappy. Throughout the winter and spring of 1944/45, the Association of Municipal Corporations had passed resolutions for the Home Secretary, Herbert Morrison, to revoke the Defence Regulations and let everything return to 'normal' at the end of the war – which appeared to be imminent.[10] Pressure was also applied through questions in Parliament by the members of the constituencies concerned. The flurry of questions to the Home Secretary on Thursday 17 May 1945, just over a week after VE Day, typified the concern.[11] Captain Leonard Plugge, Member for Chatham, asked: 'Now the emergency has passed, will he re-examine the police?' Mr Gordon Touche, Member for Reigate, asked 'whether he will now repeal the Defence Regulations which Reigate Borough Police was amalgamated into Surrey'. Mr Alfred Bossom, Member for Maidstone, and Mr William Craven-Ellis, Member for Southampton, asked similar questions about the Kent and Hampshire forces.

'I have made it clear,' replied Mr Morrison, 'that the future of the orders made under the Defence Regulations 1942 has been engaging my attention … and … I hope shortly to be in a position to put forward proposals with regard to general policy relating to the amalgamation of police forces.' He further added that the continuation of defence schemes would 'conduce to police efficiency'.

There is no doubt that Herbert Morrison would, in the fullness of time, have passed legislation to this effect. Fate, however, intervened, and just two months later he was replaced as Home Secretary. Under the 'Labour Landslide' of the 1945 General Election on Thursday 26 July, the coalition wartime government was replaced by a Labour government under Clement Attlee, which 'heralded a period of great reforming activity'.[12]

The new government set about assembling the Welfare State and groundbreaking legislation was in prospect. This, of course, included the police. The new Home Secretary, James Chuter-Ede, in realising that he had no powers to enforce the merging of police forces – which obviously did not fit well with the new Welfare State view of things – set about rectifying it.

A bill was introduced into Parliament within a 'few months' to abolish all non-county borough forces. It also sought powers to compel the amalgamation of any police force the Home Secretary thought fit 'in the interests of efficiency'.[13] However, as a 'check and balance' each forcible amalgamation would be preceded by a public inquiry.

Despite opposition from the police forces concerned,[14] the government's majority (393 against 230 combined opposition)[15] was too great, and the Police Act 1946 (9 and 10 George VI, Chapter 46) received the Royal Assent on Monday 15 April 1946. The full title of the Police Act 1946 was 'An Act to abolish non county boroughs as separate police areas; to provide for the amalgamation of county and county borough police areas; to provide for the purchase of land for police purposes by compulsory purchase order; to redefine the Metropolitan police district'. It also provided – under Section 1(2) – that no chief constable of a previous non-county borough force could be the chief constable of the new force.

Thus, on Tuesday 1 April 1947, forty-five non-county borough forces were amalgamated with their surrounding counties. Only two exceptions to the 1946 Act occurred, that of the forces of Cambridge City and Peterborough City, which were both larger than the forces of their surrounding counties, and so were treated as county boroughs. Cambridgeshire County Constabulary had an establishment of 82 and Cambridge City 120, whilst Peterborough City had 56 and the Liberty of Peterborough Police had just 10. This, by the end of 1947, left fifty-six county forces and seventy-three borough forces in England and Wales.[16]

So progress was being seen to be made in the administration of the British police service. But in 1947 something happened, the results of which every police officer has had drummed into him or her relentlessly from the second week of training – the case of Christie v. Leachinsky.

In 1942 Detective Constable Christie and Detective Sergeant Morris of the Liverpool City Police had been keeping observations on Leachinsky, who was a rag-and-bone merchant. The details are irrelevant, but Leachinsky was arrested on suspicion of theft. The case went before Mr Justice Stable at Liverpool Assizes and Leachinsky was found guilty.

Leachinsky appealed, not so much for the reason of why he was arrested, but for how he was arrested. Again the details are not needed, but eventually the appeal went right up to the House of Lords, who published their findings in 1947. This proved to be a landmark ruling, which laid down the manner of arrest to be followed by every police officer from the rawest probationer constable upwards. It is breathtaking to realise that it had taken 118 years since the birth of the 'new police' for this verging-on-an-everyday-occurrence for every police officer to come to the fore and be forensically settled.

In effect, Christie v. Leachinsky stated that when an arrest without warrant is made, the suspect must be told why he is being arrested, although that need not be in technical language. If this is not complied with, the arrest is unlawful and thus any assault made on the police officer if the culprit resists arrest is justifiable. Generations of policemen know the rulings of Christie v. Leachinsky through backwards.

In June 1946 the First Report of the Post-War Committee was published, which dealt with higher training. The idea of a police college was again mentioned,[17] and the committee was most enthusiastic about the need for a college to provide leaders for the future of the service. Lord Trenchard's scheme in the pre-war Metropolitan Police was examined, plus ideas from other sources. Much detail as to the running of the college, the types and duration of courses and so on, was all reported on and, not surprisingly, the establishment of a police college was urged without any delay.

James Chuter-Ede, the Home Secretary, was impressed and complied. The location of the college was to be at the Number 4 District Training Centre at Ryton-on-Dunsmore, near Coventry. Ryton had been a wartime hostel for the workers in the Coventry car factories, which had been turned into military vehicle factories during the war. In June 1945 it had been requisitioned as the police training centre.

However, because the anticipated influx of recruits had never materialised, Ryton was working at half steam, providing only refresher courses for those men returning from the forces, thus the decision to take over the buildings there. Number 4 District Training Centre was moved to Mill Meece, near Cannock in Staffordshire in March 1948, and Ryton-on-Dunsmore was fitted out as the first national police college.

Initially, there were two courses envisaged: the 'A' course, of six months' residential duration for substantive sergeants in preparation for the rank and duties of an inspector; and the 'B' course, of three months' residential duration in preparation for the higher ranks. Notice that the 'A' course was for substantive sergeants – men and women who had already learned the job thoroughly by walking the beat as PCs, had passed promotion exams and had been considered good enough by their chief constables to be promoted. Definitely no direct officer entry.

The college opened its doors on Monday 14 June 1948, offering the 'A' course, first of all, with the 'B' course following in September. The first course was attended by 155 sergeants and newly promoted inspectors from 103 forces, who, with an average age of 37, with all due respect, were not exactly the 'bright young things' of Lord Trenchard's aspirations. The 'B' course had 50 inspectors and chief inspectors.[18]

The choice of first commandant was unconventional in that he was not a policeman. Brigadier Piers Duncan Williams Dunn had joined the Lancashire Fusiliers in 1914, being awarded the MC and DSO during the Great War. During the Second World War, he was the colonel of the Border Regiment, awarded the CBE in 1945 and promoted to brigadier in 1948. It is a curious thing, considering the Home Office's opposition since the Police Regulations of 1920 to military men being appointed directly as chief constables, that the very first man to be placed in charge of the higher training of police officers should be a military man with absolutely no police experience whatsoever. But in the case of the police college, did police experience matter?

Both the 'A' and 'B' courses consisted of already vastly experienced police officers, many with well over ten years' service under their belts. They were not attending the police college to learn police work, as they already knew how to do that; they were attending the college to learn about leadership and, as such, did not require a policeman to teach them that. Brigadier Piers Dunn, although not a policeman, did have unrivalled experience as a lecturer on the subject of leadership. It was for this quality he was chosen, not for his expertise as a policeman. However, if he did become unstuck, his deputy commandant, Superintendent Richard Walmsley of the Birmingham City Police, was there with the necessary police knowledge.[19]

Brigadier Dunn died whilst holding office in 1957. His replacement was also a military man with no police experience. Richard Jelf had been commissioned into the Royal Artillery in 1924, had served in Europe for the whole of the Second World War and by 1957 was a major-general. Like Piers Dunn, Richard Jelf had been chosen for his leadership qualities and not for his police knowledge, although perhaps he was no stranger to the criminal law as his grandfather was Mr Justice Jelf, judge of the King's Bench.

Eventually, courses at the police college included higher command courses, as well as courses for personnel of the British Colonial Police, and even the police of independent states. Ryton had always been seen as a temporary home for the college, and so it proved. The lovely old Jacobean mansion of Bramshill, near Hartley Witney in Hampshire, had been acquired by the Home Office and, after necessary extensions had been added, the police college moved to Bramshill in the middle months of 1960, where it still remains to this day. Mill Meece was closed down and the Number 4 District Police Training Centre returned to Ryton-on-Dunsmore.[20]

All this was well and good for the chosen few, but what of the rank-and-file policeman, those content to stop as constables or unable to pass the promotion examinations? Exactly the same thing happened during the Second World War as had happened during the Great War: the cost of living rose, but police wages did not. The situation was not so dire as in 1918 and 1919, but was desperate nevertheless. The Desborough pay scales of 1919 had given the policeman over 50 per cent more pay than in industry, plus secure employment during the inter-war years.[21] By 1945 all that had gone. The government, alive to this, gave a small pay increase in April 1945, but that was soon swallowed up. The government tried again in 1946, but that was on the proviso that no more was to be forthcoming until an independent review, which would be held by the end of 1949.

The unstoppable post-war tide of inflation, however, was just that – unstoppable. Once again, industrial wages and police wages were the same, causing the inevitable drift away from the police to much 'safer' jobs which had no shift work and no risk of being assaulted by the ever-increasing number of crooks and toe-rags in an ever-escalating 'crime boom'. In short, the police were displeased.

Faced with rising discontent in the police service, coupled with the lack of recruits, the government could only do one thing. After being lobbied by the Police Federation, the government brought forward by one year the promised independent review. Appointed on Wednesday 12 May 1948, this review was to be chaired by Sir Geoffrey Lawrence, a well-respected High Court judge who had just returned from sitting at the Nuremberg Trials, and for his services had been ennobled as the first Baron Oaksey. The Oaksey Committee mandate was 'to consider in the light of the need for the recruitment and retention of an adequate number of suitable men and women for the police forces in England, Wales and Scotland, and to report on pay, emoluments, allowances, pensions, promotion, methods of representation and negotiation, and other conditions of service'. It called a range of witnesses from all interested parties from every aspect of policing. Two reports were presented, the first in April 1949[22] and the second in November 1949.[23] A working party under the chairmanship of Sir Frank Brook, the senior Inspector of Constabulary, was set up by the Oaksey Committee to look at the Aberdeen System, and his comments were included in the second Oaksey Report. His conclusions, however, were so non-committal (mainly because of the small amount of time that the committee had been in operation, thus making long-term assessment difficult) as to provoke no great interest; and although a similar scheme was tried in the West Yorkshire County Constabulary, the Aberdeen System never really caught on.

The Police Federation was lobbying for pay rises of up to 54 per cent,[24] but they were to be bitterly disappointed. Oaksey only recommended a 15 per cent pay rise, which was implemented in July 1949. But within one year, it was obvious that the rise was ineffectual and had done nothing to bolster recruitment or stop the drainage of manpower by resignation.[25] All in all, the Oaksey Report was a failure as far as pay went, and never achieved the same grandeur or gravitas as the Desborough Report undoubtedly did some thirty years earlier.

There was one beneficial effect of the Oaksey Report, however. Part 1 of the report made a recommendation that 'A statutory provision should be introduced providing that members of the police forces must not be employed on extraneous duties without the consent of the Police Authority and the sanction of the Secretary of State'. In order to achieve this there 'should be a thorough review of the extraneous duties carried out by the police'. And Home Secretary Chuter-Ede duly complied. The Committee on Extraneous Police Duties was appointed on Wednesday 30 August 1950 under the chairmanship of Mr J.H. Burrell.[26] One Inspector of Constabulary, Frederick Tarry, sat on the committee, which also included the then chief constable of Birmingham City, Edward Dodd, who would be the Chief Inspector of Constabulary between 1963 and 1966.

The Report of the Committee on Police Extraneous Duties was published in April 1953, and Paragraph 27 stated: '… we recommend that there should be substituted for Police Regulation 39, a Regulation which, subject to the Secretary of State's power to approve exceptions, will preclude the police from undertaking any of the duties in the Appendix.'

In the appendix to the report there were listed nearly forty 'duties which the police should not perform'. These included duties as Fishery Officer, Markets Inspector, Water Bailiff, Inspector of Fire Appliances, Inspectors of Domestic Servants Registers and so on. The then Home Secretary, Sir David Fyffe, accepted the Burrell Report completely and implemented its findings immediately. And so much so that in the 1951/52 annual report of the Inspectors of Constabulary (which ostensibly covered the year October 1951 to September 1952, but which was not presented to Parliament until July 1953), the inspectors could state:

> as a result of the revision of the methods of patrol, improvements in communications, relieving the police of certain extraneous duties, and the replacement of police by persons in appropriate clerical and other grades on various indoor duties, the regular police in many forces are now able to devote more time to their primary duty of preventive supervision than formerly.[27]

Perhaps as a 'sweetener' to take their minds off the bitter pill of wages, the government introduced a new and different award. In 1919 the Special Constabulary had been awarded a Long Service and Good Conduct Medal as a reward for war service,[28] but for reasons unknown the regular constabulary's war service was totally ignored, so no medal for them. Perhaps that was a sign of the government's pre-Desborough disinterest in the country's police service.

It would take another thirty-two years before this anomaly was rectified. The Police Long Service and Good Conduct Medal was established by Royal Warrant in June 1951,[29] and would be automatically awarded to all police officers, irrespective of rank (or even of good conduct), with twenty-two years' service in a recognised police force. The award was not made retrospectively and was only issued to serving officers. The qualifying period of twenty-two years remained until 2010, when it was reduced to twenty years.

Although nobody then knew it, the late 1950s would turn out to be interesting times for the British police service. The first quandary would be unique, and would not even take place in Britain.

The United Kingdom Police Unit to Cyprus 1955–60

The island of Cyprus had been a British colony since 1874. Slap bang on the route to the Middle East through the Suez Canal, Cyprus was far too valuable for Britain to give up. In July 1954 Henry Hopkinson, the Minister for Colonial Affairs, said exactly that in a speech to Parliament. Not surprisingly, the Cypriots were unimpressed by this because they wanted independence.

The resulting 'rebellion' or 'liberation struggle', depending on which view point you take, started on Friday 1 April 1955. The Greek Cypriot militia, EOKA (Εθνικι Οργανοσις Κυπριον Αγονιστον – Ethniki Organosis Kyprion Agoniston, National Organisation of Cypriot Freedom Fighters), had been formed by Archbishop Makarios III of Cyprus, together with a Greek army colonel, George Grivas, in order to mount a guerrilla campaign to gain independence. Although the British increased the number of troops on the island, its policing was in the hands of the British Colonial Police. However, it was strongly suspected that the local Cypriot police officers had been heavily infiltrated and intimidated by EOKA. So, to provide an impartial and trustworthy police force, there seemed to be only one solution: send British police officers to the troubled island.

Thus, the United Kingdom Police Unit (UKU) to Cyprus was established, and eventually 895 British police, men and women, all volunteers, were to serve on it at various times. The effect on the British police was tremendous.

Most forces were struggling with the 'crime boom' of the 1950s (where reported crimes were rising at an average yearly rate of about 15 per cent) and were chronically understrength, so to have to supply personnel to another country was a burden some forces could have done without. But the job had to be done, and the call went out for volunteers. The terms of agreement were simple: two years' attachment consisting of twenty-one months' service followed by three months' leave.

Eventually, the Cyprus emergency came to an end; the Republic of Cyprus came into existence in 1960, with Archbishop Makarios as the first President, and the UKU returned home. The price had been heavy, though. Six policemen had been murdered by EOKA and nine wounded; four had died accidentally, one had died from natural causes and twenty-five had been decorated.

Members of the UKU who lost their lives:

By terrorist activity:

Gerald Thomas Patrick Rooney (Kent County), Wednesday 14 March 1956

Reginald William Tipple (Metropolitan Police), Thursday 21 June 1956

Leonard Alfred Demmon (Metropolitan Police), Friday 31 August 1956

Hugh Brian Carter (Herefordshire County), Friday 28 September 1956

Cyril John Thoroughgood (Leicestershire and Rutland County),
   Friday 28 September 1956

Stanley Woodward (Durham County), Monday 13 October 1958

By other causes:

Maurice Eden, GM (Metropolitan Police) shooting accident,
    Monday 17 December 1956

William Edward Critchley (West Riding of Yorkshire County) shooting accident,
    Saturday 8 June 1957

Arthur James Coote (Durham County) road traffic accident, Sunday 9 June 1957

Charles Hector Brown (Cheshire County) road traffic accident,
    Tuesday 14 January 1958

William Sidney Gillett (Bristol City) leukaemia, Sunday 17 May 1959

The United Kingdom Police Unit to Cyprus was the first such unit to be constituted. It must have been favourably impressive because the tactic of supplying
British police officers to various trouble spots around the world has been used
by the British government on several subsequent occasions. There have been UK
Police Units to Anguilla, Nyasaland, Rhodesia and Kosovo.

The succeeding predicaments of this interesting decade were all home-grown,
and the first started in 1956. In that year, the attention of the Home Secretary,
Gwilym Lloyd-George (son of David), had been drawn to the antics in the
Cardiganshire County Constabulary. Disciplinary proceedings against the chief
constable, William Jones, had been instituted and had been heard before Mr John
Henderson, QC, Recorder of Portsmouth. There were eleven charges, starting
with the chief constable using police officers as caretakers and gardeners at his
private house, using police transport for his own use and driving police cars
whilst drunk. However, there were far more serious accusations.

Amongst these were allegations that two police constables had spent the night
at hotels in the company of two women and had made false entries into the hotel
registers, and a woman police constable had been made pregnant by a member of
the force. No disciplinary action had been taken by the chief constable in any of
these instances.[30]

The chief constable was eventually found guilty of gross mismanagement of
his force and was allowed to resign instead of being dismissed, but the resulting
scandal prompted the Home Secretary to use his powers under the 1946 Police
Act. In July 1958 the Cardiganshire and Carmarthenshire County Constabularies
were forcibly amalgamated, with the new chief constable being Thomas Lewis,
the chief constable of Carmarthenshire.[31]

The next scandal of the 1950s was in December 1957, when the chief constable
of Worcester City Police, Glyn Davies, was suspended by his Watch Committee
after they conducted an inquiry into the affairs of the City Constabulary Club.
Four months later, he was formally charged with false accounting and the
fraudulent conversion of £1,100 entrusted to him by members of the Worcester
Constabulary Club, of which he was treasurer.

66 Eight hundred and ninety-five British police officers, men and women, all volunteers, served in the United Kingdom Police Unit to Cyprus between 1955 and 1960. This is PS2870 Peter Holyoake in winter uniform in Ledra Street, Nicosia, which was nicknamed 'Murder Mile' because of the large number of shootings which occurred there.

Davies appeared at the Worcester Assizes in May 1958 before Mr Justice Pearson. He was found guilty on three charges and received eighteen months' imprisonment for each, to run concurrently. Eric Abbott, a superintendent of the Leeds City Police, was chosen as the next chief constable, and into his hands was placed the unenviable task of building morale back up in a force that had been shaken to its foundations.[37]

The next public embarrassment for the police also occurred in the month of December 1957. PC George Harper and PC Robert Gunn of the Caithness-shire Constabulary were patrolling near the Bay Café in Thurso. Originally a small town overlooking the Pentland Firth, Thurso had recently been much enlarged by workers from the nearby atomic energy station at Dounreay. This great prosperity had led to the inevitable increase in drunkenness and rowdiness, with the Bay Café figuring largely.

Entering the café at 10.30 p.m. on Saturday 7 December 1957, the two PCs were confronted by a gang of six youths, one of whom, John Waters, aged 15, was in a particularly vociferous mood. There then followed the usual tirade of obscenity from the foul-mouthed Waters, which virtually every police officer faces each Saturday evening from garrulous youths trying to act big in front of their cohorts. Waters was taken outside the café and spoken to, and the officers moved off. However, when Waters went back into the café he found that his coat was slightly torn. Chasing after the two PCs, he unleashed another torrent of abuse. The two officers shepherded him into a quiet alleyway, and it was what allegedly happened next that kept the nation enthralled for months.

Waters finished up with his nose bleeding and being treated by the local doctor. Not surprisingly, the parents of Waters complained and the whole rigmarole swung into action. The newspapers and media whipped up the tale of the Thurso Boy into a national story, so much so that the government was virtually brow-beaten into establishing a tribunal, headed by Lord Lorn, to look at the whole case. The tribunal published its report in April 1959 and came to the conclusion that there was insufficient evidence to convict the two constables of assault. The Caithness-shire Constabulary was also praised for the way it had handled the case, despite strident criticisms by those non-conversant with police complaint pro-cedures. The reality was that it was a disproportionate furore whipped up by the boy's parents, who were blinded by parental blinkers and refused to believe that their son could have done anything wrong.[33]

A further bombshell for the police service was dropped in February 1958. The chief constable of Brighton Borough, Charles Ridge; two members of his force, Detective Inspector John Hammersley and Detective Sergeant Trevor Heath; plus Anthony Lyons, a licensee; and Samuel Bellson, a bookmaker, all appeared at the Old Bailey before Mr Justice Donovan on charges of conspiring to obstruct the course of justice. It was alleged that, with the connivance of the chief constable, the CID officers had been running a protection racket and had suppressed pros-ecutions, and that Ridge himself had received 'backhanders' to look the other way over the capers in a particularly frisky nightclub.

The details are unnecessary. Suffice it to say that Hammersley and Heath were sent down for five years each, and Bellson for three. Ridge and Lyons were both acquitted, but received severe tongue lashings from the trial judge. Despite being found not guilty, Ridge was dismissed by the Brighton Watch Committee with-out pension.[34] Albert Rowsell, the chief constable of Exeter City Police, who had been acting as chief constable since Ridge's suspension, was confirmed as chief constable, and he was faced with exactly the same task as Eric Abbott in Worcester.

The next scandal for the British police occurred within the Metropolitan Police. On the morning of Wednesday 17 December 1958, PC Eastmond stopped a red sports car for speeding across Putney Heath. The driver turned out to be Brian Rix, the well-known actor-manager of the Whitehall Theatre. Following on behind was another car driven by a Mr Garratt, a civil servant. Recognising the driver of the sports car, Garratt was evidently the sort to be overawed by famous people such as this, and stopped his own car and proceeded to poke his nose into a matter which was none of his business whatsoever. What happened next only the three participants know, but PC Eastmond arrested Garratt for alleged assault on a police officer. However, when Eastmond arrived with his prisoner back at the station, the station sergeant refused the charge and Garratt was released.

Garratt promptly sued PC Eastmond, claiming damages for assault and false imprisonment. The fact that only the three participants know what happened is because the Metropolitan Police commissioner, Sir Joseph Simpson, promptly settled out of court by offering £300 without admission of liability, which Garratt accepted. Thus the truth was never established, as no court case or inquiry was ever made into the matter. PC Eastmond was never disciplined and continued to serve. This matter was debated in Parliament in November 1959,[35] but the whole issue was destined to become far more significant than anyone knew, because by then the last and perhaps greatest episode of the doleful 1950s had happened and was well known. The shenanigans at Cardigan, Worcester, Thurso and Brighton had all concerned individual policemen, but what happened in Nottingham was entirely different because it concerned constitutional issues of tremendous importance.

In June 1959 Athelstan Popkess, the chief constable of the Nottingham City Police, suspected that twenty members of the Labour-controlled City Council had acted corruptly. After consulting the Director of Public Prosecutions, he launched an inquiry and, to provide impartiality, asked the Metropolitan Police to undertake it. However, after receiving the report, the Director of Public Prosecutions declined to act. As a result, the Nottingham Watch Committee asked the chief constable to report to them on the investigation. Popkess refused point-blank, saying that law enforcement in the city was his responsibility and not that of the Watch Committee, and on that score he was not accountable to them. The Watch Committee immediately suspended him, as they still could do under the Municipal Corporations Act of 1835 (then still in force), on the grounds of incompetence.

'Rab' Butler, the Home Secretary, despite a deputation from the Watch Committee, ordered them to reinstate Popkess at once on the grounds that the chief constable was beholden only to the law and not to the Nottingham Watch Committee. In this he had the backing of the stated case of Fisher v. Oldham Corporation of 1930 (see Chapter 3). He also threatened to withhold the Exchequer Grant, but the Watch Committee counteracted this by saying he could only do that if the Inspectorate of Constabulary found the force to be 'inefficient' – which they had not.

Due to impending local elections, the Labour Party ordered the Watch Committee to back down, which they did. However, all this left a nasty taste, plus the realisation that the existing Municipal Corporations Act 1835, which should have defined the relationship between borough police forces and the Watch Committee, did no such thing and, as a result, it remained totally useless.[36]

The Popkess affair was known about when the case of Garratt *v.* Eastmond was debated in November 1959. And it was debated because of one thing. It was asked of the Home Secretary why £300 of public money had been paid out if PC Eastmond had done nothing wrong, and if he had been in the wrong, why had he not been disciplined?

The Home Secretary, 'Rab' Butler, glossed over the details; after all, the incident had happened a year earlier. He avoided embarrassing questions like this by playing his trump card: 'This case, though starting from a small incident, does have underlying it, a number of questions of great importance, both to the public and to the police, in which there is evidence of widespread interest and about which there is evidence of considerable anxiety.' He then referred to the questions prompted by all the 'scandals' of the previous few years (the relationship of the Police Authority to the chief constable and of the government to the Police Authority, and so on), adding: 'I do not believe that in modern conditions the police can carry out their heavy responsibilities without adequate public co-operation and the fullest measure of public confidence … The time has come to have them examined with the authority and impartiality of an independent enquiry.' So was born the Royal Commission on the Police.[37]

Appointed on Monday 25 January 1960, under the chairmanship of Sir Henry Willink, Bt, MC, QC, the wartime Minister of Health, and at that time the Master of Magdalene College, Cambridge, the Royal Commission on the Police held its first public meeting on Thursday 17 March 1960. The terms of reference for the Royal Commission (the Willink Committee) were:

> to review the constitutional position of the police throughout Great Britain, the arrangements for the control and administration, and in particular, to consider (i) the constitution and functions of local police authorities (ii) the status and accountability of members of police forces, including the chief officers of police (iii) the relationship of the police with the public and the means of ensuring that complaints by the public against the police are effectively dealt with (iv) the broad principals which should govern the remuneration of the constable, having regard to the nature and extent of police duties and responsibilities and the need to attract and retain an adequate number of recruits with the proper qualifications.

All in all, the commission sat for twenty-seven days between Thursday 17 March 1960 and Wednesday 31 May 1961. A total of 181 witnesses were heard, not only from the spectrum of law enforcement, but also from such bodies as the National Union of Journalists, the National Council for Civil Liberties, the Automobile Association and Royal Automobile Club, and the Pedestrians' Association for Road Safety.[38]

The commission also took trips to twenty-six individual police forces and several of the police training centres. The secretary of the commission was

Mr Thomas Critchley, who had been Rab Butler's Principal Private Secretary and was then a senior member of the Home Office Police Department. It was Thomas Critchley who was to write the splendid *A History of Police in England and Wales* in 1967, which was, and perhaps still is, at the forefront of the few police histories that exist, certainly on the Royal Commission – he should know, he was there.[39]

The Royal Commission presented two reports: an Interim Report, published in November 1960, and the Final Report in May 1962.[40] For the police, the Interim Report, which was awaited with trepidation, proved to be extremely well received, mainly because the commission had concentrated on the fourth part of the Terms of Reference – police pay.

Since the commission had found that the police were still 13,500 under-strength, and that, unsurprisingly, the police constables' work was incomparable to any other job in the land, bar none, the commission worked out a formula for police pay and recommended that it be implemented immediately. It was, giving the police a 40 per cent pay rise. In the year before the publication of the Interim Report, the police lost a net total of 500 men; in the two years after publication there was a net gain of 7,000. However, that was the only part of the Royal Commission that touched the rank-and-file PC; the rest concerned the political squabbles as to who controlled the police.

The commission continued to gather evidence after the Interim Report and the main thrust was to determine who should control and administer the police. The key question was whether there should be one national police force or many local police forces. Opinions, naturally, were polarised. Some witnesses from central and local government wanted no change, as they thought the present arrangements were adequate. Some chief constables wanted a national force or at least regional forces; and some chief constables said that the mutual aid and co-operation between forces then in existence made a national force irrelevant.

Some politicians were strongly in favour of the national police force, which would be answerable to the Home Secretary; therefore the Home Secretary could be hauled before Parliament and held accountable if anything went wrong. Some professors of law argued that local police forces were only a historical accident anyway, and that only local pride and tradition stood in the way of a national force.

Complaints against the police were also touched upon. Some lawyers were of the opinion that for the police to investigate complaints against themselves was wrong and what was needed was an independent body. Then the nebulous subject of police/public relations reared its head.

The Final Report, published in May 1962, did not please everybody, as they never do in these cases. In Chapter X, there were 111 paragraphs of recommendations, and in paragraphs 8–10 the commission stated that although logically there was no constitutional objection to a national police force, the changes which were envisaged for the police could be achieved under the present system, and thus a national police force was not recommended.

This resulted in furious outbursts from those who wanted a politically control-led national police force, writing in such magazines as *The Economist* and the *New Statesman*, especially when they found that one member of the commission had disagreed with the national police force recommendation.

On page 157 of the report, and filling the next twenty-five pages, was a 'Memorandum of Dissent' by Doctor A.L. Goodhart. Arthur Goodhart was Emeritus Professor of Law at Oxford University (he had been awarded the KBE, but as he was American he was not allowed to be called Sir Arthur) and had disagreed with the rejection of a national police force. As such, he put forward his own ideas of a 'Royal English and Welsh Police' and a 'Royal Scottish Police'.

His plan split the country into regions, with each region having its own force under a commissioner who would be chosen by and answerable to the Home Secretary. Although he goes into a lot more detail about the minutiae of admin-istration, the fact remains that there seemed to be nothing new about his system. If Goodhart's terms 'region' and 'commissioner' were substituted for the words 'county' and 'chief constable', the resulting system would be virtually the same as the status quo.

Irrespective of how many contrary voices were heard, the report went before Parliament in May 1963, although by that time one of the recommendations of the Royal Commission had already been acted upon, as the legislation for the recommendation was already in place and had been for the past eighteen years. The Police (HM Inspectors of Constabulary) Act, for the appointment of a Chief Inspector of Constabulary, had been passed in 1945, but for reasons unknown it had never been acted upon. After the publication of the Final Report of the Royal Commission, the appointment of a Chief Inspector of Constabulary was made immediately. On Saturday 1 December 1962, Sir William Johnson was promoted as the first HM Chief Inspector of Constabulary, a post envisaged as being one of the top advisors on police policy to the government of the day, as indeed it still is.

After debating, the government introduced the Police bill into Parliament in November 1963. Based upon the recommendations of the Royal Commission, the bill contained no surprises. Apart from the pay formula, there was only one thing that concerned the rank-and-file police officer, and this item was a 'leftover' from day one of the 'new police'. Under the old, confused police Acts of the nineteenth century, the borough PC, as well as having jurisdiction in his own borough, also had jurisdiction in the surrounding county. The county PC, on the other hand, did not have jurisdiction in any of the boroughs enclosed in his county. The 1964 Act changed all that, and from then on every police officer was to have jurisdiction everywhere. That apart, all the changes brought about by the 1964 Police Act concerned the constitution of the police and not the policeman on the beat.

After the usual procedures, the bill was passed with little or no fuss through both Houses and received the Royal Assent in June 1964, becoming known as the Police Act 1964. Through this Act, a lot of old legislation was swept away; in fact, sixty-one Acts of Parliament were repealed.

The main provisions of the Act were: counties and county boroughs were kept as the standard police areas; the functions of the Home Office, police authorities and chief constables were now legally defined; the Home Secretary was given powers to call for reports from chief constables and to compel the retirement of inefficient chief constables; and the police authorities' duties were now plainly defined and their constitutional make-up altered to two-thirds local politicians to one-third magistrates. But the power most eagerly awaited by the Home Secretary, the power to enforce the amalgamation of forces, was used immediately and continued vigorously for the next eight years.

There was to be no shilly-shallying this time, unlike with the 1946 Police Act. This had stated that any proposed amalgamations would be preceded by a public inquiry. Although the same provision was placed into the 1964 Police Act, it is clear to us now looking back that if the Home Secretary had decreed an amalgamation, then an amalgamation there would be, and the concession of a public inquiry was just a smokescreen and a sop to the forces concerned.

The first two forces to feel the wrath were Northampton Borough and Northamptonshire County, who were required to amalgamate in April 1965. A stay of execution for one year was made so that the public inquiry could be held. Despite the borough putting up a spirited defence, it is now clear that the decision had been made way before the inquiry even started. The two forces were joined in April 1966.[41]

Other forces, viewing this, knew that resistance would be futile. A welter of amalgamations followed and in three short years the 117 forces in England and Wales were reduced to 49.[42]

The 1964 Police Act set the standard. It is still in force and is still the main legislation for the administration of the police forces of twenty-first-century Britain, even though it is nearly fifty years old.

THIRTEEN

1964–2011

The 1964 Police Act concentrated on the settling of constitutional anomalies rather than on the job of the rank-and-file police officer. So much so, that in the fifty years since, no attention has been paid to the constitutional arrangements as laid down in 1964. All the legislation since then has been directed at the rank-and-file police officer and the way that he or she does the job.

These past fifty years have seen the job of a police officer placed under unprecedented pressures, both from general society and from within the police service. The cynic would say that the last fifty years have seen the death of common sense because of the disproportionate rise in paperwork, the health-and-safety straitjacket, the political correctness insanity and the continual tinkering with the system by politicians who are totally clueless as to how the police operate.

Society has changed a great deal in the last fifty years, and it all started, according to Peter Hitchens, with Roy Jenkins, the most liberal and woolly minded Home Secretary of all time.[1] The 1962 Royal Commission had found nothing wrong with the idea of the 'policeman on the beat' – if they had, it would have been commented on at least. But Roy Jenkins, in tandem with his cohort, Eric St Johnstone, chief constable of Lancashire, changed all that and changed it forever, and not for the good.

Being faced with the new town of Kirkby in Lancashire, and not having enough men to police it in the traditional way, St Johnstone resorted to what has become known as the 'Unit Beat Policing'. Instead of the town being split into walking beats, with each beat being patrolled twenty-four hours a day, the town was split into areas. Each area was then split into two 'beats', each having its own residential officer, who lived there and treated it as his own village beat.

But he would not be available round the clock, so in order to provide continual surveillance, cars would be introduced. Each car, driven by one officer, was painted in such a way as to make it stand out from the monochrome of other traffic, hence the two-colour scheme of black and white, and hence the name 'Panda Car'. This car, crewed by officers on a shift system, was to provide twenty-

67 Eric St Johnstone, chief constable of Lancashire County 1950–67, who first introduced Unit Beat Policing into Kirkby in 1966. Possibly as a reward, he was made Chief Inspector of Constabulary, with a knighthood, in 1967.

68 Frank Williamson, chief constable of Carlisle City 1961–63; Cumberland, Westmorland and Carlisle City 1963–67; and HM Inspector of Constabulary 1967–72. It was Frank Williamson who tried Unit Beat Policing in Carlisle in 1966, probably after being pressurised by the Home Office.

four-hour coverage of the one area. To provide the area's collective intelligence, the job of the so-called collator would be established at the main police station to record on a card index all the information fed back by the officers on the street. He would then publish a weekly bulletin detailing all the goings-on in the town and generally keeping everybody up to speed with the criminals of the parish.[2]

The idea was that the Panda Car would be used to convey the officer from point to point, where he would then park up, get out and patrol on foot, but could get instant mobility should an emergency arise in another part of his area. This was the theory.

Policemen being policemen, however, and all too human, never parked up and never patrolled on foot, but stopped in their nice warm cars all the time, only getting out when they were sent to a job. As a result, walking the beat, meeting the public, being a deterrent to crime by their very presence and being available for members of the public, all disappeared overnight. The downward slide had begun.

Nevertheless, statistics then materialised to 'prove' that Unit Beat Policing had worked in Kirkby and, not only that, it had reduced the manpower needed to police a town by 50 per cent. The 'magic formula' had arrived.

But the Unit Beat system had only been tried in a recently built area with a recently arrived population still in a state of flux, still regarding their new estate as a transit camp. They had no roots in the place and not enough time had passed to form much in the way of local pride or civic ethos. Could the system work in a long-established town with untold generations of local pride and traditions? To find this out, 'at the request of the Home Office', the system was introduced into Carlisle by Frank Williamson, the chief constable of the Cumberland, Westmorland and Carlisle City Joint Police, which, incidentally, had the longest title of any British police force before or since.[3]

It is perhaps unnecessary to add that the Unit Beat system was championed by two men who had no idea of 'policing at the sharp end, down in the muck and the bullets'. Both came from comfortable middle-class backgrounds. St Johnstone had joined the civil service branch of the Metropolitan Police and then transferred on to the Trenchard Scheme, so he had never walked the beat or discovered what being a real policeman meant. And Jenkins certainly hadn't.

Frank Williamson, on the other hand, had. Son of a chief constable of Northampton Borough Police, Frank Williamson had joined the Manchester City Police in 1936 and had been promoted through the ranks until appointed to Carlisle City in 1961. Perhaps the fact that Williamson also found favour in the Unit Beat system was more to do with pressure from the Home Office, and perhaps lack of time for a full evaluation or realisation of the minuses of the system. Having Roy Jenkins in the Home Office driving the system forward ensured the spread of the Panda Car to the whole of the country.

With the abandonment of the 'new police' principle of preventative patrolling, the police could only respond to incidents which had already happened – the so-called 'fire brigade' system. No one seems to have realised then, but this was exactly what the 'old police' system was, and in 1829 the 'new police' had been introduced to replace this old system. It was as though the last 130 years had not happened.

This spelt danger, as from the late 1960s onwards, society was gradually breaking down into the yob culture of today and the police service was seemingly throwing away the morals which previous generations had achieved through slow and steady progress. Coupled with a legal retribution system becoming increasingly toothless and powerless, is it any wonder that the police, being left to bear the brunt of this immense change, made mistakes? Police officers are only human and stem from the same society as everyone else. They have the same interests, fears, phobias and irrational thoughts as the rest of society. Yet we expect our policemen to be paragons, and when one slips from grace by demonstrating his human frailties, it makes headline news.

These past fifty years have been minutely described by Timothy Brain in his book *A History of Policing in England and Wales from 1974*, and his subtitle, *A Turbulent Journey*, is an accurate description.[4] Brain, an ex-chief constable of

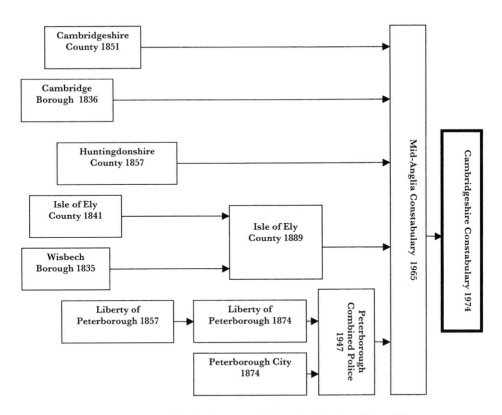

69 A 'Family Tree' of the Cambridgeshire Constabulary, showing the effects of the amalgamations after the Local Government Act of 1888, the Police Acts of 1946 and 1964, and the Local Government Act of 1972.

Gloucestershire, takes over 400 pages to describe the last fifty years. No such luxury is allowable here, so only the prominent landmarks can be described.

After Sir Robert Mark became Commissioner of the Metropolitan Police in 1972, one of his first acts was to establish the A10 Branch, which dealt specifically with complaints against the Metropolitan Police.[5] This meant that policemen were still investigating policemen. The Home Secretary, Robert Carr, established a working party to look at this, and it reported in July 1974, when Roy Jenkins had returned to the Home Office. Jenkins introduced a bill into Parliament, which eventually became the Police Act 1976, that established the Police Complaints Board. This was a complete fudge and satisfied no one; although the Police Complaints Board comprised a lay element of non-police officers and could review the findings, the investigation of the original complaint was still firmly in the hands of the police themselves.

The year 1974 saw the last great reorganisation of the British police forces. Following the Local Government Act of two years previously, it was decided that each county constabulary should be coterminous with its county council area. This was duly done, and thus the number of forces was reduced to the present forty-three, including some that were made up, such as Cleveland and Humberside.[6] These are the force areas at present in use, although thoughts about regional forces still rumble on.

By 1977 the constant war over police pay was coming to its next battle. A 7 per cent pay rise in 1974 had not kept pace with the 26 per cent inflation rate,[7] and seeing every other profession getting pay rises by striking, the Police Federation was militant. At the 1977 Federation Conference, the Home Secretary, Merlin Rees, appeared totally unsettled when he was greeted not with heckling – as being a politician he could have coped with that – but by total silence, before, during and after his speech. That seemingly did the trick, and a review body under Lord Edmund-Davis was set up. This reported in July 1978 and recommended a 45 per cent pay rise, but in instalments. For the future, a negotiating board was to be established under independent chairmen, and police pay was recommended to rise yearly in line with the 'average earnings index'. Wanting to avoid confrontation, the new incoming Conservative government under Margaret Thatcher gave the whole rise immediately.

After a series of highly publicised 'failures' of the police, including the death of Liddle Towers in Northumberland after a scuffle with police and the allegedly 'flawed' investigation into the death of Maxwell Confait in London, questions were being raised as to why the police were not following the proper procedures as laid down by the Judges' Rules. Merlin Rees, the Home Secretary, did what every politician does when he wants to postpone making a decision – he announced a Royal Commission.

The Royal Commission on Criminal Procedure was established in June 1977 under the chairmanship of Sir Cyril Philips, Professor of Oriental History at the University of London. The commission worked away quietly in the background and did not present its report until January 1981. The consequences of this report would be far-reaching, as it spawned the most important milestone in police procedure for nigh on eighty years – the Police and Criminal Evidence Act.

The Royal Commission recommended the repeal of the Judges' Rules, replacing them with a Code of Practice which would lay down strict guidelines and time limits to be followed when dealing with anyone who was in custody. The 'right of silence' was not altogether abolished, but was modified by stating that in any subsequent trial, adverse opinion could ensue if any suspect failed to mention any material fact at the interview stage.

Also recommended was the abolition of the police as the prosecuting agency as well as the investigative body. What was needed was a totally independent prosecuting service, the Crown Prosecution Service. All this, no doubt, would have been presented as a bill into Parliament, but life, as it inevitably does, intervened.

Faced with a perceived spate of lawlessness in Brixton, the Metropolitan Police introduced Operation Swamp. Brixton was saturated with police officers whose aim was to stop and search suspected criminals. The fact that the vast majority of those stopped were young black youths inevitably caused a reaction. The resulting Brixton Riots lasted for almost five days with immense property damage and physical injuries. This seemed to trigger a wave of disorder throughout that summer, and riots flared up in Southall in London, Toxteth in Liverpool, Moss Side in Manchester, and places such as Leicester, Blackburn, Bradford and, surprisingly, quiescent Cirencester. The government needed to know what had happened and what had caused all this. Lord Scarman, a judge of the Appeal Court, was instructed to find the answer.

Scarman's brief was for the Metropolitan Police only, and was published a few months later. Although he found evidence of 'racial prejudice' and 'racial harassment', he stopped short of calling the Metropolitan Police racist. He emphasised that there should be more consultation and involvement with the local community, and in real terms this had a knock-on effect on the provincial forces in looking anew at the question of race relations.

As the initial reactions to the civic riots and the Scarman Report waned, the Royal Commission came back into focus. The Police bill, which would eventually become known as the Police and Criminal Evidence Act (inevitably referred to as PACE), was set before Parliament in November 1982. It contained the majority of the commission's recommendations, as well as those of the Scarman Report. However, the bill was lost, as Margaret Thatcher, basking in 'the Falklands Effect', called a General Election and Parliament was dissolved.

Of course, the Conservatives were returned to power, with Leon Brittan as Home Secretary. His agenda included the Police bill, which was reintroduced in 1983; the Police and Criminal Evidence Act was passed in November 1984.

PACE swept away the Judges' Rules and all the old procedures, and introduced Codes of Practice, including such things as tape-recorded interviews, time limits for detention at a police station and a full paperwork system for recording every step of the process from initial arrest, or stop in the street, to the final release at the police station. A Police Complaints Authority was also created to oversee complaints investigations, with the power to direct chief officers depending on the outcome. PACE still regulates procedures and is unlikely to change in the foreseeable future.

Meanwhile, life ground on. The national miners' strike, which lasted for exactly one year from 1984 to 1985, saw the mutual aid system working at full capacity, with squads of officers spending weeks away at the collieries. More riots occurred in London, including the most notorious one at Broadwater Farm. On Sunday 6 October 1985, PC Keith Blakelock, a 40-year-old father of three, was hacked to death when he became separated from his colleagues.

Shocking as the death of a police officer on duty was, it was as astounding to discover that, with the possible exception of the Metropolitan Police, the lives of police officers dying on duty had been so little thought of; there was no list of these in existence. It is to his everlasting credit that Michael Winner, the well-known film director/producer, established the Police Memorial Trust which has since erected memorials at the scenes of the deaths of police officers.[8] It is also to his credit that Sergeant Tony Rae of the Lancashire Constabulary started researching and recording the deaths of all officers of every force. This resulted in the Police Roll of Honour Trust in 2000, which maintains the National Police Officers' Roll of Honour. It is staggering to find out that the Roll of Honour now contains nearly 4,000 names of police officers and law enforcement officers who have died in the course of duty.[9]

Prompted by the Police Federation at its 1991 conference, together with several chief constables who had seen their officers on the wrong end of serious assaults and stabbings, the Home Office was urged to review police equipment. Thus began the changing look of police officers. Gone would be the old tunics, being replaced by NATO-style pullovers and stab-proof vests. Eventually, even these would be discarded as T-shirts, being more comfortable under body armour, would be introduced. This changing style is still continuing, with blousons now being issued along with fluorescent jackets.

The 1992 General Election saw the Conservatives back in power under John Major, with Kenneth Clarke as Home Secretary. One of the party manifesto's pledges was 'community policing'. Perhaps the government had at last realised that Panda Cars had taken policemen away from the public, with the resulting deleterious effect on fighting crime. The politicians believed that yet another inquiry was needed. They apparently did not realise that the system which had worked well for nigh on 170 years would still work well if it was managed properly. The Home Secretary simply needed to tell the chief constables to abolish unnecessary squads and start putting police officers back on the streets, where the nursery of crime undoubtedly was; in other words, replace the system with what it was before the introduction of Unit Beat Policing.

The inquiry to look at police reform was headed by Sir Patrick Sheehy, the chairman of British American Tobacco, and included businessmen, civil servants and academics – all upper middle class and all only having 'received wisdom' regarding the job of a police officer. The Sheehy Report was published in 1993 and dropped two bombshells. A complex 'pay matrix' was envisaged where pay was determined not by a national scale, but by the responsibilities and qualifications of individual officers, with bonuses being awarded for good performance and reductions made for bad performance. On top of that, fixed-term contracts would be introduced, initially of ten-year durations (the failure of this scheme in the Metropolitan Police under Lord Trenchard had obviously not registered); secure tenure would end and pensions would be granted after forty, rather than thirty, years.

Not surprisingly, opposition to Sheehy was long and continuous. Although the new Home Secretary, Michael Howard, attempted to compromise, Sheehy's proposals never got to the statute books. As with Edwin Chadwick after the 1839 Royal Commission, perhaps Sir Patrick Sheehy was only guilty of naivety and ignorance of human nature. To expect a police officer to tolerate a lower wage than a colleague of the same rank doing a different but 'more important' job, who probably only got that job because of 'blue-eyes' or being in the same Masonic Lodge, shows a conspicuous lack of awareness of people's feelings.

Published in 1993, the Runciman Report was established to look at the English legal system. The report recommended a substantial raft of reforms, including the establishment of a DNA database, greater liaison between police and the Crown Prosecution Service, and video recording of charge rooms and corridors leading to them. Although no direct legislation has been passed, many of the Runciman recommendations have since come into practice.

Soon after Runciman, the Posen Report was published. This gave a modern approach to the age-old problem of ancillary duties of police officers. Although many extraneous duties had been abolished by the Burrell Report of 1953,[10] over the intervening years these had gradually crept back in, and Ingrid Posen, a senior civil servant at the Home Office, was asked to report on them. As in the Burrell Report, the Posen Report recommended the civilianisation of a lot of the tasks of police officers, such as the role of diseases of animal inspectors and acting as ushers in courtrooms. Over the years, Posen's recommendations have gradually been introduced.

The last gasp of the Conservative government was the Police Act 1997. This, in effect, gave statutory authority for the setting up of the National Crime Squad and the National Criminal Intelligence Service. It also paved the way for individuals to apply to see the record of their convictions, which would become the CRB checks much used today. It would surface again in 2000, when it was used to form the basis of the Regulation of Investigatory Powers Act, which, to put it simply, enabled telephone tapping and the collection of private emails.

The Labour Party under Tony Blair was swept into power in May 1997, and one of their manifesto slogans was 'tough on crime, tough on the causes of crime'. Far better political analysis will be found elsewhere of this last fourteen years, but these are the main outlines.

The Crime and Disorder Act was passed in July 1998. A whole range of measures was introduced, including the ASBO – the Anti-Social Behaviour Order.

On the evening of 22 April 1993, Stephen Lawrence, an 18-year-old Afro-Caribbean student, was stabbed to death in London. Two youths were charged, but the CPS dropped the case against them. The Lawrence family, however, did not drop the case and appealed to the court of public opinion. The result was an inquiry headed by Sir William Macpherson, a retired High Court judge. The report was published in February 1999, and made very uncomfortable reading for the Metropolitan Police, with the conclusion that because there was 'institutional racism', there was 'a collective failure' to provide an appropriate response to the Lawrence family 'because of their colour, culture and ethnic origin'.

Although the inquiry concerned only the Metropolitan Police, the ramifications of the Macpherson Report were soon felt throughout the whole of the British police. The Home Secretary, Jack Straw, replying to the first of Macpherson's recommendations to improve relations with the ethnic minorities of the country, set out targets for the recruitment into the police of men and women from ethnic backgrounds. Forces across the country started new measures to ensure equal responses to an increasingly diverse society.

The second Labour government was elected in 2001, and David Blunkett, who was appointed Home Secretary, quickly set about making his mark. The Police Standards Unit was established to review the performance of police forces. The Inspectorate of Constabulary, which had been doing precisely this for the previous 150 years, was pushed aside for seemingly being too close to the police. Thus, two bodies were doing exactly the same job.

Blunkett's lasting legacy would be contained in the White Paper *Policing a New Century: A Blueprint for Reform*. Written by Blunkett himself, this was published in December 2001. Dangerous thoughts were expressed when it proposed powers for the Home Secretary over selection, promotion and dismissal of chief police officers. Above all, it proposed civilian patrol officers. This White Paper eventually became the Police Reform Act 2002, and thus were introduced civilian patrol officers or Police Community Support Officers (PCSOs). Given very limited powers (not much more than the 'ordinary' citizen), PCSOs patrolled the streets in uniform not dissimilar to police uniform, and were cynically reviewed as 'policing on the cheap'.

The reaction to PCSOs has been mixed: some welcome them because they are patrolling and can report things to the police; some ridicule them as 'Blunkett's Bobbies', especially when press reports have them standing at an incident refusing to act because of health and safety regulations. It is probably too soon to make a proper evaluation of their effectiveness, although that question might be answered by the fact that by 2010, recruiting for PCSOs had stopped.

In the autumn of 2003, a man and a woman were found guilty at the Old Bailey for the murder of Holly Wells and Jessica Chapman in Soham in Cambridgeshire.

Questions were asked as to how the man had obtained a job at a school despite having several cautions for suspected child abuse in Humberside. There were clearly problems with the way forces swapped information. As a result, a public inquiry was established under the chairmanship of Sir Michael Bichard. The result was the establishment of a national Criminal Records Bureau (CRB) and recommendations for a national IT system for police intelligence.

The Bichard Report, however, criticised the chief constable of Humberside. Blunkett, by his powers under the Police Reform Act 2002, suspended him, but he refused to resign and the Humberside Police Authority refused to dismiss him. Compromise was reached when the chief constable was reinstated, but retired a few months later. In the meantime, personal revelations against David Blunkett forced his resignation in December 2004.

Charles Clark took over as Home Secretary just in time to face the horrors of 2005. On 7 July terrorist bombs were set off in London, with the loss of many lives. Islamic fundamentalists were blamed and a search was carried out for other members of the gang. On 22 July a surveillance team was keeping observations on a block of flats in London, the home of a suspected terrorist. It is interesting to note that this Metropolitan Police firearms team included two unarmed soldiers, and it is one of these soldiers who, seeing a man leave the flats, thought he bore a 'good possible likeness' to the suspect. In fact, he was not the suspect, but an innocent Brazilian electrician called John Charles de Menezes. The surveillance team followed de Menezes and relayed their location to another specialist firearms team. It was this firearms team who followed him into Stockwell Underground Station. What happened then is well known.

This incident led directly to the passing of the Terrorism Act 2006, which led to the British Parliament agreeing to a twenty-eight-day period of detention without charge for anyone suspected of terrorism.

Not everything that has happened in the past fifty years has been described in this book – only some of the landmarks, as space does not permit anything more. For the full minutiae of the past forty years, the best book is Timothy Brain's *A History of Policing in England and Wales from 1974: A Turbulent Journey*. Meanwhile, the task of the rank-and-file police officer goes on in all the forty-three forces of England and Wales, and the eight forces in Scotland. Not for them the heady light of publicity in the nationally famous cases, only the humdrum of trying to police an increasingly ill-mannered, aggressive and selfish society, whilst continually bogged down by the ill-informed demands of the nine-to-five bureaucratic statisticians and paper shufflers.

For extremely interesting (and factual) accounts of the daily life of a British police officer at the sharp end, and the modern-day workings of the criminal justice system, please read *Wasting Police Time* by 'PC David Copperfield' (a nom-de-plume); and *Perverting the Course of Justice* by 'Inspector Gadget' (another nom-de-plume). For an appraisal of the modern legal system, try *A Brief History of Crime: The Decline of Order, Justice and Liberty in England* by Peter Hitchens.

Although these three books provide a fairly cynical view of the state of the British police and justice in the first decade of the twenty-first century, they contain more common sense than all the sociology manuals put together. In 2011 continued tinkering with the system by politicians who have not the slightest idea is still going on. One of the last vote catchers was the proposal for elected police commissioners, though hard details as to what powers these would have are scarce. Would they have the power to override and dictate chief constables' operational policies? Would they replace the police authorities who are themselves elected local politicians, and if so, to what end?

Also, the 'Review of Policing' by Mr Tom Winsor, a former rail regulator, is in full swing (June 2011). The chief idea so far to emerge from this is the recommendation for five-year short-service commissions. The Review seems not to be aware of the failure of this idea after it was tried by Lord Trenchard in the Metropolitan Police; and the Sheehy Report's rejection of it in 1993. However, the Winsor Review is yet to be published in its finality, so we must wait and see. But it still seems clear that the politicians cannot grasp the fact that the 'new police' system, which has worked for the last 180 years, will still work well *if* it is administered properly.

All we can hope is that this state of affairs is the swing of the long pendulum, and sooner or later the pendulum will swing back the other way. Whether this generation will still be around to see it is anyone's guess.

FOURTEEN

SCOTLAND, IRELAND & THE SERVICES

The Scottish Police

Since England and Scotland were not under the same government until 1707, the policing system in Scotland evolved in a different way to that in England and Wales. Previously, up until the twelfth century, the law courts were the responsibility of local landowners who had been granted that land by the Crown. In return they had to maintain castles and supervise local government for their area, and this included conducting courts, both civil and criminal. These courts were then generally supervised by the King's Chamberlain on periodic tours of inspection.

In the twelfth century, however, the office of sheriff, imitating the English system, was adopted, and into the hands of the sheriff was passed the responsibility for law enforcement within his sheriffdom. The inspecting agency of the courts was the Crown Justiciar on periodic visits. The sheriff could deputise men to be his agents and sergeants, and in this way he upheld his own police force for his sheriffdom.

Ultimately, due to a weak, incompetent and minority rule from the monarchy, coupled with the never-ending wars against the English, central governmental power was eroded and the sheriffs became hereditary and very powerful. Of course, when this happened, squabbles between the sheriffs became the norm. This is what James VI inherited when he became King of Scotland in 1567, although only 1 year old. In the 1580s, when he came to direct the affairs of state, and in trying to restore the power of the monarchy over the sheriffs, he made the sheriffs and landowners responsible for the good behaviour of their tenants.

In 1597 he ordered the Highland landowners to provide sureties for their own good behaviour and to prove ownership of their land. Those who failed were dispossessed. In addition, James established special commissions to deal with lawbreakers in specific areas of the country. For example, the Border Commission of forty armed horsemen was established with the express task of obliterating cattle thieving in the Borders.

In 1603, when James also became King of England, he came across the English system of Justices of the Peace, the magistrates, which he termed 'a laudable custom'.[1] James attempted to introduce magistrates into Scotland and gave them the power to appoint parish constables. These parish constables were given exactly the same power as their English equivalents at that time: not only was the responsibility of law and order placed into their hands, but civil administration as well, such as the powers to maintain roads and bridges, and the street cleaning of their villages. In country parishes invariably two parish constables were chosen, but large cities had as many as their population required.

On the whole, the system of the justices failed. The public did not acquiesce to the magistrates as English society did, with 300 years of deference behind them, and the sheriffs were totally opposed to what they saw as their rivals.

The large cities and towns, as in England, had devised their own Watch and Ward system, although in Scotland it was often called by a different name – the Town Guard. As in England, this body eventually came to be staffed by the old and decrepit, mainly as an alternative to paying them (the equivalent of) poor relief. Edinburgh, for instance, kept its own town guards, who were nicknamed the 'Toon Rottens' by the local wags.

In 1736 the Toon Rottens disgraced themselves when they fired on a crowd at a public execution, killing several people. John Porteus, the Captain of the Guard, was sentenced to death, but was reprieved for reasons unknown. Incensed by this, a mob then broke into his prison, hauled him out and hanged him anyway. Edinburgh City, however, was subsequently fined for failing to stop this and for failing to bring the ringleaders to justice. Thereafter, the Edinburgh City Guard took its duties more seriously, but it was still inadequate when faced with large disturbances. Edinburgh was thus ineffectually policed and it is difficult to believe any other large town or city in the country was any different, with its town guard alongside the magistrate-appointed parish constables.

Meanwhile, in the rural areas, in addition to the special commissions, a sort of policing was established after the second Jacobite Rebellion of 1715. The Catholic James VII, having been ousted in 1688, spent the next thirteen years trying to get his throne back, and his son, Bonny Prince Charlie, tried to do likewise. This resulted in four Jacobite rebellions in 1708, 1715, 1719 and, the best known, in 1745.

After the 1715 rebellion had been crushed, an 'Act for the disarming of the Highlands' was passed in 1724. This allowed money to be levied for the purposes of 'apprehending, subsisting and prosecuting criminals'. The money raised was called 'rogue money', and it is known that at least three local 'police forces' were set up using this money, although the exact number is not known; what is definitely well known is that the Black Watch was recruited in 1729.

The 42nd Regiment of the Line, the Black Watch, nicknamed after the general demeanour of the tartan it wore, was established from local clans for the specific purpose of policing the disaffected parts of the Highlands. Still having some power, the large individual landowners also took to law enforcement for their districts and set up their own 'Fencible Regiments' for peace keeping and riot control. But what Scotland lacked, and England had, was the militia system. The militia was almost the equivalent of the modern Territorial Army and in England, before the county constabularies came along in the 1830s and 1840s, was often mobilised for crowd-control duties.

For various reasons, not the least of which was the four Jacobite rebellions, the militia system had never been tried in Scotland. An attempt was made to introduce the system in 1793 under a Militia (Scotland) bill, but was defeated. However, with the French Revolution of 1797, a sort of panic set in, with the realisation that if the populace could rebel in France, then it could also do so in Scotland. This, coupled with the fact that a few local Fencible Regiments could not be trusted, led to another attempt to introduce the militia system. Although facing stiff opposition, the Militia Act 1797 was passed.

The towns and cities, meanwhile, had been limping along with the system of town guards and the magistrates' constables. In 1778, however, an attempt was made to get a better organised force into Glasgow. This failed, as did an attempt in 1788. Nevertheless, in 1800 the Glasgow Police Act was passed which established Scotland's first statutory police force and had as the Police Authority the police commissioners, who were empowered to raise a levy to pay for the police. Glasgow was followed by Greenock (1800), Edinburgh (1805), Paisley (1806), Gorbals (1808), Perth (1811), Aberdeen (1818), Calton (1819), Airdrie (1822), Dundee (1824), Anderston (1824) and Dunfermline (1832), making twelve in total.[2]

Although many forces pre-date the Metropolitan Police of 1829, these Scottish burgh forces were different in that they were the local authority 'maids of all work', and their duties included paving and street lighting provision and maintenance, street cleaning and enforcement of local sanitation by-laws. In 1819, for instance, the Clerk of Police for Edinburgh was dismissed for overcharging the police commissioners £258 in one year for street-cleaning brooms.[3]

In 1833, however, in seeing the slow spread of these forces, the Royal Burghs (Scotland) Act was passed. For the self-same reasons as the English County Police Act in 1839, the Royal Burghs (Scotland) Act was not made mandatory, but advisory. It enabled the large and important burghs, those being enriched by the industrial boom, to select police commissioners who were empowered to appoint constables and levy rates to maintain them. As in England, some burghs accepted the Act and some totally ignored it. As far as can be ascertained, the following burghs indulged:

1833   Montrose
1835   Musselburgh

1836	Arbroath
1838	Kirkintilloch
1840	Cullen, Hawick and Kelsyth
1841	Thurso and Wick
1843	Dumfries
1844	Dunbar
1845	Ayr
1846	Helensburgh, Kilmarnock and Rothesay
1847	Inverness

So successful was this Act that two more amending Acts were made – the Burgh Police (Scotland) Act 1847 (10 and 11 Victoria, Chapter 39) and the Police (Scotland) Act 1850 (13 and 14 Victoria, Chapter 33) – to extend the provisions into other burghs and 'populous places'. Several more forces followed:

1850	Elgin, Galashiels
1854	Alloa
1855	Dunbarton, Hamilton, Jedburgh, Johnstone
1856	Maryhill
1857	Blairgowrie, Forfar, Haddington, North Berwick, Port Glasgow, Renfrew, Stirling, Stranraer
1858	Annan, Campbelltown, Dysart, Partick, Portobello, Pultneytown, St Andrews
1859	Ardrossan, Banff, Brechin, Burntisland, Cromarty, Cupar, Dingwall, Forres, Frazerburgh, Kirriemuir, Leith, Macduff, Maybole, Nairn
1862	Clyde
1863	Maxwelltown
1864	Govan

By the time the Inspectorate of Constabulary for Scotland came along in 1857, just one year after its English equivalent, the vast majority of burghs had police forces. The Scottish counties, however, still had the old 'rogue money' forces, plus the Fencibles, and it became apparent as the nineteenth century wore on that this was not good enough. As far as can be ascertained, there were three 'rogue money' forces: East Lothian (or Haddingtonshire) (1832); Kinross-shire (1836) and Wigtownshire (1838).

East Lothian had been established in 1832 by the local landowners who were fearful of working-class recalcitrance in the area. Thus, the situation in Scotland mirrored that of England, whose first county forces were also established through fear of public disquiet rather than concern over crime. Not only that, but Chartism was also making itself felt in Scotland as well. The Lord Lieutenant of Fife (Robert Ferguson) had similar fears and communicated them to the Home Secretary, Lord John Russell. And, as we have seen, the County Police Act was passed in August 1839, which applied to Scotland as well, making county police forces advisable but not mandatory. Exactly the same reaction occurred in Scotland as in England: some counties formed forces and some counties didn't.

The Scottish county forces formed under the 1839 Act (along with East Lothian, Kinross-shire and Wigtownshire) were:

1	Perthshire	unknown date in April 1839
2	Ayrshire	unknown date in 1839
3	Kirkcudbrightshire	unknown date in 1839
4	Dumfriesshire	unknown date in 1839
5	Roxburghshire	unknown date in March 1840
6	Banffshire	15 April 1840
7	Aberdeenshire	21 April 1840
8	Dunbartonshire	26 May 1840
9	Mid Lothian	unknown date in May 1840
10	Argyllshire	16 July 1840
11	Fife	unknown date in August 1840
12	Inverness-shire	16 October 1840
13	Forfarshire	unknown date in 1840 (renamed Angus in 1928)
14	West Lothian	unknown date in 1840
15	Renfrewshire	unknown date in 1840
16	Kincardineshire	unknown date in 1841
17	Peeblesshire	unknown date in 1841
18	Selkirkshire	13 September 1842
19	Elginshire	unknown date in 1844 (renamed Morayshire in 1890)

Although the names of the first chief constables of these counties are known, unfortunately many of their backgrounds are not, which gives an indication of the level of neglect of police history by historians. For what it's worth, however, this is the list:

Perthshire	unknown
Ayrshire	James Young, Captain, Army
Kirkcudbrightshire	unknown
Dumfriesshire	William Mitchell(?), nothing known
Roxburghshire	William Cleaver, nothing known
Banffshire	William Anderson, Captain, Army
Aberdeenshire	shared with Banffshire for the first year
Dunbartonshire	Edward Pond, nothing known
Mid Lothian	Alfred List, Metropolitan Police (an original 'Peeler' of 1829)

Argyllshire	Hugh Mackay, nothing known
Fife	Richard Adamson, nothing known
Inverness-shire	Eyre Powell, nothing known
Forfarshire	Henry Williams, nothing known
West Lothian	Adam Colquhoun, nothing known
Renfrewshire	unknown
Kincardineshire	Alexander Weir, nothing known
Peeblesshire	Ninian Notman, nothing known
Selkirkshire	James Fraser, nothing known
Elginshire	William Hay, nothing known

As in England, by the mid-1840s the first flush of enthusiasm had worn off. Chartism was receding, as was industrial and civil unrest, and with it the perceived need for a county police. However, when the Police (Scotland) Act was passed in 1850, primarily relating to the burghs and following on from the successful Royal Burghs (Scotland) Act of 1833, it also applied to the counties. Although counties were still not made compulsory, five counties were nevertheless goaded into action and in 1850 the police forces of Berwickshire, Clackmannanshire, Nairnshire, Stirlingshire and Sutherland were formed. Their respective chief constables were Samuel Underhill, Thomas Berkins, James Wilson, David Fleming and Philip McKay, about all of whom absolutely nothing is known.

The passing of the 1856 County and Borough Police Act introduced the concept of the Inspectorate of Constabulary and the annual inspection with the 'carrot' of government money. The Act did not apply to Scotland, but it was inevitable that the annual inspection idea would soon be broadened. Sure enough, the Police (Scotland) Act 1857 (20 and 21 Victoria, Chapter 72) arrived, and with it the first Inspector of Constabulary (HMI) for Scotland. Only one inspector was deemed sufficient and John Kinloch was appointed in 1857.

When Kinloch's first report was published a year later, predictably it painted the same appalling and diverse conditions in the Scottish police at that time as the first English and Welsh report had done: low rates of pay, harsh discipline, bad living conditions and inefficient forces. Kinloch started off his own campaign for the Scottish Inspectorate policy to eradicate all of this. Nevertheless, as it had done with the English and Welsh police, the Home Office proved its supreme indifference.

The 1857 Scottish Act, strangely enough, although making county forces compulsory, did not do the same for the burghs. This was probably due to the large take-up of the 1833, 1847 and 1850 Acts. In fact, in 1892 when the passing of the Burgh Police (Scotland) Act (55 and 56 Victoria, Chapter 55) made burgh police forces compulsory, only two were affected: Kinning Park and Lerwick.

All the 1857 Act said about burgh forces was that any existing burgh force would be allowed to continue (and presumably receive the Exchequer Grant)

70 Sir Percy Sillitoe (middle of front row) was chief constable of Glasgow City Police
1931–43. With a total of five appointments at this rank, Sillitoe holds the record for the highest
number of chief constableships.

if the HMI found it 'complete and efficient'. Whatever 'complete and efficient'
meant was presumably left to Kinloch to determine, along the lines of the English
inspectors. There were fifty-seven burgh forces and in 1859 two were inefficient.

However, the five backsliding counties were now obliged to form forces, and
so they did: Lanarkshire in 1857; Ross County, Bute and Caithness in 1858; and
Cromarty County in 1859. Strangely enough, the 1857 Act did not affect Orkney
and Shetland, but, not to be left out, Orkney voluntarily formed its force in 1858,
although Shetland demurred until 1883.

The 1857 Act also altered the constitution of the county police authorities.
Previously, the rural police authorities were the Commissioners of Supply, but
after 1857 the Police Authority became the Police Committee, consisting of
elected commissioners plus the county sheriff and lord lieutenant. The police
commissioners of the burghs under the 1833 Act continued as they were.

As with the English and Welsh HMIs, the Scottish HMIs were obliged to form
their own policy, the main plank of which was the abolition of the small burgh
forces. Again, no coercive legislation was forthcoming from central government,
so any amalgamations were purely voluntary. Nevertheless, by 1900 there were
thirty-five burgh forces and only eighteen by the start of the Second World War.[4]

Scottish police history now comes to shadow that of England and Wales.
Standing Joint Committees were introduced in 1889, along with the county
councils. To their everlasting credit, not one Scottish force came out on strike in
1918 and 1919, and they received the benefit of the Desborough Report and 1919
Police Act, which also applied to Scotland.

Scottish chief constables started to hold their own conferences and the HMIs
of Scotland provided the conduit to the Home Office. Sir Percy Sillitoe, when

chief constable of Glasgow (1931–43), introduced many innovations, such as radio systems and radio cars, fingerprint and photographic departments, and such like.

Although a Police Consolidation Committee in 1933 had recommended the reduction of the Scottish forces from forty-eight to fourteen, this was not carried through, and it was left to the powers under the Police Act 1964 to compel amalgamations. As such, there were thirty-three forces in 1950, but by 1968 there were twenty-two. Under the Scottish Local Government Act of 1975, the number was further reduced to the eight forces there are today, each coterminous with local authority boundaries.

The above has been a very quick resume of a very complicated subject. A full, all-inclusive history of the policing of Scotland is not possible in the space available and reference should be made to the lamentably few Scottish police history books. The same can be said of Irish police history.

The Irish Police

The Irish Police, being established in 1822, is therefore seven years older than the Metropolitan Police. Sir Robert Peel became the Chief Secretary in Ireland in 1812,[5] and in 1814 passed the Peace Preservation Act. Although Peel left Ireland in 1818, his successor, Henry Goulbourn, passed legislation for the setting up of the Irish Police proper in 1822. It was organised along provincial lines and the four Irish provinces each had its own chief officer (Sir Richard Willcocks in Munster, Major Thomas Powell in Leinster, Major John Warburton in Connaught and Major Thomas D'Arcy in Ulster).[6]

This original force was reorganised in 1836 to become the Irish Constabulary under one chief officer, Sir James Kennedy, a veteran of Waterloo, with the rank of inspector-general. As a result of the loyalty shown by the force after severe political upheaval, Queen Victoria bestowed the title 'Royal' in 1867, and in 1870 it also took over the policing of Derry, which had previously policed itself. After the declaration of the Irish Free State in 1922, the force was split into two: the Royal Ulster Constabulary and the Garda Siochana. The Dublin Metropolitan Police, which had policed Dublin since 1836, also endured a name change to Dublin Metropolitan Garda.

The Garda Siochana and the Dublin Metropolitan Garda promptly joined up three years later to become the Garda Siochana, which it still remains.

The Royal Ulster Constabulary, because of the political situation in Ireland, became the Police Service of Northern Ireland in 2001. Just before being disbanded, however, it was awarded the George Cross for the collective gallantry of its personnel.

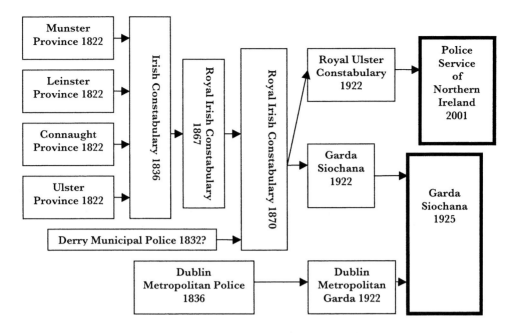

71 Policing Ireland. A 'Family Tree' of the present-day police forces of Ireland.

The Ministry of Defence Police

Also still awaiting a more complete history, the Ministry of Defence Police is an amalgam of the police forces of the three armed services. In the early nineteenth century, the Royal Dockyards started organising their own system of watch-keepers. These, not having been of a recognised police establishment, had to be sworn in as special constables.

In 1860 it was recognised that this arrangement was not the best, so by the Metropolitan Police Act of that year (23 and 24 Victoria, Chapter 135), the Metropolitan Police were given the responsibility of policing the Royal Dockyards. This arrangement lasted until just after the Great War, when the Admiralty, alongside other government departments, was given the power to form its own police forces and not just use special constables as it had previously had to do. Consequently, the Royal Marine Police was started in 1922, and by 1934 had assumed control of all twenty-one dockyards from the Metropolitan Police, with a total strength of 900 men.

With the expansion of the Admiralty in the early part of the Second World War, the Admiralty Civil Police and the Royal Marine Police (Special Reserve) were established, which augmented the Royal Marine Police and took over

72 Before becoming chief constable of Norfolk in 1928, Stephen Van Neck was the first chief constable of the War Department Constabulary 1925–28.

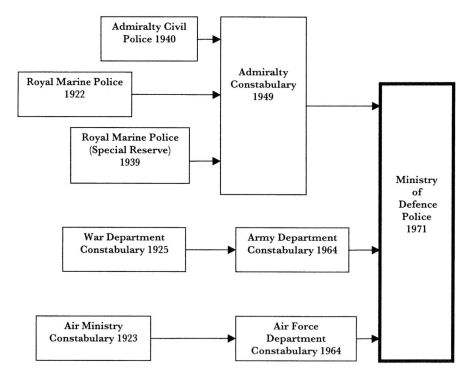

73 A 'Family Tree' of the Ministry of Defence Police.

some of their duties. However, come peacetime these three forces were logically combined to form the Admiralty Constabulary in 1949.[7] The army and Royal Air Force also received the same powers in 1922 as the Admiralty. Consequently, the Air Ministry Constabulary was formed in 1923 and the War Department Constabulary in 1925. Apart from a change of name in 1964, these two police establishments were amalgamated with the Admiralty Constabulary in 1971 to form the present-day Ministry of Defence Police (nicknamed the 'Modplods').

The present MoD Police comprises 3,500 officers, all with full police powers. About 100 Ministry of Defence establishments are policed, including the Royal Mint and, by arrangement, some American air bases.

NOTES

1 The Previous System

1 Critchley, T.A., *A History of Police in England and Wales* (London: 1979), all unreferenced facts come from this splendid book.

2 Goddard, Henry, *Memoirs of a Bow Street Runner*, ed. Patrick Pringle (London: Museum Press, 1956); again, all facts about the Bow Street Runners come from this book.

3 Pringle, Patrick, *Hue and Cry: The Birth of the British Police* (London: Museum Press, 1955).

2 1829–34

1 Ascoli, David, *The Queen's Peace: The origins and development of the Metropolitan Police 1829–1979* (London: Hamish Hamilton, 1979), p. 80.

2 Reith, Charles, 'Charles Rowan 1783–1852', *The Police Review* (9 May 1952), p. 326.

3 Ascoli, David, op. cit., p. 80.

4 Browne, Douglas G., *The Rise of Scotland Yard: A History of the Metropolitan Police* (London: George G. Harrap & Co. Ltd, 1956), p. 79.

5 Moylan, J.F., *Scotland Yard and the Metropolitan Police* (London: G.P. Putnam's Sons Ltd, 1929), p. 317.

6 Melville-Lee, Captain W.L., *A History of Police in England* (London: Methuen & Co., 1901), p. 236.

7 Browne, Douglas G., op. cit., p. 89.

8 Fido, Martin & Skinner, Keith, *The Official Encyclopaedia of Scotland Yard* (London: Virgin Books, 1999), p. 12.

9 The National Archives website, www.nationalarchives.gov.uk, for conversions.

10 www.policeoracle.com.

11 Ascoli, David, op. cit., p. 89.

12 Ibid., p. 85.

13 Browne, Douglas G., op. cit., p. 93.

14 Howard, George, *Guardians of the Queen's Peace: The development and work of Britain's Police* (London: Odhams Press, 1953), p. 135.

15 Dilnot, George, *Scotland Yard: Its history and organisation 1829–1929* (London: Geoffrey Bless, 1929), p. 91.

16 Details come from the Police Roll of Honour Trust (www.policememorial. org.uk); and Cobb, Belton, *Murdered On Duty: A chronicle of the killing of policemen* (London: W.H. Allen, 1961).

17 Ascoli, David, op. cit., p. 89.

18 Fido, Martin & Skinner, Keith, op. cit., p. 210.

19 Browne, Douglas G., op. cit., p. 105.

20 Ascoli, David, op. cit., p. 107.

21 Ibid., p. 109.

22 Fido, Martin & Skinner, Keith, op. cit., p. 293.

23 Powicke, Maurice & Fryde, E.B., *Handbook of British Chronology* (London: The Royal Historical Society, 1961), p. 109.

24 *Dictionary of National Biography.*

25 Police Roll of Honour Trust (www.policememorial.org.uk).

3 1835

1 Powicke, Maurice & Fryde, E.B., *Handbook of British Chronology* (London: The Royal Historical Society, 1961).

2 Ascoli, David, *The Queen's Peace: The origins and development of the Metropolitan Police 1829–1979* (London: Hamish Hamilton, 1979), p. 107.

3 Webb, Sidney & Beatrice, *The Manor and the Borough* (London: Frank Cass, reprinted 1963), Part II, p. 713.

4 Critchley, T.A., *A History of Police in England and Wales* (London: 1979), p. 63.

5 Stallion, Martin & Wall, David S., *The British Police: Police Forces and Chief Officers 1829–2000* (Bramshill, Hampshire: The Police History Society, 1999).

6 Critchley, T.A., op. cit., p. 64.

4 1836–39

1 Critchley, T.A., *A History of Police in England and Wales* (London: 1979), p. 69.

2 James, R.W., *To the best of our Skill and Knowledge. A Short History of the Cheshire Constabulary 1857–1957* (Chester: 1957), p. 32.

3 Critchley, T.A., op. cit., p. 74.

4 *Dictionary of National Biography.*

5 Elliott, Douglas J., *Policing Shropshire 1836–1967* (Studley, Warwickshire: 1984), p. 14.

6 Stallion, Martin & Wall, David S., *The British Police: Police Forces and Chief Officers 1829–2000* (Bramshill, Hampshire: The Police History Society, 1999), p. 53.

7 Greater Manchester Police, *The Police! 150 years of policing in the Manchester area* (1989), unpublished.

8 Reilly, John W., *Policing Birmingham. An account of 150 years of police in Birmingham* (Birmingham: 1989), p. 12.

9 Critchley, T.A., op. cit., p. 79.

10 Blake, Robert, *Disraeli* (London: 1978), p. 162.

5 *1839–56*

1 Rumbelow, Donald, *I Spy Blue. The Police and Crime in the City of London from Elizabeth I to Victoria* (London: 1971), p. 133.

2 *Police Review* (24 May 1929).

3 Jones, D., *Crime, Protest, Community and Police in 19th Century Britain* (London: 1982), p. 153.

4 Reiner, Robert, *The Politics of the Police* (Brighton: 1985), p. 9.

5 Storch, Robert D., 'The Policeman as Domestic Missionary: Urban discipline and popular culture in Northern England 1850–1888', *Journal of Social History* IX (1976), pp. 481–509.

6 *Stone's Justices' Manuals* (various editions).

7 Moriarty, C.C.H., *Police Law. An Arrangement of Law and Regulations for the Use of Police Officers* (London: various editions from 1929).

8 Ibid.

9 Storch, Robert D., 'The Plague of Blue Locusts: Police Reform and Popular Resistance in Northern England, 1840–1857', *International Review of Social History* XX (1975), pp. 72–8.

10 *Dictionary of National Biography*.

11 Jones, Glyn, 'Who Was First?', *Journal of the Police History Society*, No 6 (1991), p. 22.

12 Stallion, Martin & Wall, David S., *The British Police: Police Forces and Chief Officers 1829–2000* (Bramshill, Hampshire: The Police History Society, 1999).

13 Wall, David S., *The Chief Constables of England and Wales. The socio-legal history of a criminal justice elite* (Aldershot, Hampshire: 1998), passim.

14 Cowley, Richard, *Policing Northamptonshire 1836–1986* (Studley, Warwickshire: 1986).

15 Emsley, Clive, *The English Police. A Political and Social History* (Hemel Hempstead, Hertfordshire: 1991), p. 43.

16 Ritcher, Andrew Francis, *Bedfordshire Police 1840–1990* (Bedford: 1990), p. 22.

17 Powicke, Maurice & Fryde, E.B., *Handbook of British Chronology* (London: The Royal Historical Society, 1961).

18 Philips, David & Storch, Robert D., *Policing Provincial England 1829–1856. The Politics of Reform* (Leicester: 1999), p. 213.

19 Ibid., p. 215.

20 Critchley, T.A., *A History of Police in England and Wales* (London: 1979), p. 101.

21 Ibid., pp. 102–4, where it is quoted in full.

22 Ibid., p. 98.

23 Ibid., p. 105.

24 Philips, David & Storch, Robert D., op. cit., p. 216.

25 Ibid., p. 217.

26 Parliamentary Papers (1852/53), XXXVI, p. 92.

27 Trinder, B.S. (ed.), *A Victorian M.P. and his Constituents: The correspondence of H.W. Tancred 1841–1859* (Banbury, Oxfordshire: Banbury Historical Society, Volume 8, 1967), pp. 95–6, letters 126 & 127.

6 1856–74

1 Cowley, Richard, *Policing Northamptonshire 1836–1986* (Studley, Warwickshire: 1986), p. 12.

2 Stanley, Clifford R., 'A Profile of General William Cartwright DL JP. Soldier, Magistrate and Britain's First H.M. Inspector of Constabulary, 1856–1869', *Northamptonshire and Bedfordshire Life* (September 1974), p. 23.

3 Parliamentary Papers (1875), (352) XIII, p. 367, *Minutes of Evidence.*

4 Parliamentary Papers (1852/53), XXVI, p. 92.

5 Parliamentary Debates, 3rd Series, Vol. CXXXIII, Col. 1267 (Friday 2 June 1854).

6 Steedman, Carolyn, *Policing the Victorian Community. The formation of English provincial police forces, 1856–80* (London: 1984), p. 2.

7 Critchley, T.A., *A History of Police in England and Wales* (London: 1979), p. 118.

8 Steedman, Carolyn, op. cit., p. 29.

9 Stanley, Clifford R., op. cit., p. 24.

10 Steedman, Carolyn, op. cit., pp. 38, 40.

11 Ibid., p. 40.

12 Northamptonshire Record Office, reference ZA 4691.

13 Dobson, Bob, *Policing in Lancashire 1839–1989* (Blackpool: 1989), p. 16.

14 Ibid., p. 29.

15 *Report of HM Inspectors of Constabulary* for 1856/57. Parliamentary Papers (1857/58), (20) XLVII, p. 657 (referred to below as First Report 1856/57).

16 Critchley, T.A., op. cit., p. 119 footnote.

17 Hewitt, Eric J., *A History of Policing in Manchester* (Manchester: 1979), p. 58.

18 First Report 1856/57.

19 Parris, Henry, 'The Home Office and the Provincial Police in England and Wales 1856-1870', *Public Law* (1961), p. 233.

20 Steedman, Carolyn, op. cit., p. 26.

21 Ibid., p. 26.

22 Critchley, T.A., op. cit., p. 123.

23 Ibid., p. 79.

24 Parris, Henry, op. cit., p. 231.

25 Hart, Jenifer, 'The County and Borough Police Act, 1856', *Public Administration*, XXXIV (winter 1956), p. 413.

26 Midwinter, E.C., *Law and Order in Early Victorian Lancashire* (York: 1968), p. 39.

27 First Report 1856/57.

28 Parris, Henry, op. cit., p. 243.

29 Hutchins, Walter J., *Out of the Blue. A History of the Devon Constabulary* (Devon: 1975), p. 49.

30 Elliott, Douglas J., *Policing Shropshire 1836–1967* (Studley, Warwickshire: 1984), pp. 64–6.

31 Yearnshire, John, *Back on the Borough Beat. A brief illustrated history of Sunderland Borough Police Force* (Sunderland: 1987), p. 16.

32 Parris, Henry, op. cit., p. 232.

33 Hart, Jenifer, 'Reform of the Borough Police', *The English Historical Review*, LXX (July 1955), pp. 420–1.

34 The National Archives website, www.nationalarchives.gov.uk, for conversions.

35 Maddox, W.C., *A History of the Radnorshire Constabulary* (Llandrindod Wells: 1981), p. 12.

36 First Report 1856/57.

37 Parris, Henry, op. cit., p. 231.

38 Ibid., pp. 231–2.

39 Hart, Jenifer (1956), op. cit., p. 412.

40 Hart, Jenifer, *The British Police* (London: 1951), p. 33.

41 Dobson, Bob, op. cit., pp. 16–17.

42 Elliott, Douglas J., op. cit., p. 22.

43 Parris, Henry, op. cit., p. 238.

44 *Report of HM Inspectors of Constabulary* for 1861/62, Parliamentary Papers (1863), (20) L, p. 181.

45 Parris, Henry, op. cit., p. 238.

46 Ibid., p. 231.

47 Critchley, T.A., op. cit., p. 123.

48 Ibid.

49 Jones, J. Owain, *The History of the Caernarvonshire Constabulary 1856–1950* (Caernarvon: 1963), p. 42.

50 Parris, Henry, op. cit., p. 241.

51 First Report 1856/57, p. 657.

52 Critchley, T.A., op. cit., p. 126.

53 Parris, Henry, op. cit., p. 241.

54 Parliamentary Papers (1859), (17 Session 1) XXII, p. 399.

55 Parris, Henry, op. cit., p. 248.

56 Ibid., pp. 249–52.

57 Waller, Stanley, *Cuffs and Handcuffs: The Story of the Rochdale Police Through the Years 1252–1957* (Rochdale: 1957), photograph 11.

58 Ford, Richard, *They Guarded Guildford. The History of the Guildford Borough Police Force 1836–1947* (Guildford: 1969), p. 14.

59 Yearnshire, John, op. cit., p. 16.

60 Hart, Jenifer (1956), op. cit., p. 407.

61 Parris, Henry, op. cit., p. 234.

62 Ibid., p. 242.

63 Savill, Stanley, *The Police Service of England and Wales* (London: 1901), p. 80.

64 Hart, Jenifer (1955), op. cit., p. 425.

65 *Report from the Select Committee on Police Superannuation Funds.* Parliamentary Papers (1877), (158) XV, p. 101, paragraph 7.

66 Steedman, Carolyn, op. cit., pp. 109–12.

67 Ibid., p. 26.

68 Parliamentary Papers (1860), (30) LVII, p. 527.

69 Midwinter, E.C., *Victorian Social Reform* (London: 1976), p. 36.

70 Steedman, Carolyn, op. cit., p. 39.

71 Ibid., p. 16.

72 Ibid., p. 54.

73 Parris, Henry, op. cit., p. 235.
74 Ibid., p. 236.
75 Powicke, Maurice & Fryde, E.B., *Handbook of British Chronology* (London: The Royal Historical Society, 1961).
76 Parris, Henry, op. cit., p. 234.
77 Hart, Jenifer (1951), op. cit., p. 87.
78 Ibid., p. 88.
79 Parris, Henry, op. cit., p. 234.
80 Ibid., pp. 234–5.
81 Pellew, Jill, *The Home Office 1848–1914: From Clerks to Bureaucrats* (London: 1982), p. 148.
82 Hart, Jenifer (1956), op. cit., p. 409.
83 Pellew, Jill, op. cit., p. 148.
84 Ibid., p. 148.
85 Parliamentary Papers (1859), (17 Session 1) XXII, p. 399.
86 Parliamentary Papers (1860), (30) LVII, p. 527.
87 Parliamentary Papers (1861), (67) LII, p. 641.
88 Powicke, Maurice & Fryde, E.B., op. cit.
89 Parliamentary Papers (1862), (28) XLV, p. 443.
90 Parliamentary Papers (1863), (20) L, p. 181.
91 Parliamentary Papers (1865), (32) XLV, p. 393.
92 Parliamentary Papers (1864), (26) XLVIII, p. 605.
93 Hart, Jenifer (1951), op. cit., pp. 34–5.
94 Savill, Stanley, op. cit., p. xiii.
95 Steedman, Carolyn, op. cit., p. 7.
96 Parliamentary Papers (1866), (54) XXXIV, p. 1.
97 Parliamentary Papers (1867), (14) XXXVI, p. 147.
98 Parliamentary Papers (1867/68), (132) XXXVI, p. 1.
99 Parliamentary Papers (1871), (25) XXVIII, p. 345.
100 Parliamentary Papers (1874), (25) XXVIII, p. 1.
101 Parris, Henry, op. cit., pp. 241–2.
102 Hart, Jenifer (1956), op. cit., p. 408.
103 Whitmore, Richard, *Victorian and Edwardian Crime and Punishment from Old Photographs* (London: 1984), Introduction, unpublished.
104 Ford, Richard, op. cit., p. 19.
105 Pellew, Jill, op. cit., List of Home Secretaries.

7 1874–90

1 Pellew, Jill, *The Home Office 1848–1914: From Clerks to Bureaucrats* (London: 1982), List of Home Secretaries.
2 Blake, Robert, *Disraeli* (London: 1978), p. 539.
3 Ibid., p. 665.
4 Ibid., p. 543.
5 *Dictionary of National Biography*.
6 Critchley, T.A., *A History of Police in England and Wales* (London: 1979), p. 126.

7 *Dictionary of National Biography.*

8 Midwinter, E.C., *Victorian Social Reform* (London: 1976), p. 44.

9 Critchley, T.A., op. cit., p. 127.

10 Parliamentary Papers (1877), (158) XV, p. 101.

11 Parliamentary Papers (1878), (33) XL, p. 1.

12 Critchley, T.A., op. cit., p. 130.

13 Ibid.

14 Ibid.

15 Ibid.

16 Pellew, Jill, op. cit., List of Home Secretaries.

17 Webb, R.K., *Modern England from the Eighteenth Century to the Present* (London: 1981), p. 427.

18 Ibid., p. 429.

19 Ibid., p. 428.

20 Parliamentary Debates, 3rd Series, Vols CCCXXIII–CCCXXX.

21 Critchley, T.A., op. cit., p. 133.

22 Ibid., p. 133.

23 Stallion, Martin & Wall, David S., *The British Police: Police Forces and Chief Officers 1829–2000* (Bramshill, Hampshire: The Police History Society, 1999).

24 Ibid.

25 Parliamentary Papers (1890), (35) XXXVI, p. 345.

26 Parliamentary Papers (1890/91), (171) XLII, p. 1.

27 Parliamentary Debates, 3rd Series, Vol. CCCLXVI, Column 20 onwards.

28 Parliamentary Papers (1890), (C.6065) LIX, p. 329.

29 Parliamentary Papers (1894), (83) XLII, p. 1.

30 Parliamentary Papers (1901), (200) XXXII, p. 1.

31 Hart, Jenifer, *The British Police* (London: 1951), p. 36.

32 Savill, Stanley, *The Police Service of England and Wales* (London: 1901), pp. 258–62.

33 Ibid., pp. 225–40.

34 Wilson, J.P. & Martin, Gail, *The Police: A Study in Manpower. The Evolution of the Service in England and Wales 1829–1965* (London: 1969), p. 20.

35 Steedman, Carolyn, *Policing the Victorian Community. The formation of English provincial police forces, 1856–80* (London: 1984), p. 54.

36 Devlin, J. Daniel, *Police Procedure, Administration and Organisation* (London: 1966), p. 60.

37 Ford, Richard, 'Police Firemen', *Journal of the Police History Society*, No 4 (1989), pp. 55–6.

38 *Reports of His Majesty's Inspectors of Constabulary for the Year ended 29 September 1939* (9 May 1940) (124).

39 *The Times* (Thursday 12 March 1891), obituary notice.

8 *1890–1914*

1 Based on the article 'Catherine Gurney – Beloved Benefactor', *Police Review* (Friday 30 March 1990), pp. 648–9.

2 *Police Review*, Centenary Edition (1993), p. 6.

3 Critchley, T.A., *A History of Police in England and Wales* (London: 1979), p. 171.

4 *Police Review and Parade Gossip* (13 November 1925), from where all this information is taken.

5 Hibbert, Christopher, *The English. A Social History 1066–1945* (London: 1987), p. 599.

6 *Report of the Select Committee on the Police Forces (Weekly Rest Day) together with the Proceedings of the Committee, Minutes of Evidence and Appendices*, Parliamentary Papers (1908), (353 and 354) IX, pp. 679ff.

7 *Dictionary of National Biography.*

8 Fido, Martin & Skinner, Keith, *The Official Encyclopedia of Scotland Yard* (London: 1999), p. 242.

9 *Derby Evening Telegraph* (7 August 1980).

10 Abbott, P.E. & Tamplin, J.M.A., *British Gallantry Awards* (London: 1981), p. 186.

11 *Judges' Rules and Administrative Directions to the Police*, Home Office Circular HO 31/1964.

12 *Police Review* (30 August 1929).

13 Critchley, T.A., op. cit., p. 173.

9 1914–19

1 Poolman, Kenneth, *Zeppelins over England* (London: 1960); and *Police Review* (April 1997).

2 Critchley, T.A., *A History of Police in England and Wales* (London: 1979), p. 183.

3 Reynolds, Gerald W. & Judge, Anthony, *The Night the Police went on Strike* (London: undated, 1968?); and Sellwood, A.V., *Police Strike – 1919* (London: 1978). All unattributed facts on the police strikes come from these two excellent books.

4 Fido, Martin & Skinner, Keith, *The Official Encyclopedia of Scotland Yard* (London: 1999), p. 153.

5 *Who Was Who 1941–1950* (London: 1952).

6 *Report of the Committee on the Police Service of England, Wales and Scotland*, Part 1 (1919), Cmd. 253, XXVII, p. 709; Part 2 (1920), Cmd. 574, XXII, p. 539; Minutes of Evidence (1920), Cmd. 874, XXII, p. 573.

7 Fido, Martin & Skinner, Keith, op. cit., pp. 205ff.

8 Not a derogatory remark, far from it; it is taken from the memoirs of Joan Lock, *Lady Policeman* (London: Michael Joseph, 1968), which, together with another of her books, *The British Policewoman. Her Story* (London: Robert Hale, 1979), provides the majority of information about our policewomen.

9 Fido, Martin & Skinner, Keith, op. cit., p. 291.

10 1919–39

1 *Report of the Committee on the Police Service of England, Wales and Scotland*, Part 1 (1919), Cmd. 253, XXVII, p. 709; Part 2 (1920), Cmd. 574, XXII, p. 539; Minutes of Evidence (1920), Cmd. 874, XXII, p. 573 (referred to below as *Desborough Report*).

2 *Desborough Report*, paragraph 17.

3 *Desborough Report*, paragraph 18.

4 *Desborough Report*, paragraph 18.

5 *Desborough Report*, paragraphs 19–22.

6 Critchley, T.A., *A History of Police in England and Wales* (London: 1979), p. 194.

7 Judge, Anthony, *The First Fifty Years. The Story of the Police Federation* (London: The Police Federation 1968), Chapter 1.

8 Ibid., p. 11.

9 *Desborough Report*, paragraph 91.

10 *Report of HM Inspectors of Constabulary* for 1919/1920, Parliamentary Papers (1921), (39).

11 *Report of HM Inspectors of Constabulary* for 1920/1921, Parliamentary Papers (1923), (5).

12 Ripley, Howard, *Police Forces of Great Britain and Ireland – Their Amalgamations and their Buttons* (Henley-on-Thames: R. Hazell & Co., 1983).

13 Critchley, T.A., op. cit., p. 197.

14 *Report of HM Inspectors of Constabulary* for 1919/1920, op. cit., paragraph 17.

15 *Police Review* (October 1925), passim.

16 Yorkshire, North Riding, *The First Hundred Years of the North Riding of Yorkshire Constabulary 1856–1956* (North Yorkshire Police, reprinted 2004).

17 Ritcher, Andrew Francis, *Bedfordshire Police 1840–1990* (Bedford: Paul Hooley & Associates, 1990), p. 132.

18 *Police Review* (Friday 19 July 1940).

19 *Police Review* (Friday 23 June 1944).

20 *Police Review*, various editions.

21 Fido, Martin & Skinner, Keith, *The Official Encyclopedia of Scotland Yard* (London: 1999), p. 37.

22 Stallion, Martin & Wall, David S., *The British Police: Police Forces and Chief Officers 1829–2000* (Bramshill, Hampshire: The Police History Society, 1999).

23 *London Gazette* (2 January 1939), p. 21.

24 *London Gazette* (25 April 1941), p. 2339.

25 *London Gazette* (25 September 1888), p. 5328.

26 *London Gazette* (3 March 1916), p. 2349.

27 All details have been culled from the *Police Review* and *Police Chronicle*.

28 *Police Review* (Friday 13 July 1945).

29 Emsley, Clive, *The English Police. A Political and Social History* (Hemel Hempstead, Hertfordshire: 1991), p. 135.

30 Critchley, T.A., op. cit., p. 199.

31 *Report of the Royal Commission on Police Powers and Procedures* (16 March 1929), Cmd. 3297.

32 Fido, Martin & Skinner, Keith, *The Official Encyclopedia of Scotland Yard* (London: 1999), p. 232.

33 *Police Review* (Friday 5 March 1930), 'Stop-Press Supplement'.

34 *Report of the Sub-Committee of the Police Council appointed to consider and report upon the scheme for the establishment of a Police College, submitted to the Council at their meeting on 4th March, 1930, 34–296.*

35 Fido, Martin & Skinner, Keith, op. cit., p. 267.

36 Ibid., p. 269.

37 Critchley, T.A., op. cit., p. 207.

38 *Report of HM Inspectors of Constabulary* for 1921/1922, ibid., paragraph 14.

39 *Reports of HM Inspectors of Constabulary.*

40 *Report of HM Inspectors of Constabulary* for 1920/1921, op. cit., paragraph 9.

41 *Report of HM Inspectors of Constabulary* for 1937/1938, Parliamentary Papers (1939), (83) paragraph 21.

42 Popkess, Captain Athelstan, CBE, *Traffic Control & Road Accident Prevention* (London: 1957), p. 8.

43 *Report of HM Inspectors of Constabulary* for 1920/1921, op. cit., paragraph 28.

44 Ibid., paragraph 9.

45 Road Traffic Act 1930 (20 and 21 Geo 5, cap 43).

46 Fido, Martin & Skinner, Keith, op. cit., p. 75.

47 *Report of HM Inspectors of Constabulary* for 1921/1922, Parliamentary Papers (1923), (55).

48 Stallion, Martin & Wall, David S., op. cit., p. 119.

49 *Report of HM Inspectors of Constabulary* for 1921/1922, op. cit., paragraphs 15 & 16.

50 *Report of the Committee on Police Extraneous Duties*, Parliamentary Papers (1953), (627).

51 *Report of HM Inspectors of Constabulary* for 1920/1921, op. cit., paragraph 6.

52 Critchley, T.A., op. cit., p. 197.

53 *Report of HM Inspectors of Constabulary* for 1927/1928, Parliamentary Papers (1929), (50).

54 *Report of HM Inspectors of Constabulary* for 1930/1931, Parliamentary Papers (1932), (36) paragraph 5.

55 *Report of HM Inspectors of Constabulary* for 1932/1933, Parliamentary Papers (1934), (26) paragraph 5.

56 *Report of the Select Committee on Police Forces' Amalgamations*, Parliamentary Papers (1934), (106).

57 Jeffries, Sir Charles, *The Colonial Police* (London: 1952), p. 1.

58 *Who Was Who 1961–1970.*

11 1939–45

1 Moriarty, C.C.H. & Whiteside, J., *Emergency Police Law* (London: 1940), p. 1.

2 Ibid., p. 2.

3 *Report of HM Inspectors of Constabulary* for 1937/38, Parliamentary Papers (1939), (83) paragraph 21.

4 Critchley, T.A., *A History of Police in England and Wales* (London: 1979), p. 226.

5 Ibid., p. 227.

6 *Who Was Who*, various editions.

7 *Report of HM Inspectors of Constabulary* for 1939/45, Parliamentary Papers (1946), (168) p. 3.

8 *Who's Who 1940* (London: 1940).

9 Stallion, Martin & Wall, David S., *The British Police: Police Forces and Chief Officers* (Bramshill, Hampshire: 1999).

10 Critchley, T.A., op. cit., p. 229.

11 Ripley, Howard, *Police Forces of Great Britain and Ireland – Their Amalgamations and their Buttons* (Henley-on-Thames: R. Hazell & Co., 1983).

12 Abbott, P.E. & Tamplin, J.M.A., *British Gallantry Awards* (London: 1981), pp. 138, 144.

13 Ibid.

14 *The Register of the George Cross* (London: 1985), p. 96.

15 Ibid.

16 *Police Review* (Friday 11 May 1945).

17 *Police Review* (Friday 24 December 1943).

18 *First Report of the Police Post-War Committee*, Parliamentary Papers (1946), (51360), p. 3.

19 Ibid.

20 *Second Report of the Police Post-War Committee*, Parliamentary Papers (1947), (C59820).

21 *Third Report of the Police Post-War Committee*, Parliamentary Papers (1947), (56071).

22 *Fourth Report of the Police Post-War Committee*, Parliamentary Papers (1947), (C20360).

12 *1945–64*

1 The Police (His Majesty's Inspectors of Constabulary) Act 1945 (8 and 9 George VI, cap 11).

2 Ingleton, Roy, *The Gentlemen at War: Policing Britain 1939–45* (Maidstone: 1994), p. 174.

3 *Report of HM Inspectors of Constabulary* for 1939/1945, Parliamentary Papers (1946), (168).

4 Ibid., p. 8.

5 *Report of HM Inspectors of Constabulary* for 1945/1946, Parliamentary Papers (1947), (134) Statistical Table, p. 20.

6 *Report of HM Inspectors of Constabulary* for 1946/1947, Parliamentary Papers (1948), (143) Statistical Table, pp. 18–20.

7 *Police Review* and *Police Chronicle*, passim.

8 *Police Review* (Friday 22 April 1949), Letters to Editor.

9 *Police Review* and *Police Chronicle*, and see also: Whitcombe, George, *Bullet. Rope. Guillotine. A Hereford Lad's Nail-Biting Police Experiences* (Hereford: 1995), who served with the Special Police Corps.

10 Critchley, T.A., *A History of Police in England and Wales* (London: 1979), p. 242.

11 *Hansard*, 5th Series, Vol. 410, p. 2619.

12 Cootes, R.J., *The Making of the Welfare State* (London: 1968), p. 98.

13 Critchley, T.A., op. cit., p. 243.

14 Ibid.

15 Cootes, R.J., op. cit., p. 98.

16 *Report of HM Inspectors of Constabulary* for 1946/1947, op. cit., Statistical Table.

17 *First Report of the Police Post-War Committee*, Parliamentary Papers (1946), (51360).

18 Scollan, Maureen, *Ryton Revisited. The Police Training Centre's Tale* (Chelmsford: 1982), p. 20.

19 Ibid.

20 Ibid.

21 Critchley, T.A., op. cit., p. 250.

22 *Report of the Committee on Police Conditions of Service*, Part 1, Parliamentary Papers (1949), Cmd. 7674.

23 *Report of the Committee on Police Conditions of Service*, Part 2, Parliamentary Papers (1949), Cmd. 7831.

24 Critchley, T.A., op. cit., p. 251.

25 Ibid.

26 *Report of the Committee on Police Extraneous Duties*, Parliamentary Papers (1953), (627).

27 *Report of HM Inspectors of Constabulary* for 1951/1952, Parliamentary Papers (1953), (216), p. 5.

28 Mackay, James & Mussell, John W. (eds), *The Medal Yearbook 2002* (Honiton, Devonshire: 2002), p. 234.

29 *Royal Warrant instituting the Police Long Service and Good Conduct Medal*, Parliamentary Papers (14 June 1951), Cmd. 8270.

30 *Report of Enquiry into the Administration and Efficiency of the Cardiganshire Constabulary and the State of Discipline in the Force*, Parliamentary Papers (August 1957), Cmd. 251.

31 *Report of Inquiry into the Proposed Compulsory Amalgamation of the Police Forces of the County of Carmarthen and the County of Cardigan*, Parliamentary Papers (February 1958), Cmd. 374.

32 *Police Chronicle* (Friday 3 January to Friday 30 May 1958).

33 Minto, G.A., *The Thin Blue Line* (London: 1965), Chapter 15.

34 Minto, G.A., op. cit., p. 157.

35 *The Times* (Friday 6 and Thursday 19 November 1959).

36 Critchley, T.A., op. cit., pp. 270–1.

37 Ibid., p. 274.

38 *Royal Commission on the Police 1960, Interim Report*, Parliamentary Papers (November 1960), Cmd. 1222.

39 Critchley, T.A., op. cit. As he was the secretary of the Royal Commission, perhaps it is not surprising that Thomas Critchley devotes twenty pages (274–95) to it, and from which all the facts in this chapter are derived.

40 *Royal Commission on the Police 1962, Final Report*, Parliamentary Papers (May 1962), Cmd. 1728.

41 Cowley, Richard, *Policing Northamptonshire 1836–1986* (Studley, Warwickshire: 1986), Chapter 17.

42 Ripley, Howard, *Police Forces of Great Britain and Ireland – Their Amalgamations and their Buttons* (Henley-on-Thames: R. Hazell & Co., 1983).

13 1964–2011

1 Hitchens, Peter, *A Brief History of Crime. The Decline of Order, Justice and Liberty in England* (London: 2003), p. 50.

2 From the personal experience of the author, having sat through lectures on the system, and then actually working it, 1968 onwards.

3 Hitchens, Peter, op. cit., p. 62.

4 Brain, Timothy, *A History of Policing in England and Wales from 1974. A Turbulent Journey* (Oxford: Oxford University Press, 2010). All facts not otherwise referenced are derived from this book.

5 Fido, Martin & Skinner, Keith, *The Official Encyclopedia of Scotland Yard* (London: 1999), p. 52.

6 Ripley, Howard, *Police Forces of Great Britain and Ireland – Their Amalgamations and their Buttons* (Henley-on-Thames: R. Hazell & Co., 1983).

7 Brain, Timothy, op. cit., p. 48.

8 Police Memorial Trust, 219 Kensington High Street, London, W8 6BD.

9 Police Roll of Honour Trust, PO Box 999, Preston, PR4 5WW.

10 *Report of the Committee on Police Extraneous Duties*, Parliamentary Papers (1953) (627).

14 Scotland, Ireland & the Services

1 Gordon, Paul, *Policing Scotland* (Glasgow: 1980), p. 13.

2 Ripley, Howard, *Police Forces of Great Britain and Ireland – Their Amalgamations and their Buttons* (Henley-on-Thames: R. Hazell & Co., 1983).

3 Gordon, Paul, op. cit., p. 19.

4 Ripley, Howard, op. cit., p. 5.

5 Powicke, Maurice & Fryde, E.B., *Handbook of British Chronology* (London: 1961).

6 Stallion, Martin & Wall, David S., *The British Police: Police Forces and Chief Officers* (Bramshill, Hampshire: 1999).

7 McLennan, A.N., 'The Origins of the Admiralty Constabulary', *Police Chronicle and Constabulary World* (Friday 17 October 1958), p. 9.

BIBLIOGRAPHY

Books

Abbott, P.E. & Tamplin, J.M.A., *British Gallantry Awards* (London: Nimrod Dix & Co., 1981)

Appleby, Pauline, *A Force on the Move. The Story of the British Transport Police 1825–1995* (Malvern: Images Publishing, 1995)

Ascoli, David, *The Queen's Peace: The origins and development of the Metropolitan Police 1829–1979* (London: Hamish Hamilton, 1979)

Best, Geoffrey, *Mid-Victorian Britain 1851–75* (London: Fontana Press, 1987)

Blake, Robert, *Disraeli* (London: Methuen & Co. Ltd, 1978)

Bordua, D. (ed.), *The Police: Six Sociological Essays* (New York: Wiley, 1967)

Brain, Timothy, *A History of Policing in England and Wales from 1974. A Turbulent Journey* (Oxford: Oxford University Press, 2010)

Brogden, Mike, *On the Mersey Beat. Policing Liverpool between the Wars* (Oxford: Oxford University Press, 1991)

Browne, Douglas G., *The Rise of Scotland Yard: A History of the Metropolitan Police* (London: George G. Harrap & Co. Ltd, 1956)

Bunker, John, *From Rattle to Radio* (Studley, Warwickshire: Brewin Books, 1988)

Butcher, Brian David, *'A Movable Rambling Police'. An Official History of Policing in Norfolk* (Norwich: Norfolk Constabulary, 1989)

Carmichael, Evelyn G.M., *The County and Borough Police Acts 1831–1900* (London: William Clowes & Sons Ltd, 1900)

Clay, Ewart W. (ed.), *The Leeds Police 1836–1974* (Leeds: Leeds City Police, 1974)

Cobb, Belton, *Murdered on Duty: A chronicle of the killing of policemen* (London: W.H. Allen, 1961)

Cootes, R.J., *The Making of the Welfare State* (London: Longmans, 1968)

'Copperfield, David', *Wasting Police Time. The crazy world of the war on crime* (Wolvey, Leicestershire: Monday Books, 2009)

Cowley, Richard, *Policing Northamptonshire 1836–1986* (Studley, Warwickshire: Brewin Books, 1986)

———, *Guilty M'Lud! The Criminal History of Northamptonshire* (Kettering, Northamptonshire: Peg & Whistle Books, 1998)

———, *Policing EOKA: The United Kingdom Police Unit to Cyprus 1955–1960* (Kettering, Northamptonshire: Peg & Whistle Books, 2008)

———, *A History of the Northamptonshire Police* (Stroud, Gloucestershire: Sutton Publishing, 2008)

———, *Outrage and Murder! 800 Years of Criminal Homicide and Judicial Execution in Northamptonshire*, Vol. 1: 1202–1850 (Kettering, Northamptonshire: Peg & Whistle Books, 2010)

Cowley, Richard & Todd, Peter, *The History of Her Majesty's Inspectorate of Constabulary: The first 150 years* (London: HM Inspectorate of Constabulary, 2006)

Cramer, James, *The World's Police* (London: Cassell, 1964)

———, *A History of the Police of Portsmouth* (Portsmouth: The Portsmouth Papers, 1983)

Critchley, T.A., *A History of Police in England and Wales* (London: Constable, 1967; reprinted 1979)

Devlin, J. Daniel, *Police Procedure, Administration and Organisation* (London: Butterworths, 1966)

Dilnot, George, *Scotland Yard: Its history and organisation 1829–1929* (London: Geoffrey Bless, 1929)

Dixon, Michael V., *Constabulary Duties. A History of Policing in Picture Postcards* (Market Drayton, Shropshire: S.B. Publications, 1990)

Dobson, Bob, *Policing in Lancashire 1839–1989* (Blackpool: Landy Publishing, 1989)

Elliott, Douglas J., *Policing Shropshire 1836–1967* (Studley, Warwickshire: Brewin Books, 1984)

Emsley, Clive, *The English Police. A Political and Social History* (Hemel Hempstead, Hertfordshire: Harvester Wheatsheaf, 1991)

———, *The Great British Bobby. A history of British policing from the 18th century to the present* (London: Quercus, 2009)

Fairhurst, James, *Policing Wigan. The Wigan Borough Police Force 1836–1969* (Blackpool: Landy Publishing, 1996)

Fido, Martin & Skinner, Keith, *The Official Encyclopedia of Scotland Yard* (London: Virgin Books, 1999)

Forbes, G.J. & Capstick, G.R., *A History of the Burnley Police Force* (Burnley: Burnley County Borough Libraries, 1980)

Ford, Richard, *They Guarded Guildford. The History of the Guildford Borough Police Force 1836–1947* (Guildford: Surrey Constabulary, 1969)

Forrest, Gordon & Hadley, Ted, *Policing Hereford and Leominster. An Illustrated History of the City of Hereford Police 1835 to 1947 and Leominster Borough Police 1836 to 1889* (Studley, Warwickshire: Brewin Books, 1989)

Foster, David, *The Rural Constabulary Act 1839* (London: Standing Council for Local History, 1982)

'Gadget, Inspector', *Perverting the Course of Justice* (Wolvey, Leicestershire: Monday Books, 2009)

Gardiner, Juliet & Wenborn, Neil, *The History Today Companion to British History* (London: Collins & Brown Ltd, 1995)

Goddard, Henry, *Memoirs of a Bow Street Runner*, ed. Patrick Pringle (London: Museum Press, 1956)

Gordon, Paul, *Policing Scotland* (Glasgow: Scottish Council for Civil Liberties, 1980)

Grant, Douglas, *The Thin Blue Line. The Story of the City of Glasgow Police* (London: John Long, 1973)

Griffiths, Sir Percival, *To Guard my People. The History of the Indian Police* (Bombay: Ernest Benn Ltd, 1971)

Hallett, Penny, *150 Years Policing of Bristol* (Bristol: Avon & Somerset Constabulary, 1986)

Hardwicke, Glyn, *Keepers of the Door. The History of the Port of London Authority Police* (London: Port of London Authority, undated)

Hart, Jenifer, *The British Police* (London: George Allen & Unwin, 1951)

Hewitt, Eric J., *A History of Policing in Manchester* (Manchester: E.J. Morten, 1979)

Hibbert, Christopher, *The English. A Social History 1066–1945* (London: Grafton Books, 1987)

Hitchens, Peter, *A Brief History of Crime. The Decline of Order, Justice and Liberty in England* (London: Atlantic Books, 2003)

Holberry, Steve, *A Pictorial History of the Huddersfield and District Police Force, from the earliest records to the present day* (Huddersfield: Print City, undated)

Howard, George, *Guardians of the Queen's Peace: The Development and Work of Britain's Police* (London: Odhams Press, 1953)

Hunt, Walter William, *'To Guard My People'. An Account of the Origin and History of the Swansea Police* (Swansea: Swansea Borough Police, 1957)

Hutchings, Walter J., *Out of the Blue. History of the Devon Constabulary* (published privately, 1957)

Hyndman, David, *Nottingham City Police. A Pictorial History*, 2 Volumes (Nottingham: published privately, 1968)

Ingleton, Roy, *The Gentlemen at War. Policing Britain 1939–45* (Maidstone: Cranbourne Publications, 1994)

———, *Police of the World* (London: Ian Allan Ltd, 1979)

Jacob, Leslie C., *Constables of Suffolk. A Brief History of Policing in the County* (Ipswich: Suffolk Constabulary, 1992)

James, R.W., *To the Best of our Skill and Knowledge. A Short History of the Cheshire Constabulary 1857–1957* (Chester: Cheshire Constabulary, 1957)

Jeffries, Sir Charles, KCMG, OBE, *The Colonial Police* (London: Max Parrish, 1952)

Jones, D., *Crime, Protest, Community and Police in 19th century Britain* (London: Routledge, 1982)

Jones, J. Owain, *The History of the Caernarvonshire Constabulary 1856–1950* (Caernarvon: Caernarvonshire Historical Society, 1963)

Judge, Anthony, *The First Fifty Years. The Story of the Police Federation* (London: The Police Federation, 1968)

Lock, Joan, *Lady Policeman* (London: Michael Joseph, 1968)

———, *The British Policewoman. Her Story* (London: Robert Hale, 1979)

Lucas, Norman, *WPC 'Courage'. The Heroism of Women of the British Police Forces* (London: Weidenfeld & Nicolson, 1986)

————, *Heroines in Blue. Stories of Courage by Women of the British Police Forces* (London: Weidenfeld & Nicolson, 1988)

Mackay, James & Mussell, John W. (eds), *The Medal Yearbook 2002* (Honiton, Devonshire: Token Publishing Ltd, 2002)

Maddox, W.C., *A History of the Radnorshire Constabulary* (Llandrindod Wells: The Radnorshire Society, 1981)

Madigan, T.J., *'The Men who wore Straw Helmets'. Policing Luton 1840–1974* (Dunstable: The Book Castle, 1993)

Marshall, Geoffrey, *Police and Government. The Status and Accountability of the English Constable* (London: Methuen & Co. Ltd, 1965)

Martin, J.P. & Wilson, Gail, *The Police: A Study in Manpower. The Evolution of the Service in England and Wales 1829–1965* (London: Heinemann Educational Books, 1969)

Melville-Lee, W.L., *A History of Police in England* (London: Methuen & Co., 1901)

Midwinter, E.C., *Victorian Social Reform* (London: Longman, 'Seminar Studies in History', 1976)

Minto, G.A., *The Thin Blue Line* (London: Hodder & Stoughton, 1965)

Moriarty, C.C.H., *Police Law. An Arrangement of Law and Regulations for the Use of Police Officers* (London: Butterworth & Co., various editions from 1929)

Moriarty, C.C.H. & Whiteside, J., *Emergency Police Law* (London: Butterworth & Co., 1940)

Moylan, J.F., *Scotland Yard and the Metropolitan Police* (London: G.P. Putnam's Sons Ltd, 1929)

Osborn, Neil, *The Story of Hertfordshire Police* (Letchworth: Hertfordshire Countryside, undated)

Pellew, Jill, *The Home Office 1848–1914: From Clerks to Bureaucrats* (London: Heinemann Educational Books, 1982)

Philips, David & Storch, Robert D., *Policing Provincial England 1829–1856. The Politics of Reform* (Leicester: Leicester University Press, 1999)

Pooler, Bob, *From Fruit Trees to Furnaces. A History of the Worcestershire Constabulary* (Pershore: Blacksmith Publishing, 2002)

Popkess, Captain Athelstan, CBE, *Traffic Control & Road Accident Prevention* (London: Chapman & Hall, 1957)

Poulsom, Neville, Rumble, Mike & Smith, Keith, *Sussex Police Forces* (Midhurst, West Sussex: Middleton Press, 1987)

Powell, James A., Sutherland, Graham & Gardner, Terence, *Policing Warwickshire. A Pictorial History of the Warwickshire Constabulary* (Studley, Warwickshire: Brewin Books, 1997)

Powicke, Maurice & Fryde, E.B., *Handbook of British Chronology* (London: The Royal Historical Society, 1961)

Pringle, Nik & Treversh, Jim, *150 Years Policing in Watford District and Hertfordshire County* (Watford: Radley Shaw Publishing, 1991)

Pringle, Patrick, *Hue and Cry: The Birth of the British Police* (London: Museum Press, 1955)

Radzinowicz, Leon, *A History of English Criminal Law and its Administration from 1750*, 4 Volumes (London: Stevens & Sons, 1956)

Rawlings, Philip, *Policing. A Short History* (Cullompton: Willan Publishing, 2002)

Reilly, John W., *Policing Birmingham. An account of 150 years of police in Birmingham* (Birmingham: West Midlands Police, 1989)

Reiner, Robert, *The Politics of the Police* (Brighton: Wheatsheaf Books, 1985)

Reith, Charles, *The Police Idea. Its History and Evolution in England in the Eighteenth Century and After* (Oxford: Oxford University Press, 1938)

Reynolds, Gerald W. & Judge, Anthony, *The Night the Police went on Strike* (London: Weidenfeld & Nicolson, 1968?)

Ripley, Howard, *Police Forces of Great Britain and Ireland – Their Amalgamations and their Buttons* (Henley-on-Thames: R. Hazell & Co., 1983)

Ritcher, Andrew Francis, *Bedfordshire Police 1840–1990* (Bedford: Paul Hooley & Associates, 1990)

Rose, Geoffrey, *A Pictorial History of the Oxford City Police* (Oxford: Oxford Publishing Co., 1979)

Rumbelow, Donald, *I Spy Blue. The Police and Crime in the City of London from Elizabeth I to Victoria* (London: Macmillan London Ltd, 1971)

Sample, Paul, *'The Oldest and The Best'. The History of the Wiltshire Constabulary 1839–1989* (Salisbury: No Limits Public Relations, 1989)

Savill, Stanley, *The Police Service of England and Wales* (London: 'Police Review' Publishing, 1901)

Scollan, Maureen, *Ryton Revisited. The Police Training Centre's Tale* (Chelmsford: published privately, 1982)

———, *Sworn to Serve. Police in Essex 1840–1990* (Chichester: Phillimore & Co. Ltd, 1993)

Sellwood, A.V., *Police Strike – 1919* (London: W.H. Allen, 1978)

Shaw, Barry, *The History of the West Riding Constabulary* (Tadcaster: published privately, 1970)

Sillitoe, Sir Percy, *Cloak without Dagger* (London: Cassell & Co. Ltd, 1955)

Sinclair, Georgina, *At the End of the Line. Colonial Policing and the Imperial Endgame 1945–80* (Manchester: Manchester University Press, 2006)

Smith, David J., *Policing West Mercia 1967–1988* (Studley, Warwickshire: Brewin Books, 1989)

Stallion, Martin & Wall, David S., *The British Police: Police Forces and Chief Officers 1829–2000* (Bramshill, Hampshire: The Police History Society, 1999)

Steedman, Carolyn, *Policing the Victorian Community. The formation of English provincial police forces 1856–1880* (London: Routledge & Kegan Paul, 1984)

St Johnstone, Eric, *One Policeman's Story* (Chichester: Barry Rose Ltd, 1978)

Taylor, Michael Bradley & Wilkinson, Victor Legender, *Badges of Office. An Illustrated Guide to the Helmets and Badges of the British Police 1829 to 1989* (Henley-on-Thames: R. Hazell & Co., 1989)

Taylor, Denis, *999 and All That. The Story of the Oldham County Borough Police Force* (Oldham: Oldham Corporation, 1968)

Thomas, Harry, *The History of the Gloucestershire Constabulary 1839–1985* (Gloucester: Alan Sutton, 1987)

Thomas, R.L. (ed.), *The Kent Police Centenary. Recollections of a Hundred Years* (Maidstone: Kent County Constabulary, 1957)

Thomson, David, *England in the Nineteenth Century 1815–1914* (London: Penguin Books, 1969)

Tobias, J.J., *Against the Peace* (London: Ginn & Company, 1970)

Trinder, B.S. (ed.), *A Victorian M.P. and his Constituents: The Correspondence of H.W. Tancred 1841–1859*, Volume 8 (Banbury: Banbury Historical Society, 1967)

Tunstall, Alf, *The Borough Men. The Story of the Newcastle Borough Police* (Leek, Staffordshire: Churnet Valley Books, 1995)

Turnbull, George, *The Isle of Man Constabulary. An Account of its Origins and Growth* (Onchan, Isle of Man: Mansk-Svenska Publishing Co. Ltd, 1984)

Walker, Peter N., *The Story of the Police Mutual Assurance Society* (Lichfield, Staffordshire: Police Mutual Assurance Society, 1992)

Wall, David S., *The Chief Constables of England and Wales. The socio-legal history of a criminal justice elite* (Aldershot, Hampshire: Ashgate Publishing Ltd, 1998)

Waller, Stanley, *Cuffs and Handcuffs. The Story of the Rochdale Police Through the Years 1252–1957* (Rochdale: Rochdale Borough Police, 1957)

Walters, Roderick, *The Establishment of the Bristol Police Force* (Bristol: Historical Association (Bristol Branch) Local History Pamphlets, 1975)

Watson, Alan S. & Harrison, Derek, *Policing the Land of the Prince Bishops. The History of Durham Constabulary 1840–1990* (Exeter: Wheaton Publishers Ltd, 1990)

Watt, Ian A., *A History of the Hampshire and Isle of Wight Constabulary 1839–1966* (Winchester: Hampshire & Isle of Wight Constabulary, 1967)

Webb, R.K., *Modern England from the Eighteenth Century to the Present* (London: George Allen & Unwin, 1981)

Webb, Sidney & Beatrice, *The Manor and the Borough* (London: Frank Cass, reprinted 1963)

Whitaker, Ben, *The Police in Society* (London: Eyre Methuen, 1979)

Whitbread, J.R., *The Railway Policeman. The Story of the Constable on the Track* (London: George G. Harrap & Co. Ltd, 1961)

Whitcombe, George, *Bullet. Rope. Guillotine. A Hereford Lad's Nail-Biting Police Experiences* (Hereford: Aintree Publishing, 1995)

Whitmore, Richard, *Victorian and Edwardian Crime and Punishment from Old Photographs* (London: B.T. Batsford Ltd, reprinted 1984)

Wilson, J.P. & Martin, Gail, *The Police: A Study in Manpower. The Evolution of the Service in England and Wales 1829–1965* (London: 1969)

Withers, Bill, *Nottinghamshire Constabulary. 150 Years in Photographs* (Huddersfield: Quoin Publishing Ltd, 1989)

Woodgate, John, *The Essex Police* (Lowerham, Suffolk: Terence Dalton Ltd, 1985)

Wyles, Lilian, *A Woman at Scotland Yard. Reflections on the struggles and achievements of thirty years in the Metropolitan Police* (London: Faber & Faber Ltd, 1952)

Wyness, Fenton, *The Diced Cap. The Story of Aberdeen City Police* (Aberdeen: Aberdeen City Corporation, 1972)

Yearnshire, John, *Back on the Borough Beat. A Brief Illustrated History of Sunderland Borough Police Force* (Sunderland: published privately, 1987)

Unattributed Force Histories & Other Works

Bacup Borough Police, *Jubilee Souvenir 1887–1937* (1937)

Brighton Borough Police, *Brighton Police Centenary 1838–1938* (1938)

Cardiganshire Constabulary, *Rules, Orders and Guides to Constables also a Short History of the Force* (1897)

Derbyshire Constabulary, *A Short History of the Derbyshire Constabulary* (1981)

Greater Manchester Police, *The Police! 150 years of policing in the Manchester area* (1989)

Lerwick Burgh Police, *Regulations and Instructions* (1896)

Macclesfield Borough Police, *A Short History of the Macclesfield Borough Police Force* (1947)

Oldham Borough Police, *The Borough Police* (1949)

Peterborough City Police, *Commemorating 100 Years of the Peterborough Police 1857–1957* (1957)

Register of the George Cross (London: This England Books, 1985)

Register of the Victoria Cross (London: This England Books, 1981)

Southend-on-Sea Borough Police, *The Borough Men. The Police in Southend-on-Sea 1840–1969* (Essex Police Museum, 1992)

Yorkshire, East Riding, *East Riding of Yorkshire Police 1857–1957* (1957)

Yorkshire, North Riding, *The First Hundred Years of the North Riding of Yorkshire Constabulary 1856–1956* (North Yorkshire Police, reprinted 2004)

Reference Works

Burke's Peerage

Dictionary of National Biography

Hansard

Journals of the Police History Society

London Gazette

Parliamentary Debates

Police Chronicle

Police Journal

Police Review

Stone's Justices' Manual (various editions)

The Times

Who Was Who (various dates)

Articles

Cowley, Richard, 'The First H.M.I.', *Police Review* (7 March 1986), pp. 522–3

———, 'Catherine Gurney – Beloved Benefactor', *Police Review* (30 March 1990), pp. 648–9

Foster, D.M., 'The East Riding Constabulary in the Nineteenth Century', *Northern History* XXI (1985), pp. 193–211

Gillespie, W.H., 'An Old Force: The History of the Deal Borough Police', *Police Journal* XXVII (1954), pp. 306–17

Hart, Jenifer, 'Reform of the Borough Police', *The English Historical Review* LXX (July 1955), pp. 411–27

————, 'The County and Borough Police Act, 1856', *Public Administration* XXXIV (Winter 1956), pp. 405–17

Jones, D.J.V., 'The New Police, Crime and People in England and Wales 1829–1888', *Transactions of the Royal Historical Society* XXXIII (1983), pp. 151–68

McLennan, A.N., 'The Origins of the Admiralty Constabulary', *Police Chronicle and Constabulary World* (17 October 1958), p. 9

Parris, Henry, 'The Home Office and the Provincial Police in England and Wales 1856–1870', *Public Law* (1961), pp. 230–55

————, 'Police History: A Bibliography', *Police Journal* XXXIV (1961), pp. 286–90

Storch, Robert D., 'The Plague of Blue Locusts: Police Reform and Popular Resistance in Northern England, 1840–1857', *International Review of Social History* XX (1975), pp. 61–90

————, 'The Policeman as Domestic Missionary: Urban Discipline and Popular Culture in Northern England 1850–1888', *Journal of Social History* IX (1976), pp. 481–509

Swift, Roger, 'Urban Policing in early Victorian England, 1835–1856: a reappraisal', *History* (June 1988), pp. 211–37

Wren, Pauline, 'The Police Inspectorate', *Police Review* (14 May 1971), pp. 619–20

Parliamentary Reports

Report from the Select Committee on Police Superannuation Funds (1877), (158) XV, p. 101 and the *Minutes of Evidence* (1875), (352) XIII, p. 376

Memorandum in Explanation of the Police Bill, 1890 (C.6065) LIX, p. 329

Report of the Select Committee on the Police Forces (Weekly Rest Day) together with the Proceedings of the Committee, Minutes of Evidence and Appendices (1908), (353 and 354) IX, p. 679

Report of the Committee on the Police Service of England and Wales and Scotland ('The Desborough Committee')
     Part 1 (1919), Cmd. 253, XXVII, p. 709
     Part 2 (1920), Cmd. 574, XXII, p. 359

Minutes of Evidence (1920), Cmd. 874, XXII, p. 573

Report of the Royal Commission on Police Powers and Procedures (1928–1929), Cmd. 3297 IX, p. 127

Report of the Select Committee on Police Forces' Amalgamations (1931–1932), (106) V, p. 123

First Report of the Police Post-War Committee, PP 1946 (51360)

Second Report of the Police Post-War Committee, PP 1947 (C59820)

Third Report of the Police Post-War Committee, PP 1947 (56071)

Fourth Report of the Police Post-War Committee, PP 1947 (C20360)

Report of the Committee on Police Conditions of Service ('The Oaksey Report')
     Part 1, PP 1949 (Cmd. 7674)
     Part 2, PP 1949 (Cmd. 7831)

Report of the Committee on Police Extraneous Duties, PP 1953 (627)

Final Report of the Royal Commission on the Police, PP 1962 (Cmd. 1728)

INDEX

Other titles published by The History Press

Crime and Criminals of Victorian England
ADRIAN GRAY

978-0-7524-5280-7

£14.99

This thrilling book recounts classic murders, by knife and poison, and much more, and explores the less familiar parts of Victorian life, uncovering the criminal world of the nineteenth century. Gray journeys through the cities, villages, lanes, mills and sailing ships of the period, showing how our laws today have been shaped by what the Victorians considered acceptable or made illegal.

Mysteries of Police and Crime: Victorian Murders
MAJOR ARTHUR GRIFFITHS

978-0-7524-5524-2

£14.99

This richly illustrated, fascinating volume also includes every other case of note in the annals of Victorian crime. From Elizabeth Brownrigg, who whipped her domestic into an early grave, to the horrific tale of Henry Wainwright, who attempted to transport the dismembered body of his lover across London, it is not for the faint of heart.

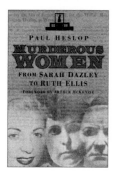

Murderous Women: From Sarah Dazley to Ruth Ellis
PAUL HESLOP

978-0-7509-5081-7

£14.99

Serial poisoners, crimes of passion, brutal slayings and infanticide – this book examines the stories and trials behind the most infamous cases of British female killers between the early part of the nineteenth century and the 1950s. Including post-trial material, as well as the executions of the offenders, Heslop also offers his 'verdicts', at times putting justice itself on trial.

Murderers' Row: An International Murderers' Who's Who
ROBIN ODELL

978-0-7509-4404-5

£8.99

Beginning in 1885 with the execution of Henry Kimberley and ending in 1955 with Ernie Harding, the last man hanged for child murder, this highly readable account of Winson Green Gaol features each of the forty cases in one volume for the first time and is fully illustrated with rare photographs, documents, news cuttings and engravings.

Visit our website and discover thousands of other History Press books.

www.thehistorypress.co.uk